THE FBI'S WAR AGAINST THE MAFIA

THE FBI'S WAR AGAINST THE MAFIA

FRANK STOREY

CITADEL PRESS
Kensington Publishing Corp.
kensingtonbooks.com

CITADEL PRESS BOOKS are published by

Kensington Publishing Corp.
900 Third Avenue
New York, NY 10022

Library of Congress Control Number: 2026937442

First hardcover printing: September 2026
ISBN: 978-0-8065-4469-4

ISBN: 978-0-8065-4471-7 (e-book)

10 9 8 7 6 5 4 3 2 1

Printed in the United States of America

DISCLAIMER

In accordance with my obligations as a former FBI employee and pursuant to my FBI employment agreement, this book has undergone a prepublication review for the purpose of identifying prohibited disclosures, but has not been reviewed for editorial content or accuracy. The FBI does not endorse or validate any information that I have described in this book. The opinions expressed in this book are mine and not those of the FBI or any other government agency.

CONTENTS

FOREWORD BY JOE PISTONE

In the early 1970s, the FBI was just beginning to intensify its investigative efforts against the Mafia. At that time, I had been an agent for several years and had some experience working on organized crime cases. I was approached to work as an undercover agent in New York and attempt to penetrate the Bonanno Mafia family. After much thought, I agreed to accept this challenge. I assumed a new identity—Donnie Brasco—and developed a cover as a jewel thief from Miami.

Over a six-year period, I was successful in penetrating a Bonanno crew headed by capo Alphonse "Sonny Red" Indelicato. During many of my contacts, I wore a body recorder and critical conversations were recorded regarding their criminal activities. My actions were closely monitored by an FBI team of agents who were assigned to the investigation, as my life was in constant danger.

At one point, I was about to become a member of the family. Before doing so, I was ordered to murder a rival Mafia member. The decision was made to end my assignment and all the associates I had been working for were advised of my true identity. The FBI then arrested all those I had encountered in my undercover role. Philip "Rusty" Rastelli, the boss of the Bonanno family, held several members of Indelicato's crew responsible for accepting me as a member and ordered their murders. Sonny himself was brutally killed. The evidence I was able to develop led to the indictment of numerous high-level family members, but the enterprise continued.

I first met Frank Storey shortly after he arrived in the New York office as the Agent in Charge of the Organized Crime Program in 1981. There were only a few executives in the FBI who had the experience and willingness to take on the Mafia. Frank Storey was one of them.

He had the vision to go after the Five Families simultaneously, which many superiors in the FBI believed was an impossible task. I wanted to be part of this effort. My undercover assignment was over, and my penetration of the Bonanno family was well-known within Mafia circles. Frank realized this, but we reached an accommodation whereby I would assist with the investigative effort, consulting with the supervisors and agents regarding the inner workings of a Mafia family. This was extremely helpful to them in identifying the key Mafia figures in each family.

In this book, Frank has skillfully portrayed the methods and techniques the agents adopted in conducting their investigative assault against the Five Families. This book identifies specific Mafia families, chapter by chapter, that the FBI investigated. It's all here: the undercover scenarios that were employed, the interceptions of critical conversations among Mafia members, the development of informants and cooperative witnesses, and the finality—the trial of the bosses who were all convicted of RICO violations and sentenced to life imprisonment.

This work will give the reader a real understanding of how evil the Mafia was during this period and a hands-on view of how the FBI took down the entire leadership of the five Mafia families in New York. It is a must-read for those who want not only a clearer understanding of the Mafia, but also an insider's view of the inner workings of the FBI and how they conduct investigations of this magnitude.

Joe Pistone is a former undercover FBI agent who infiltrated the Bonanno family between 1976 and 1981. He is also the author of Donnie Brasco: My Undercover Life in the Mafia, *which was adapted into the 1997 film starring Johnny Depp and Al Pacino.*

THE FBI'S WAR AGAINST THE MAFIA

INTRODUCTION

The Mafia has a long and storied history. Charles "Lucky" Luciano organized the Mafia in the United States in the mid-1930s. He realized that the numerous gangs that had risen in New York and other major cities along the East Coast and Chicago were constantly at odds with one another over control of illegal activities. This rivalry resulted in many gang wars and one boss after another was assassinated. Due to this constant unrest, opportunities to earn more profits and control legitimate businesses were squandered. At that time, Luciano, who was born in Sicily, had considerable authority and respect from the leaders of organized crime in New York. He decided to act.

He called together a meeting with the bosses of the major gangs. They all agreed to create five separate Mafia families, which would be overseen by a Commission. In the 1960s, the families would eventually be identified by the last names of the reigning bosses: Gambino, Lucchese, Colombo, Genovese, and Bonanno.

Joseph Valachi was a member of the Genovese family who was convicted of drug trafficking in 1959. He was sentenced to fifteen years in prison and became involved in a dispute with a fellow inmate, whom he then murdered. After receiving a life sentence, he contacted the FBI, became a cooperative witness, and testified before the United States Senate Subcommittee. He disclosed detailed information about the Mafia regarding its members and operations. He became the first member of the Mafia to come forward and violate the code of silence, "omertà," that all Mafia members had to abide by or face death. The Commission would be composed of each family's boss or, in his absence, his underboss. They would now operate under the codes established by the Sicilian Mafia. The New York families would have influence and interaction with other Mafia families located along the East Coast and in Chicago. The Commission would settle any disputes that occurred within the families. Each family would be designated to control certain unions and legitimate businesses, and the competition and rivalry would end. If the agreement was violated, the Commission would take appropriate action.

The traditional meaning of the term "family," taken in its true essence, by no means reflects the inherent viciousness and evil intent of the members of a Mafia family. When each candidate is inducted into Cosa Nostra, they must take an oath before the leaders of a particular family. As their hand holds a burning holy card, they pledge allegiance to the group to honor a code of silence relative to their participation in the family's business. Breaking this code of honor is punishable by death. In many ways, the entire philosophy of the Mafia is similar to a religious cult. It is a cult of men who only care about one thing: earning significant profits by any means necessary.

The five New York Mafia families that Luciano created became a powerful force, and local and federal law enforcement agencies were not equipped to investigate and prosecute their members. Individual arrests were made, highlighted by front-page headlines, but the family enterprises survived and continued to prosper. In addition to controlling traditional illegal activities such as gambling, prostitution, and loan-sharking, the Mafia Luciano organized was able to infiltrate and control all major labor unions and thus extort and, in some cases, take over legitimate businesses. They were now operating as a million-dollar criminal enterprise almost with impunity. In effect, they were functioning as a separate government entity.

The FBI did not begin to focus on these organizations until the early 1970s, with minimal success. Their primary approach was to collect intelligence information regarding all the families, as they did not have the federal statutes to fight this cancer effectively. Finally, Congress responded by passing the Racketeer Influenced and Corrupt Organizations (RICO) statute in 1970. This law now gave the FBI the authority to investigate organizations such as the Mafia that were engaged in illegal activities in interstate commerce. They now had the opportunity to develop new investigative strategies to attack organized crime; however, there were initial delays in moving forward due to a lack of understanding of the opportunity that the provisions of the RICO statute afforded.

As a young supervisor newly appointed to the FBI headquarters to monitor organized crime investigations, I directed several field offices to utilize the RICO statute to investigate a corrupt labor union controlled by the Mafia. The case, entitled UNIRAC, was the first RICO investigation undertaken by the FBI. It was a success and resulted in the convictions of members of the Gambino and Genovese families and union representatives of the International Longshoremen's Association (ILA). Subsequently, I was transferred to New York and again decided to utilize the RICO statute to investigate the five Mafia families created by Luciano.

In New York, I led a workforce of over 140 agents exclusively assigned to investigate the Five Families. This book portrays a firsthand account of the methods these agents—the "game changers"—utilized to develop the necessary evidence that resulted in the convictions of the bosses of these five Mafia families in New York. We utilized undercover agents and informants to penetrate specific families. The evidence they developed was utilized in obtaining extensive electronic court-authorized interceptions of conversations of the highest-ranking members of each family. I was an eyewitness to all the events that occurred, and I am honored to finally tell the story of how the game changers won their battle against the Mafia.

CHAPTER 1
The Indictments

On February 25, 1985, after an unprecedented investigation by the FBI, a federal grand jury indicted the bosses of the five Mafia families in New York. As the agent in charge of the investigation, I directed a workforce of over 140 agents who worked tirelessly over three years to accomplish this remarkable achievement. After all the arrests that day, I left the command center of the New York office at approximately 8:00 p.m. and returned to my office. I felt exhausted, could barely keep my eyes open, and was elated simultaneously. I paused momentarily and glanced through the office window at the city before me. I took a long sigh and shouted to myself, "Son of a bitch! We finally did it."

I called my wife Susan to let her know I was okay. She had learned of the arrests from the breaking news accounts. Her response was a loud "yes, yes" as she softly cried tears of relief. There were times when events had gone wrong during the investigation and on many occasions, I would bring my stress home as I walked in the door. Sue was always there when I needed her and guided me through many rough spots. One of her "squeezy hugs" always did the trick. A special dinner with champagne was in order. We could worry about the hangover in the morning. It was time to celebrate tonight.

Earlier that afternoon, Jim Kossler, my coordinating supervisor, had walked into my office and announced, "Frankie, it's done—the grand jury just returned sealed indictments."

I couldn't believe it was finally happening. We planned to arrest the five Mafia bosses at 8:00 a.m. the following morning. After the arrests, United States Attorney Rudy Giuliani and FBI Director William Webster had scheduled a noon press conference. We were anticipating national media coverage. Everything seemed to be in place—or so I thought. Suddenly, events began to turn seriously in the wrong direction.

Around 5:30 p.m., Kossler returned to my office with a worried look and blurted out, "The damn press knows about the indictments."

"What?" I dropped the file I had been reading and stared at him in disbelief. "What the fuck!" I jumped to my feet. "How did this happen?"

The leak certainly did not come from our office, as only a few knew the indictments had been returned. This was not good. If one or more of the subjects indicted became aware of a public announcement of their fate, they could flee and we would lose the opportunity to seize potential evidence incidental to their arrests. Kossler was waiting for me to make a decision. I told him to call the supervisors immediately to alert their agents. We were going to take the bosses down tonight.

I angrily stalked into the office of Tom Sheer, Special Agent in Charge (SAC) of the Criminal Division, to whom I directly reported. As soon as Tom heard of the latest developments, he agreed that we should proceed immediately. Tom said he would call US Attorney Rudy Giuliani and advise him that we had to make our move tonight due to a possible leak to the press. He also intended to call Bill Baker at headquarters, who would be coordinating a national press release and accompany the director to New York the next day. At this point, our press officer, Joe Valiquette, had not received any inquiries from the press.

The agents executed the arrest warrants that night without incident, and within a couple of hours, all the Mafia bosses were in custody. Anthony "Fat Tony" Salerno, the boss of the Genovese family, faked a heart attack on the way to the federal lockup, but after a quick check by medical staff, he found himself in an uncomfortable cell. We advised headquarters of our action and they confirmed that the director would fly up in the morning for a noon press conference with Guiliani. The director hoped to meet with the supervisors privately and a few agents assigned to the investigation, if his schedule permitted.

Later that evening, I left my office and saw Kossler in the hallway. Sheer was also leaving, and after greeting us, we walked together to the elevator that would take us to the garage twenty-seven floors below. We did not say much to one another as we rode down those many floors to the basement. We were just worn out. The elevator doors opened and we began to walk toward our cars.

Sheer suddenly turned and remarked, "Do you realize what we accomplished today?" I stared at him for a moment, too exhausted to reply. He then nodded and, with a smile on his face, quietly said, "See you tomorrow."

We had just arrested the leaders of the New York Mafia, and it all seemed like just another day on the job. I began driving home, reviewing the day's events. It was not just another day on the job. The arrests were the culmination of diligent and, at times, dangerous work by so many dedicated agents, the game changers who took down the Mafia. I had traveled a long road to arrive at this moment and started to ponder how all this began.

CHAPTER 2
The New Recruit

My journey in the FBI began in 1962 when I was a sophomore at La Salle College in Philadelphia. To stay enrolled, I had to have a steady income to help pay tuition. I took the bus one day into the city and visited several banks with the hope that they might hire college students to work in the evening. None of the banks seemed interested, and I began meandering down Broad Street, feeling somewhat rejected, heading for the bus depot. A thought suddenly occurred to me. A classmate had mentioned that his father played golf with an FBI agent who worked in Philadelphia. The agent had stated that if his son ever needed part-time work while attending college, to let him know, as the FBI hired students.

As I continued walking, I saw a police officer directing traffic at the corner of Broad and Chestnut Streets. On impulse, I approached the officer and asked if he knew the location of the FBI office. He stared at me with a puzzled look and wondered what I was up to.

He abruptly responded, "It's right there in the Widener Building," as he pointed his baton toward a building on Chestnut Street. I walked to the building's lobby without wasting a moment and noted that the directory listed the FBI office on the fifth floor. Unsure of my next move, I jumped on the elevator.

I entered the office and the official nature of the reception area caused me to pause. Our country's flag was proudly displayed in the corner of the room, with a large FBI seal on the wall depicting the words: FIDELITY, BRAVERY, INTEGRITY. The entire room had been paneled in dark mahogany. I approached the receptionist and she pleasantly greeted me.

"Hello, my name is Mary. How can I help you?"

I nervously responded, mumbling about being in college and coming into town looking for a job. Mary smiled and commented, "The FBI does hire college students to work odd shifts to handle administrative duties."

She handed me an application and a brochure about the FBI. I thanked her several times, went home, and completed the application. I mailed it the next day, never expecting a response. I knew nothing about the FBI besides media references or a television drama about a sensational case they solved.

The document was very detailed and probed into your background and education. A pointed question surprised me: "Have you ever been arrested?" I had to answer yes, as I had been arrested just a few months before. I could explain the arrest. It was a simple disturbance of the peace incident at a neighborhood school.

A number of us had bought a case of beer on a hot August night and were hanging out drinking the cold beer. Naturally, we got a little boisterous. The school custodian called the police, who hauled us away to the local precinct. They did not charge us with any crime, and we were all released after a stern lecture from the sergeant on duty.

A few weeks passed, and I had not heard from the FBI and wondered if the arrest would affect my chances of employment. One afternoon, FBI Agent Bill Naylor called and requested that I come into the office for an interview. I was surprised, excited, and apprehensive all at once.

Agent Naylor greeted me in the reception room when I arrived at the office the following week. As we wandered through the hallways, I noticed several gambling tables and equipment lining the walls. He saw my inquisitive look and commented, "We had several raids last night at illegal gambling locations throughout the city." This impressed me.

As we began the interview, he leaned back in his chair and commented, "Tell me about this big arrest you mentioned in your application." I rambled on about it being "a hot summer night and we were just hanging out, and things got out of hand."

He said, "We know all about it. We interviewed the arresting police officer." This comment caught me off guard, but he did not elaborate. The interview lasted about an hour, and he appeared very interested in how I perceived current events and the political landscape. I freely offered my opinions on various topics, and it seemed to be a good exchange.

He concluded the interview by simply saying, "I will be in touch."

Within a few weeks, a few of our neighbors contacted my mother and said the "FBI was in the neighborhood checking up on Frank" and wanted to know if I was in trouble. Agent Naylor called within a couple of weeks and offered me an administrative position working the four-to-twelve shift, which I immediately accepted. I reported for work two weeks later. Two additional employees were assigned to this shift, and an agent was also on duty to respond to criminal complaints.

Over the next year or so, I enjoyed the position and was able to keep up with my studies. Although the job severely reduced my social schedule, I felt fortunate to have this opportunity. At this point, I still had yet to decide if I wanted to apply for the position of special agent when I graduated. I enrolled in accounting courses at La Salle and entertained the thought of pursuing a law degree. However, the events on November 22, 1963 convinced me otherwise.

On that dreaded day, around 1:30 p.m., I had just left the college library and was walking to my car. I had intended to stop at home for lunch before reporting to work. I suddenly noticed a friend driving toward me in front of the main entrance to the campus in an erratic manner. He brought the car to a screeching halt and shouted, "Frank, they just shot Kennedy!"

I will never forget those words. For some reason, I began running to my car. I don't know why—where was I going? I started the car, turned on the radio, and headed toward the Schuylkill Expressway.

What had just happened? This couldn't be true. The news from Dallas was not good. The president had been shot while riding in a motorcade with his wife, Jackie. They had rushed him to the hospital, with his condition still not known. For a moment, I felt relieved and prayed that he had not suffered severe wounds. I robotically worked my way down the expressway, concentrating solely on the voices on the radio. It soon became apparent that the president had been seriously wounded, as they reported that two priests had arrived at the hospital.

Within minutes, they announced the president had been pronounced dead. I almost lost control of the car. I could not drive any further, so I pulled over to the side of the expressway and wept. I wept for the president and his family, but I also wept for the country. At that time, I did not know what the ramifications of the assassination meant. Gaining my composure, I proceeded to the FBI office, thinking I might be of some help. The agents and staff would be reacting to the assassination, and I suspected that some investigation would be in progress and they would need administrative support.

I reported to my supervisor, Bill Phillips, who seemed surprised to see me. I usually did not report for work until much later in the afternoon. Phillips seemed upset and not himself. He pointed to the door and told me, "Report to Hartenstein and his squad—they've got the ticket."

As I later found out, two college professors who were employed at a Philadelphia university had a relationship with Marina Oswald, the wife of the alleged assassin Lee Harvey Oswald. The agents had to flush out the details of that connection. Throughout the evening, other support personnel and I handled administrative duties to assist the agents in their investigation. Teletypes were coming in from headquarters and Dallas all night, advising field offices of updates and requesting that leads be covered.

It was incredible how quickly the FBI sprang into action in response to the assassination. Everyone went about their assignments with an eerie and compelling sense of purpose. The agents' dedication and focus convinced me that the FBI would get the answers to this tragedy. Agents approached their assignments as if they were in the military serving their country. You could sense that being a special agent was not just another job. To them, it was more than that. How they approached the assassination investigation clearly demonstrated to me how they felt.

I did not leave work until four o'clock the following morning. The agents completed their work over the weekend and assembled their findings in a report, which I mailed to Dallas and FBI headquarters the following Monday evening. What I witnessed that day and evening convinced me I wanted to make the FBI my career.

While working the four-to-twelve shift, I had the opportunity to develop casual relationships with the agents who, on many occasions, were still out on the street working cases. Friday nights were always busy, since, for whatever reason, a bank robbery always seemed to occur. I would respond to their radio transmissions if they needed assistance or requested that I call their wives and inform them their husbands would be home late. Occasionally, they would arrest a suspect and escort him to the office for interrogation. Several squads of agents handled different types of crime, but one particularly fascinated me. It was the organized crime squad led by Supervisor David Breen.

Breen was a World War II veteran and a former Marine. He also had graduated from La Salle College and was a down-to-earth guy. His squad comprised a great group of agents whom, over time, I got to know personally. They often worked at night surveilling local Mafia members. Angelo Bruno, head of the Philadelphia Mafia family, was their primary target, along with his top associates. They appeared to be compiling intelligence information about the family's activities.

Almost daily, Agent J.R. Pearce would hand me a sealed manila envelope to be mailed to a particular unit at FBI headquarters. On one occasion, Agent Pearce told me, "Frank, I don't know why we keep sending this down to DC, because Hoover does not believe there is a Mafia. We have the evidence to prove it, but headquarters ignores the obvious." I could sense the frustration in his voice, but of course I did not know the facts that led him to that conclusion. Sometimes, the agents would develop sufficient evidence to arrest an individual member, but Bruno was never arrested. My experiences interacting with the agents reinforced my desire to apply for the special agent position. Breen's squad had a sense of camaraderie and purpose, which jumped out at me.

Over the next several months, I anxiously waited to take a series of tests to be considered for the special agent position. Time passed and I could think of nothing else but being notified that I was eligible. An applicant had to be at least twenty-three years of age. That day was approaching, and finally I was allowed to take the exams. As the weeks passed, I was still in limbo, waiting for the results. One afternoon, I was notified to report to the SAC (Special Agent in Charge), Joe Jamieson. This was highly unusual. As I nervously wandered through the hallways toward his office, I sensed this could only mean one thing. When I was escorted into his office, he stood behind his desk with Supervisor Breen.

Mr. Jamieson handed me a sealed envelope and said, "Congratulations, Frank."

I ripped open the envelope. It was my appointment letter for a position as a special agent in the FBI. As I read the letter, I became speechless. The whole idea of actually becoming a special agent seemed surreal at that moment. I thanked Mr. Jamieson, shook Dave's congratulatory hand, and stumbled out the door.

I had only two weeks to get my things in order. My last day in Philadelphia was fast approaching. The FBI Training Academy was at the Marine Corps Base in Quantico, Virginia. My wife Doris intended to move in with her father until my training was completed.

On my final day, many employees I had worked with these past three years gathered to give me a send-off. They also gave me a nice leather suitcase with a handwritten note on the front, *Quantico or Bust*. I choked up a bit, which was quite noticeable. Frankly, I was still overwhelmed by the appointment. Breen was there and invited me for a drink after work at the bar in the basement of the building. It was their place to unwind after a tough day.

Dave had previously been a new agents counselor at Quantico and was in charge of a class of newly recruited agents. He was on track for an executive position, but when he learned one of his parents had become seriously ill, he requested a transfer to Philadelphia. The Bureau was compassionate in these types of personal concerns and would honor a hardship transfer request by an agent if possible. Dave took me aside and gave me a quick overview of what to expect during my training. As a counselor, he spent all his time with the agents' class he was assigned to and guided them through their training.

As I left the bar that night, he gave me a few additional words of advice: "Frank, keep your head down and your mouth shut, and you will be fine."

I did not sleep all night—how could I? I had to be in room 5231 at the Department of Justice to be sworn in as an FBI agent at 9:00 a.m. It would be my first day of training and the start of my new career. The anticipation and nervousness were suffocating. I was lying in bed in a room on the fifth floor of the Hotel Harrington in downtown Washington, staring at the ceiling at 1:00 a.m. The room did not have a TV that worked. I finally dozed off after reading the Sunday paper for the third time.

I went out the door at 7:00 the following morning and after having a quick breakfast, I was on my way to be sworn in. Within minutes, I arrived at the Department of Justice, only two blocks from the hotel. The serenity and vastness of the building struck me. There were so many corridors and people moving about that I had to pause momentarily to get my bearings. A security guard approached and after asking me for some identification, he directed me to the fifth floor. Several other men began congregating outside room 5231, and we all moved inside cautiously, glancing at one another.

There were nineteen of us, and specific seats had already been assigned alphabetically. An FBI official entered the room and introduced himself as Joseph Casper, assistant director in charge of the training division. He instructed us to raise our right hand, and we were sworn in as probationary special agents of the FBI. Our group was designated New Agents Class Number 14. At this point, another official, George Benjamin, entered the room and introduced himself as our class counselor. He had a self-assured demeanor with a broad smile. He told us to take a deep breath and relax.

"This is going to be easy," he said. I needed some assurance, as I felt very unsure of myself. The group comprised eighteen white males and an Asian American, Calvin Shishido. At the time, the FBI did not hire women, and there were very few black or Hispanic agents in the Bureau. We took turns introducing ourselves. Many of the men in our class were veterans, lawyers, or accountants. Their average age was about thirty. I was the youngest at twenty-three, had no worldly experience to offer, and felt out of place. Did I belong here? The day was spent reviewing administrative matters, filling out forms, and discussing what was expected of us during the training period. After we were dismissed for the day, we boarded a bus and headed to the Marine Corps base for fourteen weeks of training.

Over the next several weeks, we studied manuals and regulations in the classroom and there were many presentations by FBI officials. I had no issue with this phase; my problem was learning to fire a weapon accurately. I almost did not make the cut, as I had the distinction of being the poorest shot in the class. I had to undergo individual training with a firearm. The head firearms instructor, George Zeiss, who stood at least six foot six and had a bellowing voice, joked one day on the range in front of my fellow recruits. "We'll have to issue Storey a machine gun to wear on his hip. It seems he cannot hit the broad side of a barn." I didn't find his remarks humorous, but you didn't argue with George Zeiss. I eventually qualified and shot a respectable score on the firing range.

There was one final bridge to cross. As a class, we had to gather outside J. Edgar Hoover's office and greet him personally. We formed a line outside his office according to our height. Being the shortest class member, I would lead the parade. There had been rumors that this could be trickier than it appeared. Clyde Tolson, the deputy director, allegedly would lurk somewhere in the room, focusing on each of us as we passed to greet Mr. Hoover. If he had some issue with your appearance, he would reportedly make a comment to Hoover. Not knowing if this was true or not, we knew it didn't matter. The rumor was enough to put us all on edge.

The procession began and I walked straight up to Mr. Hoover and quickly said, "Frank Storey, sir, pleased to meet you." Hoover nodded his head but did not respond. We were all in and out in less than two minutes without repercussions. If Tolson was in his office, I would not have noticed.

Upon graduation, I was ordered to report to a five-man resident agency in Asheville, North Carolina. As the state was so huge, several smaller offices had been established statewide and reported to our headquarters in Charlotte. Agents assigned to Asheville covered ten counties, and I was assigned to investigate cases in Marion and Rutherford. As a first-office agent, less complicated cases were usually assigned to me until I acquired enough experience. The territory was rural and Asheville was a small, sleepy little town in a dry county. The topography, of course, was beautiful, as we were located in the Blue Ridge Mountains. Two memorable events occurred during my assignment. My firstborn son Trip arrived and a bloodhound named Lulabelle helped us capture three bank robbers.

It was a scorching summer day and I had been on the job less than a year. I had an applicant investigation in Rutherford County, a long distance from Asheville. A young man was being considered for a government position. An urgent transmission came across my car radio from headquarters that a bank had been robbed in the town of Ellenboro, and I was ordered to report to the bank immediately. I proceeded to the bank as fast as the 1964 Ford I drove would allow me.

As I pulled up to the bank, Agent George Wilson came running out and shouted, "A possible getaway car has been found on a dirt road about two miles out of town! Get out there right away!" Wilson had arrived at the bank first and assumed supervision of the investigation. Another first office agent, Jim Dunn from Charlotte, also had responded to the bank robbery. We proceeded directly to the site of the abandoned car. The only description of the bank robbers available indicated we were searching for three white males driving a white Chevrolet and armed with a shotgun. When Dunn and I arrived at the location where the car had been abandoned, we observed a white Chevy parked off the side of the road.

A nearby resident informed us, "I saw three men run into those woods from that car." Deputy Sherrif Gene Biggerstaff from the Rutherford County Sheriff's Office soon arrived.

We brought Biggerstaff up to date. He immediately stated, "I will call the prison farm and request that a trainer and bloodhound be sent to the scene." A truck soon arrived, the trainer opened the back, and Lulabelle, a bloodhound, jumped out. He walked Lulabelle to the car and she immediately began leading the four of us toward a relatively dense wooded area.

The trainer turned to us and said, "She has picked up their scent."

A clearing with a narrow creek running through the terrain

could be seen a short distance away. Freshly made footprints were visible in the sand along the creek, and it appeared the bank robbers had made a sharp turn upstream. As we continued for about a quarter of a mile, I noticed that the trainer began to trot to keep up with Lulabelle, who increased her gait as she plowed through the brush.

The trainer suddenly yelled, "Look, there they are!"

I saw three white males running about fifty yards ahead of us. Our pace quickened and I drew my gun as we began the chase. Seconds later, I stumbled to the ground, but thankfully, my gun did not discharge. I immediately got to my feet and pursued the robbers. My heart was pounding; I had no time to think. Within seconds, one of the robbers also fell to the ground and Dunn quickly handcuffed him. The second robber soon surrendered and we secured him in cuffs. However, the third bank robber with the shotgun hid behind a tree. I stood firm about fifteen yards from the tree with my gun drawn, along with Biggerstaff. Things were happening so fast that I had to rely on my training and instincts. Dunn was guarding the other two bank robbers.

We began barking commands for the third suspect to surrender, but he did not budge. I shouted every expletive I could imagine while ordering him to come out, but he still did not move. I cannot remember what commands came out of my mouth; I was that scared. Biggerstaff became impatient and fired two or three shots, which bounced off the tree. If the bank robber came out with the shotgun drawn on us, I would have shot him. He decided otherwise, threw the shotgun to the ground, and surrendered. The whole encounter could not have lasted more than a few minutes. It was a long walk back to the road where other agents and state police officers had gathered. The press was also present and began taking pictures. I was exhausted and just wanted to sit down and rest.

I turned to Dunn and asked, "Jim, what the hell happened back there?" He paused for a moment and responded, "I have no fucking idea." We then parted and unfortunately, I never had the opportunity to work with him again. Reflecting on this event while driving back to Asheville, I realized this was a "what-if" moment. When I arrived home, I did not go into much detail about what had occurred that day. Doris was seven months pregnant and I did not want to upset her.

The next day, the local media ran a front-page story of the event, as Ellenboro had never had a bank robbery take place. The headline appropriately read: LULABELLE CAPTURES BANK ROBBERS. I kept the newspaper clipping for many years, but it has been misplaced. I have told this story to my kids and grandkids on many occasions. They loved to hear about Lulabelle. While a close call, this event had a happy ending and I was glad Lulabelle was there that day. Shortly afterward, a transfer letter arrived from headquarters and I was headed to Gary, Indiana, and assigned to work on organized crime cases.

CHAPTER 3
Gary, Indiana

Gary had a reputation for having a high crime rate, a corrupt political machine, and a poor law enforcement presence. It bordered Chicago, Illinois, the home of United States Steel. Our office occupied the first floor of a federal building only half a mile from the steel plant. There were only a few good neighborhoods in the immediate area. Since I could not afford to buy a home in the suburbs, we were able to locate an excellent rental that would do for the time being. I knew nothing about organized crime or the Mafia, so I had much to learn as I started my new assignment.

Agents Bob Johnson and Orville Watts had been assigned to the program for several years. Johnson drove me around town and gave me an overview of the criminal problems in Gary. I noted that the city had very few office buildings or commercial businesses as we drove through the downtown area. It appeared run-down and in need of serious upgrading. In some of the areas, I observed open prostitution houses on Washington Avenue, with prostitutes standing in the doorways in broad daylight, beckoning us as we drove past. I mean, the solicitations were wide open. We then drove further down Washington and observed several bars, such as the Venus Café and Frisco Tavern.

Bob mentioned that they were all controlled by the Greek Mob and only employed white prostitutes. He also indicated that the

Chicago Mafia controlled all organized crime–related activities in Lake County, comprising three cities: Gary, East Chicago, and Hammond.

After our little tour, I asked Johnson, "What the hell is going on here? I never saw anything like this."

Bob shrugged his shoulders and replied, "What can I say? It's been this way for a long time." There was a lot to take in on the first day.

I noticed Bob didn't discuss any arrests they had made. He had a vast knowledge of the organization's workings, but that was all he had to offer. He did not mention any pending investigations or the overall plan to combat this type of criminal activity. On the other hand, Orville had a few cases he appeared to be actively working on but, for some reason, would not discuss them. I realized I would have to go it alone; there would be no tutoring period.

Orville suggested we visit the US Attorney's Office in Hammond. Two federal prosecutors were assigned to this office. They made prosecutorial decisions on our investigation and determined if there was enough evidence to make an arrest. One of the attorneys, Frank Kimbrough, was recently assigned to the office, so he and I had something in common. He was around my age and appeared to approach his work aggressively.

He had a warm greeting, "Welcome aboard, Frank." I liked that—he would be my go-to guy. Orville then gave me a quick tour of the area and pointed out several locations, which he described as illegal gambling operations that had been in existence for quite some time. He cautioned me, "Frank, you cannot trust the police." Hammond bordered Calumet City, Illinois, which was also wide open to organized crime–related activity and had little law enforcement oversight. The tour of Hammond was beneficial.

I reviewed the intelligence that had been accumulated through previous analysis. Frank Zizzo, a reputed member of the Chicago Mafia, was their representative who oversaw all illegal activities in Lake County. He was assisted by Angelo Cardinale, also known as Andy Raymond. Zizzo owned the Pepper Pot Pizza located on a main road just south of downtown. Cardinale operated from a pool hall on Broadway Avenue, just a few blocks from our office. He also ran a high-stakes Greek dice game called *barbotte* in East Chicago. They were the two principal Chicago Mafia representatives who controlled Lake County.

After doing independent research and poring over some files, my first thought was, *Where do I start?* Even to a newcomer, it was apparent that the Mafia was making a lucrative profit from illegal gambling operations in Gary and Hammond without any concern that local or federal law enforcement authorities would shut them down. What existing federal statutes could be applied to investigate this illegal activity?

The Interstate Travel in Aid of Racketeering Act was passed by Congress in 1961 at the urging of Attorney General Robert Kennedy to provide law enforcement with the means to investigate organized crime. The act made it unlawful for an individual traveling in interstate commerce to engage in an illegal activity, such as operating a gambling establishment. This law might be the vehicle we needed to investigate the many bookmaking operations in Hammond, which bordered Illinois. This entire process was new to me, as investigating organized crime had not been mentioned during our training. I would have to take this one step at a time and learn my craft on the job.

One of the locations Orville pointed out on our tour was an alleged illegal bookmaking operation run by Paul Erlenbaugh, located not far from the federal courthouse. The location was on the first floor of an older building. An open parking lot was adjacent to the structure, enabling us to observe those entering and leaving. So, what was the plan? If possible, we could develop an informant to verify that illegal activities were taking place. The option of sending an undercover agent or cooperative witness into the location to observe the illicit activity could also be considered. This would enable us to obtain a search warrant and seize evidence of an illegal bookmaking operation. This could lead to possible indictments and shutting down the operation.

I opened an investigation on Erlenbaugh under the new anti-racketeering law. As his operation was located so close to the Illinois state line, there was a possibility that he or his employees were traveling in interstate commerce. I elicited the support of agent Ed Jenkins and we began conducting frequent surveillance of the location. A pattern emerged that seemed unusual. An elderly man driving a car with an Illinois license plate showed up frequently at Erlenbaugh's location, and we observed him leaving and returning a short time later several times during the day. His car was registered to Ralph Hugo Meiswinkel at an address in Calumet City. As he left the parking lot one morning, we followed Meiswinkel to a pool hall run by another bookmaker named Ray Goodman. He stayed but a few minutes and returned to Erlenbaugh's location.

Jenkins, who had more experience, suspected that "Meiswinkel was a runner for Erlenbaugh and was likely furnishing betting odds to Goodman, who was part of Erlenbaugh's operation." He believed that Erlenbaugh must have had access to a third party who was directly giving him the odds, and he then relayed them to Goodman through Meiswinkel. As our investigation discovered, Ed was right.

Late one afternoon, I drove by Meiswinkel's home in Calumet City and observed his car in the driveway. A search of the city directory and a check with the utility companies established that he lived there. Meiswinkel, an employee of Erlenbaugh, was traveling in interstate commerce to facilitate an illegal gambling operation.

The bookmaking activity appeared wide open, with customers entering freely without a doorman serving as a lookout. One of the agents assigned to the office agreed to work undercover and attempt to enter the location to make bets, which he did successfully.

He reported that the bookmaking operation "took in large

amounts of cash." We were also able to repeat the same scenario at Goodman's location. Meiswinkel had been accepting what appeared to be betting slips from Goodman, which tied him directly into the Erlenbaugh operation. I met with prosecutor Kimbrough, and he drafted a search warrant for both locations.

I had never executed a search warrant before and was unsure how this would all turn out. We had a team of eight agents and assumed that Erlenbaugh and his employees would be uncooperative. He usually had a man at the door to check on customers attempting to enter. We approached the front door with some hesitation just before three in the afternoon, as the racetracks had been open for several hours. I reached for the door handle and shouted, "FBI, we have a warrant! Do not move!" Thankfully, the door was not locked and we were all inside in seconds. We met no resistance. Simultaneously, Jenkins and his team successfully executed a search warrant at Goodman's location.

The searches resulted in the seizure of thousands of dollars in cash and extensive records, establishing that both operations were lucrative. Meiswinkel agreed to testify and the subjects were eventually prosecuted and convicted but received probationary sentences, which we expected. I felt empathy toward Meiswinkel, as he—in a way—had just gotten caught up in the web of our investigation. More than likely, he was only trying to make some extra money to augment his monthly Social Security check. We never had any intention of prosecuting him. For Erlenbaugh and Goodman to operate, they had to pay a percentage of their earnings to Mafia representative Frank Zizzo. He was our real target, the first step in confronting his criminal enterprise in Lake County.

I learned much from this initial investigation. It provided me with a framework on how to investigate illegal bookmaking activities. We identified similar operations in both Gary and Hammond. With the support of several agents in the office, we made a significant number of arrests for interstate gambling violations, but this highlighted an obvious deeper problem. The gambling networks had been in business for so long that the players we arrested were quickly replaced. Zizzo was still in charge, running the operations with impunity. This became frustrating, as our investigative approach did not end the criminal activity. We then turned our sights on Zizzo.

Zizzo spent most of his time at the Pepper Pot Pizza but did not run the business; it was all a front. I would drive by the location periodically and observe known bookmakers and suspected organized crime figures parked in the driveway or entering the restaurant. I surmised they were meeting with Zizzo. I checked on his background further and determined he was on federal parole, which stipulated that he could not associate with members of the criminal element. My plan was simple: All agents love pizza, so why not send them into the restaurant to have some on me? We had authorized funds available to cover the expenses.

I ran my idea by a few guys: "Does anybody want to eat free pizza on me?" They quickly responded, "Count me in." Over a month or so, we made numerous sightings in the restaurant, establishing that Zizzo was meeting with criminals we could positively identify. I contacted the federal parole official for our region and advised him of our findings. A formal hearing was subsequently held, and I testified regarding the details outlined in the report I had prepared. As I did so, Zizzo sat about fifteen feet from where I was sitting and never took his eyes off me. If looks could kill, I would not be writing this account.

The federal parole board declared that Zizzo was in violation of his parole and sent him back to federal prison to serve the remainder of his sentence. We all thought this was a significant accomplishment; however, it did not negatively impact organized crime activities in the region. The illegal enterprise continued, and the Chicago Mob quickly appointed Angelo Cardinale to oversee its operations. This experience left an impression on me. We arrest one boss and another quickly replaces him; nothing changes. My conclusion led me to believe there must be a better way to address this situation.

In 1968, politics played a role in reducing the threat the Mafia represented. That year, a young attorney, Richard G. Hatcher, announced his candidacy for the office of mayor of Gary. He was a primary challenger against the incumbent Democratic mayor, A. Martin Katz. He won the nomination and was running against the Republican nominee, Joseph Radigan. Lake County had been controlled politically by the Democratic Party for years, and the current chairman, John Krupa, called all the shots. Krupa advised Hatcher that the party would only support him if he could select the next chief of police, city attorney, and other essential administrators. Hatcher refused to negotiate with Krupa. Krupa would not take no for an answer and began a series of moves to neutralize Hatcher. He began supporting the candidacy of Radigan, which was unprecedented politically.

We believed that one of the vehicles the Mafia implemented to control illegal activities in Lake County was their ability to compromise government officials responsible for enforcing local and state laws. Angelo Cardinale and his confederates did not want to see Hatcher win. He had vowed that if elected, he would close the red-light district on Washington Avenue and shut down all illegal gambling operations. Our informants had told us Cardinale intended to support Krupa in his attempts to elect Radigan. Both groups joined forces and vowed to resort to whatever means necessary to accomplish their objective. Hatcher and his team filed a civil rights complaint with the Department of Justice, alleging acts of voting fraud and voter intimidation on the part of the Krupa machine.

Within days, a Department of Justice attorney arrived at our office and informed us that the FBI would be the lead agency in investigating Hatcher's complaint. For several weeks, all the agents assigned to the office worked day and night, tracking down leads related to extortion, bribery, and outright voter fraud allegations to sway the election in Radigan's favor. There was no indication that Radigan was aware of or part of this scheme. He enjoyed a stellar reputation. All attempts to steal the election failed and

Hatcher barely won by 2,000 votes. Hatcher would keep his campaign promise. He appointed a chief of police who adopted a no-nonsense policy, shut down the red-light district, and ran the bookmakers out of town. Hatcher would remain in office for the next twenty years. There was, however, one more bell to answer: Angelo Cardinale. He was now our number one target.

We intended to penetrate Cardinale's barbotte dice game in East Chicago. We had an informant, a regular and trusted player who had suffered considerable losses and owed Cardinale a lot of money. He could not pay and had been threatened by a couple of enforcers who worked for Cardinale, and he was naturally concerned about his safety. He agreed to cross the line, become a cooperative witness, and introduce one of our agents to the game as a player.

Headquarters approved a budget for the operation, but we had a limit on how much we could spend. The game was usually held on the weekend at an isolated building near the East Chicago police department. We were sure the department knew of the game's existence and might even provide some protection for the operation. It was not open to the general public. This assignment for our undercover agent was tricky and his safety was our biggest concern. I insisted he wear a body recorder so we could monitor his movements. If he encountered a problem, we would make immediate entry.

We first had to acquaint the agent with the game itself. It was simple, but he had never played it before. Our informant had advised that one of the dealers was from Calumet City, and a limo driver would bring players from Chicago to the game. It was played in very few locations in the area. The agent we selected was brought up from Indianapolis, as we wanted to avoid the risk of one of the players identifying any of our agents assigned to the office in Gary. Late one Saturday night, we were ready to make our first move.

The informant accompanying the agent was well-known to Cardinale's people. As they entered the location, we listened in over the wire and were somewhat concerned by the doorman's reaction to our undercover agent: "Who the fuck is this guy?" Not a warm welcome. The informant handled it well and our guy was accepted. The agent made all the necessary observations we needed and won $500 his first night. After his second entry was successful, we were ready to move and obtain the necessary search warrant.

We intended to execute the warrant when the informant and agent were present to draw suspicion away from them temporarily. They would also be our eyes and ears if we had difficulty entering, which was precisely what happened. At 1:00 a.m. on a Sunday, we gathered a team of ten agents and were ready to take down the door to enter, as we knew Cardinale and his associates would not welcome us with open arms. We were also concerned that the game operators might be armed due to the high stakes being wagered.

East Chicago was usually a bitterly cold place during the winter. Most establishments had an outer storm door protecting the main entrance. The lead agent in our raiding party had a sledgehammer and, in an anxious moment, slammed it into the outer door, the inner panel of which was glass. It shattered into a thousand pieces and caused a severe wound to his hand, which had to be attended to immediately. We escorted the agent off to the side of the building and called for an ambulance. At the same time, the remaining team members took down the main door, entered the game, and executed the warrant without incident. A few women who were attendees became hysterical and began to scream, but everyone else, including Cardinale, just froze. Several of the players were belligerent and uncooperative. The agents would take none of that and forcefully let them know if they kept it up, their "asses would be hauled off to jail for obstructing justice." They got the message and we were out of there. Over $25,000 was seized during the raid. The barbotte game was history and so was Cardinale.

* * *

Although each agent assigned to our office usually worked a specific type of federal crime, it was "all hands on deck" when an event required the entire office to mobilize. Such was the case with the kidnapping of little Sarah. Two individuals whom we later found out were heavily in debt due to their chronic gambling debts had borrowed considerable funds from loan sharks. They could not make the excessive interest payments. They feared reprisals by the organized crime network in Gary and out of desperation, they kidnapped Sarah. A telephone call to our office was received from a frantic mother that her baby girl Sarah had been abducted. The kidnappers had been in touch with the child's father, who was a local businessman, and a ransom demand had been made. The father had determined that at least two kidnappers were involved and a woman was guarding the child. He was reluctant to notify the FBI, as he feared for his daughter's life and wanted to pay the ransom.

We sat down with the father and advised him we would discreetly follow him to the site where he had been instructed to leave the ransom. He was naturally nervous and seemed reluctant to cooperate fully. He just wanted the ordeal to be over. A ransom package was assembled and the father left for the site drop. We initiated our surveillance and had agents in a surveillance plane able to observe the entire landscape.

The ensuing movements were difficult to control. The father began to take evasive action to avoid our surveillance and wanted to meet the kidnappers on his own. We thus had to be more aggressive in our surveillance movements, as we did not want to lose sight of him. He suddenly pulled into a strip mall and approached two males standing by a pay phone. I heard the words "Goddamn it" come over the radio from one of the agents. This was not our plan. Unfortunately, the suspects noticed our surveillance vehicles and began to flee the area. We had to move in right away and arrest both individuals. But we had a problem. The two kidnappers were in custody, but we did not have Sarah.

At times like this, you have to make adjustments. There was no point in formally interviewing the subjects and reading them their Miranda rights. We were only interested in one thing: Where was Sarah? At that moment, we demanded, as forcibly as legally possible, that they tell us of her location. One of the subjects began to swear at us, but his partner had the fear of God in his eyes, so we walked him to the other end of the parking lot.

He instantly blurted out, "I will tell you everything, just let me go." He told us of the general neighborhood where they left the child in a house with their woman accomplice, but he did not have an address. We had no intention of letting him go anywhere.

We then began a block-to-block grid search requiring us to knock on every door. Chuck Keenan and I were assigned to cover a three-block area, and we searched with a sense of urgency. We were fearful that the woman who had the child would panic when her two associates did not return with the ransom money. Keenan and I frantically knocked on the doors of at least fifty homes and came up with no leads, and then it suddenly happened: Just like that, we got our break.

A young woman responded to our fifty-first knock and told us she had seen "a woman with a baby in the house across the street." She thought this was "highly unusual, as the house was up for sale, and the owners had already moved." The woman showed up yesterday with the baby and was dropped off by a man she did not know. The man left, but the woman felt the baby may still be in the house.

Keenan and I briskly moved toward the house across the street and drew our weapons. Keenan peered around the side of the house and said, "All clear." I remained by the front door. There was total silence in the house and no movement of any kind. We were both concerned that if the suspect was in the house, she may have observed us talking to the witness across the street.

I whispered to Chuck, "We got to go in; we can't wait. Let's kick the fucking door down and move fast." We had no idea where the hell the other agents were. We still had our guns drawn and were ready to move. My heart was pounding, unsure of what we would find behind the door. Keenan stood back and hit the door with his right foot with everything he had. The door sprung open, but the glass frame exploded into tiny pieces.

I heard a little girl scream. It was a piercing sound that echoed in my ears. As we raced inside, I prayed that the flying pieces of glass had not harmed the little girl. I saw the helpless two-year-old standing in the middle of the living room, crying her eyes out. She was no older than my daughter Karen Elizabeth. I holstered my weapon, quickly scooped her into my arms, and headed for the front door. I still didn't know if the suspect was in the house. Chuck covered me as we made our exit. I guarded Sarah with my body. The woman across the street had notified the police of our presence and they soon arrived. I handed Sarah to one of the arriving police officers. She was immediately taken to the hospital for an examination and a reunion with her parents. The woman who guarded Sarah was captured a short time later.

The next day, upon reflection, I began to wonder. If the two kidnappers had not been chronic gamblers who had to borrow money from organized crime loan sharks, this kidnapping might have never happened. Who knows? This was a harrowing experience, one that I will never forget. I think of Sarah occasionally and wonder where she is today. I hope she is okay and has led a good life.

My tour in Gary was winding down. We had a new addition to the family: Karen Elizabeth had arrived.

Headquarters soon ordered me to report to New Orleans, the home of the Marcello Mafia family.

CHAPTER 4
The Big Easy

After a long trip, our family arrived in New Orleans. The kids were grumpy and hungry and had been in the car for hours. Traveling like this was rough on them. I cannot remember how often Trip asked, "Daddy, are we there yet?" We checked into a Holiday Inn and after settling down and ordering room service, I turned on the TV to catch up on the news.

A group of eight politicians were on a stage arguing over who would be the next governor of the State of Louisiana. I was unaware of any governor's race that ever had eight candidates. This struck me as odd—why was there such interest in that position? I would get the answer to my question much later. The next day, we found temporary quarters until we could move into our new home.

I reported to the office for my assignment and sat down with my supervisor, Assistant Special Agent in Charge Joseph Sylvester. He immediately impressed me as a throwback to the FBI of the past. He dressed as they did in the 1940s, with a five-button vest, a gold link watch chain on his side, and a blue-striped narrow lapel suit. I thought momentarily that he resembled Eliot Ness from the TV series *The Untouchables*. (The actor Robert Stack.) I was very impressed. He had a warm, friendly manner, and I immediately liked him. He walked me out to the squad area, and I met Agents Tom Duhadway and Dick Voyles, who welcomed me. We went to lunch after I got settled, and they gave me a short overview of the issues they were facing with the Carlos Marcello crime family. It was a good beginning.

Over the next few days, I researched available files for background information regarding Marcello. His family had immigrated to the United States in 1911 and settled in the city's suburbs. His first arrest was related to drug trafficking, but he received a reduced sentence. His criminal activities continued and he soon was accepted as a member of the Mafia family headed by Silvestro Carollo. He assumed control of the family in 1947 when then-boss Carollo was deported to Sicily. He quickly recognized business opportunities and formed a relationship with the New York Mafia financier Meyer Lansky to invest in the casino industry. He was able to rule as the boss of the family for an extended period and operated his illegal enterprise without interference. He also had a quick and sometimes violent temper.

On two occasions, Marcello was called before the Senate Committee Investigating Organized Crime. He pleaded the Fifth on both occasions and even refused to acknowledge his name. The committee concluded that due to his past associations with the top leaders of the Mafia, he was one of the most significant Mob bosses in the country. Robert F. Kennedy, the lead counsel on the committee, eventually deported Marcello to Guatemala, but within three months, he was back in New Orleans.

In 1966, the office determined that there was a dispute within the family. At that time, an active intelligence investigation was underway and assigned to Special Agent Pat Collins. He had determined through informant information that Anthony Carollo, a highly placed leader in the family and the son of the former boss Silvestro Carollo, wanted to succeed Marcello as boss when he stepped down. He argued that he was the rightful heir to be the next boss. Marcello, on the other hand, favored naming his brother Joseph as his successor. Due to Carollo's stature, he demanded a sit-down meeting with the Commission in New York to settle the matter.

What was the Commission? This was the first I had heard this term. I needed to do more research. In 1931, Charles "Lucky" Luciano, the most powerful Mafia boss in New York, decided he had to make changes in the makeup of the Mafia. There had been several feuds within the loosely knit Mafia groups, resulting in the assassination of one leader after another. He also recognized there was constant chaos regarding which group controlled certain territories and specific illegal enterprises. Luciano had significant influence and decided to create five families with certain rights and responsibilities. It was as though he was setting up a governmental body, which was precisely what he was doing. He assembled what is now referred to as the Commission. There would be seven members, the current boss of each Mafia family in New York, plus those of Buffalo and Chicago. They would be authorized to settle disputes within the Five Families and other issues that arose in families located in different parts of the country. This gave the Commission enormous authority, and they continued to govern precisely as Luciano envisioned. He believed that there had to be order and structure for the Mafia to operate successfully, or it would eventually destroy itself from within.

On the afternoon of September 22, 1966, the New York police organized crime squad was notified by an anonymous caller that a group of mobsters were holding a meeting at the La Stella Restaurant in Queens. A team of officers was dispatched to the restaurant and observed thirteen individuals gathered around a table in the dining room located in the basement. None of the participants identified themselves or responded to questions. The subjects were transported to the police lockup and the identities of those charged were like reading the who's who in Mafia circles.

Arrested were Carlo Gambino, boss of the Gambino family; Thomas Eboli and Mike Miranda, acting bosses of the Genovese family; Jerry Catena, member of the Genovese family; Joseph Colombo, boss of the Colombo family; Aniello Dellacroce, underboss of the Gambino family; Joseph Gallo, consigliere of the Gambino family; and Dominick Alongi and Anthony Cirillo, members of the Genovese family. Santo Trafficante, Jr., the boss of his family in Tampa, Florida; Carlos Marcello and his brother Joseph Marcello; and Anthony Carollo, who originally called for the meeting, were also arrested.

Thirteen Mafia leaders were arrested and several were members of the Commission, so clearly, significant matters had to be discussed. All were released after posting bail of $100,000. They were charged with consorting in a public place with known criminals, but the charges were later dismissed. Marcello later explained to the press: "I was just meeting with some old friends."

The FBI in New Orleans was notified of the arrests and anticipating his arrival at the airport, Agent Pat Collins and his partner waited to greet Marcello and his brother. When Marcello arrived, he was angry at the presence of the press. When he observed Agent Collins, he shouted, "I am the boss here!" and punched Collins in the face. He previously had been contacted by Collins and thus knew he was an FBI agent. He was arrested and charged with assaulting a federal officer, later convicted, and sentenced to two years in federal prison. He was released after serving only six months. While in prison, his brother took over as acting boss and upon his release, Carlos resumed his role as boss of the family.

After reading this account, I needed clarification about why there was no active investigation into Marcello. He had to be one of the top Mafia bosses in the country if he could demand a sit-down with the Commission in New York to settle a family dispute. Our files also revealed that, in addition to his involvement in traditional organized crime activities, the Marcello enterprise was heavily invested in private business and had a significant interest in the Las Vegas casino industry.

The squad's investigative activity revolved around the players who worked for the family, such as the bookmakers and loan sharks. As in Gary, the tools we had to investigate a Mafia family were limited; however, that was no excuse for not having an active investigation directed at the entire family. It made no sense to me. I spoke to Agent Harold Hughes, who collated intelligence information regarding the family's structure. I wanted to know if we were actively investigating the Marcello organization.

We spent considerable time discussing each member's status, and I asked him pointedly, "What investigations are pending on Marcello and the major players in the family?" He replied, "Several ongoing illegal gambling investigations are pending, with the hope that they would lead to the major players in the family."

I thought that was something, but I was looking for more. I got my answer to why eight candidates were running for governor. Agent Hughes confirmed that the state and city had a history of systemic corruption, and "everyone wanted to get in on the action." He concluded our meeting by stating that "the media referred to New Orleans as 'the city that care forgot' and that branding was well deserved."

My fellow agent, Dick Voyles, cared. He was working on a sizable bookmaking operation run by Donald Melancon. He ran the largest gambling business in the city. It included a network of bookmakers that gave customers instant information about the betting odds regarding horse racing at the Fairgrounds, one of the largest tracks in the Southeast. Melancon was part of the Marcello enterprise and a worthwhile target. Dick had accumulated a great deal of information through reviewing telephone toll records and had identified where they were operating. He and another agent conducted surveillance at the location, identifying Melancon's associates working the phones. We had to develop additional and conclusive evidence to identify all the players in this network. The only way to accomplish this was to submit an affidavit to a federal judge setting forth the probable cause to wiretap Melancon's telephones. Dick was able to prepare the affidavit and it was approved.

Within a couple of weeks, we were in business. Melancon had several phones at his location and three associates helped him run the business. We ran the wire for several weeks and identified the network of bookmakers in the operation. They constantly laid off bets and frequently changed the line on sporting events, particularly football. The phones never stopped ringing. Many subjects were caught up in the investigation, and search warrants were issued for half a dozen locations. One afternoon, teams of agents began kicking down doors and executing the warrants. Thousands of dollars were recovered and all the necessary evidence to prosecute Melancon and his associates was seized.

The case set an example of what could be accomplished, but again, we arrested lower-level criminals who were part of the Marcello enterprise. This approach continued, additional cases and electronic surveillance were developed, and the illegal gambling business in the city was starting to feel the heat agents were generating. They were doing an excellent job when you factored in the limited federal statutes available to them. We were beginning to dent the illegal operations of the Marcello enterprise, and we got good feedback from our informants that the players were now a little uneasy with our sudden interest in their affairs.

My family was in bed, sound asleep. It was around 1:00 a.m. My wife Doris suddenly screamed, "The car is on fire!" She had heard a loud noise and saw the flames reflecting in the vanity mirror. I jumped out of bed and shouted, "Leave the house now! I'll get the kids!" I grabbed Trip and Karen as fast as possible, headed for the stairs, and we got out.

A neighbor must have called 911. Within minutes, the fire department and police arrived. We stood barefoot, shivering across the street from our home, praying that the car would not explode and cause extensive damage. The fire was extinguished, but our only car was destroyed. It was now safe to return and put the children back in bed. My wife and I sat with them until they fell asleep. Doris was unsettled, to say the least, as was I. What had just occurred and why? I was very concerned as I tossed and turned, trying to get back to sleep,

When I arrived in the office the following morning, I advised my boss, Joseph Sylvester, of what had occurred. He called Reed Jensen into his office to sit in on our discussion. Reed was the most experienced agent on the squad and had a network of highly placed informants providing information pertaining to the Marcello family. He also had Dick Voyles and Tom Duhadway join the conversation. Sylvester's immediate concern related to whether or not this was a planned act by the Marcello family to send a message.

Sylvester commented, "You have developed a higher profile due to all the arrests that have been made recently, and it may be their way of fighting back, because that's what they do." He referred to the assault on Agent Pat Collins by the boss himself, Carlos Marcello. I was not sure if this was an overreaction on his part, but he was my boss, and I had no intention of questioning his judgment.

Sylvester ordered Voyles and Duhadway to "contact the residents in Frank's neighborhood to determine if anyone saw something suspicious before the firebombing." He requested Jensen to "get ahold of all your guys for any rumblings that would be helpful." I was now beginning to feel uneasy about this incident.

The follow-up neighborhood inquiry did not develop any relevant information, nor did Jensen's contacts with his informants. The police report indicated that the subjects smashed the driver's-side window and threw a Molotov cocktail into the car, which caused the fire. The police had no leads to follow. The investigation hit a dead end. In the following days, several neighbors asked me what had happened and why the FBI had asked them so many questions.

They were uneasy about what had occurred and pointedly asked me, "Are you the target because you work for the FBI?" I responded, "Of course not," but honestly, I was not sure that was the case. We may never know. I told Doris that this was a random act and had nothing to do with my job. She was not convinced. Doris was tired of all this FBI drama, the late hours, missing time with the children, and the constant worry that something could happen to me.

Raising her voice, she shouted, "I have had it with the FBI!"

Her frustration was very telling and sincere. I had to focus more on what was happening at home. I had never seen her so upset, and I would have to concentrate on ensuring that I did not let my responsibilities with the FBI ruin my marriage.

Despite the success we seemed to be having with our illegal gambling investigations, I was still troubled by the fact that we were not investigating the entire Marcello enterprise. They practically ran the city. We had determined that Marcello had connections with local judges, prosecutors, politicians, and labor leaders. Family members and associates allegedly received favorable treatment from the district attorney's office. Local prosecutions brought against members of the Marcello family were frequently dismissed. Marcello's younger brother, Joseph Marcello, was the family's underboss and he owned several restaurants. Where did he obtain the finances to own four of the finest restaurants in the area? The answer, of course, was evident.

When reviewing the history of family members, I realized how entrenched they were in the city's fabric. Frank Caracci, a made member, owned several nightclubs on Bourbon Street in the French Quarter. Kent "Frenchy" Brouillette, a family associate, was a cousin of Governor Edwin Edwards, who had just been elected. I remember Edwards being one of the candidates I saw debating on television when we arrived in New Orleans. Coincidentally, when state authorities convicted Caracci for illegally running a gambling business and sentenced him to prison, Governor Edwards promptly granted him a pardon. At this point, I stopped with my research; I had learned enough. I was convinced we had to open a broad anti-racketeering investigation targeting the entire enterprise. If we didn't, the family would continue to dominate the community's soul with impunity.

The Old Absinthe House bar was located in the French Quarter at the intersection of Iberville and Bourbon Street. It was just down the street from one of Joseph Marcello's restaurants and a favorite hangout for members of the Marcello family. It was a "man's drinking bar" at the time. Mob figures, sports personalities, and local and state politicians frequented the establishment. A few select agents from the organized crime squad, including yours truly, would also drop by occasionally. Contrary to the initial concerns of Director Hoover, to find out what was going on with the Mafia you had to penetrate their meeting places, either discreetly or out in the open. In this case, we did not broadcast to everyone who we were, but several regulars got to know us. My main focus was developing a relationship with the bartender, Happy.

He had been tending bar for years at this location and knew everyone coming and going. Happy was about five feet five inches tall, had a robust build, to say the least, and always greeted you with a broad smile. When we walked in, he usually commented, "Here come my boys." You had to like him. He knew the Marcello brothers, Joseph and Sammy, who were consistent visitors. On occasion, they held meetings in the back bar.

Happy indicated that the back was closed to the general public when they met. Nevertheless, when we observed either brother entering and walking to the back bar, we had the opportunity to identify key business leaders and politicians who entered and then walked directly to the back. We assumed they were attending a scheduled meeting. They felt comfortable with this arrangement. There was no reason to fear local law enforcement or the FBI spying on them, or so they thought. We could not take any action. Installing a listening device in the bar was out of the question. The information we developed, however, was beneficial from an intelligence standpoint. This chain of events reinforced what some of us had already realized. Marcello and his top people felt they were above the law and untouchable.

I brought my concerns to Sylvester's attention during the next squad conference. He intently listened to what I had to say, but needed clarification on my position. He thought the squad was doing an outstanding job and had many statistical accomplishments. I agreed, but pointed out that "our successes had only dented the Marcello operation."

I suggested, "We should consider investigating the entire Marcello family." He did not respond, but his body language told me he did not want to pursue this idea. He seemed more concerned with obtaining statistical accomplishments that would make him look good. Maybe he was looking for a promotion—who knows? I was totally frustrated, but let the matter drop.

After working on lower-level cases in Gary and New Orleans, I believed that the FBI had adopted the wrong approach in investigating illegal activities controlled by the Mafia and that this error was systemic throughout the organization. I wanted to dig a little deeper into the history of the Mafia and the FBI's response over the years to its existence. The FBI began investigating organized crime as a priority only after J. Edgar Hoover was forced to admit publicly that it was a threat to our society. For years, he had refused to acknowledge its existence. His reluctance was never fully explained, but internally, a perception had developed that he was more concerned about his agents rubbing elbows with Mafia members and that they would be susceptible to corruption.

In 1963, Arkansas Senator John McClellan chaired the Permanent Subcommittee on Investigations. Joseph Valachi, who had been convicted of murder and was a member of the New York Genovese family, testified before a nationally televised audience. His testimony was explosive, as it was the first time a member of the Mafia had testified in any public forum. He identified many members and expressly referred to the Mafia Commission in New York that oversaw all the families throughout the country. He was the first member of the Mafia to use the term "La Cosa Nostra" to acknowledge how they referred to their organization.

The senators had never heard this term before and questioned Valachi, "What does La Cosa Nostra mean?" He responded, "our thing," and continued, "Once you are a member, there is no turning back." His testimony was highlighted in all the major newspapers as the Valachi hearings and, for the first time, identified organized crime as a national problem.

During this period, the FBI finally began investigating organized crime as a priority. Robert F. Kennedy was appointed attorney general and had served on the McClellan Committee. Hoover did not get along with Kennedy and initially resisted his efforts to get the FBI involved. However, Kennedy insisted and Hoover had no choice. After all, Hoover had to report to Kennedy, and his brother John just happened to be president. It had long been Hoover's practice to never abide by the chain of command, but that was not going to work for him this time,

During Robert Kennedy's tenure, Congress passed several interstate anti-racketeering laws that gave the FBI additional investigative tools. As I completed my research and reviewed the provisions of the new regulations, it still did not appear that they were designed to go after the Mafia as a criminal enterprise, but merely targeted individuals who engaged in illegal activities. It was a start, however, and a move in the right direction.

After considering these facts as I knew them and the limitations of my current assignment, I requested a transfer to FBI headquarters in Washington, DC. I wanted to pursue a management position and attempt to develop a new solution to attack the Mafia. I certainly did not have all the answers, but I was determined to help find a more effective way forward. Hoover died in 1972 and I sensed that the FBI might be ready to move in a new direction. I wanted to encourage such a move. I had limited experience in the field and had just been appointed a relief supervisor. If I did receive a transfer, there was no guarantee that I would be assigned to organized crime cases.

Donald Moore was the office's SAC and frequently interacted with our squad. I had a good relationship with him and on one occasion, I mentioned my desire to move to headquarters and become involved in policy issues.

FBI headquarters had decided to hold a conference in New Orleans, and every field office SAC and many officials from headquarters would be in attendance. Moore and his staff would host the conference, which would be held at the Roosevelt Hotel, not far from the French Quarter. Several agents, myself included, were part of a detail to pick up those attending at the airport and escort them to the hotel. We were to provide some security if they wanted to tour the French Quarter when not attending meetings.

One night, after our detail had finished, I stopped in the Old Absinthe House bar with Voyles before heading home. Happy greeted us, "What do my boys want?" I saw Moore standing at the bar with two officials from headquarters. I knew neither one, but had observed them at the conference. Moore waved us over to say hello. He introduced us to Bill Cleveland, assistant director of the Criminal Division. The Organized Crime Section was in his division. Moore told Cleveland I had many years of experience working Mafia-related cases and would like to transfer to headquarters. Cleveland nodded, took a napkin off the bar, wrote down my name, and placed it in his pocket.

Voyles and I finished our drink and left the bar. Dick turned to me and said, "Frank, are you crazy? You want to leave New Orleans?" Three weeks later, I received my transfer to headquarters and was assigned to the Organized Crime Section. I was shocked that this had happened so quickly. You never know where the path you take will lead. I might not be writing this story if I had not stopped in the Old Absinthe House bar that night and had the opportunity to meet Mr. Cleveland. The only downside of the transfer was my wife's reaction. Doris did not want to leave New Orleans, which further added to the tension in our marriage.

CHAPTER 5
UNIRAC

Within a short period, I received a transfer to headquarters and a promotion to a supervisory position in the Organized Crime Section. We purchased a home in a Virginia suburb near a good school for Trip and Karen. Several agents lived in the community, so it seemed like an ideal location. Fortunately, I reunited with my former new agents counselor, George Benjamin, who had shepherded me through the training academy. He remembered the guy who was the poorest shot in his class. An experienced supervisor, Benjamin oversaw all investigations by our East Coast offices. I was assigned to monitor the programs of the three Florida divisions and our office in Savannah.

In my initial discussions with Benjamin, I vented my frustrations with the piecemeal investigative approach we had adopted regarding the Mafia families throughout the country. "This is just not working." He recognized my concerns and responded, "I want you to sit down and read this fairly new law enacted by Congress, the Racketeer Influenced and Corrupt Organizations (RICO) statute." He continued that the new law had the primary purpose of eliminating racketeering enterprises operating in interstate commerce, such as the Mafia. The FBI had never utilized this statute as the basis to investigate a Mafia family, which was inherently an illegal enterprise. I took his advice and began to read the provisions of the law in detail. I quickly realized that this might be the vehicle we needed to finally go after the Mafia and its ability to operate as a continuing criminal enterprise. I had met a new friend—his name was RICO.

One morning, I got a call from Gene McKinney, the supervisor of the Labor Racketeering Squad in Miami. He started the conversation by saying, "Frank, we have just had a tremendous breakthrough." His squad had been investigating corruption allegations on the Miami waterfront and had made little progress. One of his agents, Ray Maria, had just developed a cooperative witness named Joey Teitelbaum, who owned a shipping supply company. Teitelbaum's employees were members of the ILA. He was making labor peace payments to William Boyle, an ILA official. Boyle worked for George Barone, an alleged Mafia member from New York. Barone was also an official of the ILA; thus, he had the authority to force a work stoppage at any time. If Teitelbaum stopped making payments, Barone would shut down his company. McKinney observed, "This could be a big opportunity to move against the ILA."

According to Teitelbaum, Barone was directly connected to Anthony Scotto, a capo in the Gambino family who controlled the New York waterfront. Teitelbaum had agreed to wear a transmitter during future meetings with Boyle and be a cooperative undercover witness. This would put Teitelbaum in grave danger if his cooperation became known, but he was willing to go forward. I told McKinney, "This is great news; proceed with the investigation. I will contact the New York office regarding the Scotto connection."

Before going further, I began independent research to learn more about the ILA. The union had a reputation for corruption dating back at least forty years. Investigative journalist Malcolm Johnson wrote an explosive exposé about the Mob's influence on the New York waterfront and won a Pulitzer Prize for his work. The Johnson reporting became the basis for the award-winning film *On the Waterfront*. At one time, the union had a membership of over 100,000 dockworkers.

In 1937, Mafia boss Albert Anastasia, also known as "Mad Hatter" and "Lord High Executioner," took control over the ILA locals along the Brooklyn waterfront. His brother Anthony "Tough Tony" Anastasio became the president of Local 1814. When Tough Tony died, Anthony Scotto succeeded him. ILA Local 1814 had over 5,000 members. Scotto was, in fact, a *caporegime* (capo) in the Gambino family. *Capo* is a term the Mafia confers on a member who controls a crew of soldiers. A soldier is a term designated for a crew member who reports directly to the capo. In Scotto's case, he had multiple crew members that controlled the waterfront. The designation of a member as a capo in the Mafia is significant, as that individual holds a key position of trust and respect—he reports directly to the boss of the family.

I dug a little deeper into our files at headquarters. I determined that George Barone was a member of the Genovese family and reported to Michael Clemente, a capo and an official of the ILA in New York. He was known as an enforcer and hit man for the boss of the family, Anthony "Fat Tony" Salerno. Through their influence in the ILA, the Genovese family controlled the docks in New Jersey and Manhattan, and the Gambino family controlled the docks in Brooklyn and Staten Island. Barone negotiated this arrangement. It appeared that Clemente wanted to establish the Mafia's influence in the South and requested Barone to relocate to Miami and establish a foothold.

Barone quickly became an official of the ILA local in Miami and was now directly involved in extorting waterfront business owners such as Joey Teitelbaum. With this information in hand, I realized we had a rare opportunity to pursue an investigation of the corrupt infrastructure of the ILA, which had been under the Mafia's control for almost half a century. I intended to contact my friend RICO to see if he could lend a hand.

The next day, I contacted the New York office and spoke to Bob Reutter, the squad supervisor responsible for investigating corrupt union practices. I briefed Bob regarding my conversation with McKinney. He told me, "Scotto had been under investigation for some time, and this new information from Miami appears worth pursuing." He was aware of the Barone and Clemente connection, but now saw the need for the squad to intensify its coverage of Scotto. I suggested I would attempt to coordinate both investigations, as we did not want to step on one another's toes. Bob, seemingly noncommittal to this approach, commented, "I have never worked with the Miami office; I am not sure that will work." He had concerns they would take actions that would jeopardize New York's ongoing investigation. I understood his concerns.

I then reached out to McKinney and emphasized that due to the importance and potential scope of the investigation, it would have to be coordinated between both offices. McKinney expressed the same concerns as Reutter. I briefed Gene on the background information I had developed regarding Barone, Clemente, and Scotto. "There seems to be some concern between you and Reutter that working together is an issue. Let me be clear: That is the direction we are going to take." I ended the call by telling him I would be in touch.

After these discussions, it was clear that the Miami and New York investigations should not be conducted separately. They had to be considered as one. The investigation could involve every FBI division along the East Coast with an active waterfront industry. I also realized I had another problem. My unit had no responsibility for overseeing cases in New York. I approached Benjamin and gave him a briefing on the potential of this case and the need for close coordination between two of our premier field offices. I emphasized to him that "our goal would be to pursue all areas of criminality by the union and the Mafia operating as a criminal enterprise. We have to target the entire group." He agreed and called a meeting with Section Chief Bob McCarthy and Unit Chief Bill Baker, who had oversight responsibility for the New York office.

Due to my recent assignment to the section, I did not know much about McCarthy. He impressed me as a no-nonsense guy with an aggressive style who wanted to get the job done. He "managed by walking around" the section and going from office to office. He always had his sleeves rolled up and his tie loose at the collar. I liked his style. He reminded me of a managing editor at a major newspaper. We all met in his office and I presented the issues. Baker pushed back at my suggestion to assign me as the sole coordinator of the investigation. He implied I "needed more experience handling such an expansive and potentially important case." I did not take this lightly, as I had more investigative experience in field operations than Baker did. He had been in the section for half his adult life. After a lengthy discussion, McCarthy gave me the responsibility to coordinate the investigation between both divisions. His blunt comment at the end of the meeting put me ill at ease: "Storey. Do not screw this up." I politely responded, "There's no way that will happen." With that, I now had the go-ahead to manage one of the most important labor racketeering investigations ever initiated by the FBI.

While sitting home nursing a nightcap after the family had gone to bed that night, I began reviewing the day's events. At times, the quiet of the night allowed me to focus more clearly. I had two of our principal field offices conducting a turf battle over which office would control the investigation. What was the answer to this dilemma? Usually, an office that initiates an investigation designates itself as the office of origin, and the case agent and supervisor assigned to that office make all investigative decisions. In the current situation, Miami and New York considered themselves the office of origin. My instincts told me this was not going to work. We would spend more time arguing over investigative strategies rather than on what steps had to be taken to achieve our goals. While McCarthy had given me the green light to coordinate both investigations, was there an established policy to make that happen? There was not.

After my second nightcap, I kicked my thoughts into high gear.

I decided the case hereinafter would be titled UNIRAC, an acronym for *union racketeering*. Headquarters would be designated as the office of origin. We would work the case as a potential violation of the RICO statute. All major decisions affecting each office's investigation would be coordinated through headquarters. I drafted the recommendations setting forth my reasoning and went to bed wondering if the brass at headquarters would buy into such an unusual proposal. I tossed and turned all night and did not sleep well.

On my way to work the next morning, I thought this proposal had better work, or I might be returning to New Orleans. Being fairly new in the section, I was taking a calculated risk. I had done that a few times before as a brick agent and would not change my approach because I was now in a supervisory position. I met with Benjamin when I arrived and presented the proposal; he liked the idea's boldness. We subsequently met with McCarthy and Baker and they jumped on board. Baker commented that New York would object because they had a built-in philosophy: "We'll do it our way." McCarthy observed that due to the unusual nature of the proposal, "you will have to obtain approval from Deputy Associate Director Jim Adams."

That afternoon, I met with Mr. Adams, who held the third-highest executive position in the FBI. As I sat opposite his vast desk, he seemed to be looking down at me. After reading the proposal, he surprised me by his reaction. "I have heard from McCarthy that this case is about taking a new approach to our investigative strategies." He paused momentarily and then requested, "Give me more details about the status of the investigation and the provisions of the RICO statute." I gladly gave him a detailed overview of the case and why we were employing the RICO statute as the foundation of the investigation. He quickly said, "I like it." He was not concerned about taking a new path that would ruffle some feathers and remarked, "That comes with the territory."

Mr. Adams approved the proposal and stated he would personally contact the special agents in charge in Miami and New York and advise them of his decision. He concluded our meeting with the comment, "Keep me advised of developments when you believe appropriate." I felt emboldened and confident when I left his office and thought this might work.

Damn, he approved my proposal, yes. I immediately forwarded the document to New York and Miami. My phone started ringing the next day and did not stop ringing for the next two years.

Within a few days, I realized I had to address another potential problem. The investigation would cross several jurisdictional lines. There would have to be a central chain of command at the Department of Justice (DOJ) to arbitrate disputes and make tactical prosecutorial decisions. I contacted David Margolis, who was responsible for the section overseeing organized crime prosecutions throughout the country. The department had established a strike force in all the major cities that exclusively prosecuted organized crime cases. I briefed him on the case status. He was vaguely familiar with the New York and Miami initiatives, but not the potential for a broader investigative effort along the East Coast. He suggested we meet, which we did the following morning. Attending the meeting was prosecutor Gerald McGuire. Margolis and McGuire listened intently as I outlined the facts as we knew them and our intention to utilize the RICO statute as the basis for the UNIRAC investigation. It was like an alarm had suddenly been turned on in their heads.

Dave enthusiastically responded, "I love it. No organized crime case has ever been prosecuted using this statute." He committed to coordinating all prosecutive decisions directly impacting other jurisdictions. Margolis assured me there would be "no mavericks acting independently." He appointed McGuire as my counterpart.

I met separately with Gerry to brief him on the direction of the investigation. Gerry was born and raised in Brooklyn and was familiar with the Mafia's reputation and influence in the city and on the waterfront. He had graduated from St. John's University and obtained his law degree from the same institution. He also worked in the Manhattan District Attorney's Office before joining the department.

McGuire advised me, "I have already contacted the strike force chiefs in Miami and New York and informed them of my new role in the investigation and the project's scope." He also planned a trip to both districts to ensure they had competent attorneys assigned to the case, which was to receive top priority. I left our meeting feeling reassured that I had the right partner to help me navigate the difficulties we would most likely face. I would be the Lone Ranger and Gerry would be my Tonto. Gerry left the meeting with the comment, "Frank, I assure you, this is going to work."

I called Reutter and arranged to travel to New York and meet with him and his squad. I had never been to the New York office. I hopped on the Amtrak and headed north. Bob and I sat down for an hour to get acquainted and discuss the case in general, and we quickly hit it off. He had an aggressive style and was not at all laid-back. I liked that—it was the approach we would need in this case. He introduced me to Jack Barrett and Louis Freeh, whom he had designated as the primary agents to run the investigation. Both were from the New York area; Freeh had recently graduated from Rutgers Law School. The meeting went well and my trip to New York reassured the agents of the Bureau's commitment to the case and its future success. My parting advice was, "Gentlemen, failure is not an option." My next stop would be Miami.

When I returned to headquarters, I contacted Gene McKinney and booked a flight to Miami. I met with McKinney and the case agent, Ray Maria, who impressed me. He was as sharp as a tack and totally into the investigation. Gene had Atlee Wampler, the chief of the strike force, attend the meeting. McGuire had already reached out to Wampler and told him of his role. It was clear that McKinney, Maria, and Wampler were on the same page. I then caught a quick flight back to DC. We had touched all the bases and were now ready to play hardball.

New York focused on Anthony Scotto, intending to develop sufficient probable cause to prepare an affidavit requesting a federal judge to authorize the interception of conversations in Scotto's union office or on his telephone. After several weeks of investigation, this was finally accomplished. Scotto frequently contacted William "Sonny" Montella, the general manager of Quinn Marine Services, which had business relationships with various shipping companies. Montella was unknown to the FBI at the time. The conversations were incriminating and it appeared that Montella could be a critical cooperative witness.

It was decided that Montella should be approached in an attempt to flip him. It was risky, as he might reject any overture and our investigation could be compromised. Nevertheless, Reutter was willing to take that risk and I agreed with the move. Agents Barrett and Freeh visited Montella's business unannounced. I am sure he was shocked when he observed two FBI agents walking through the door. Their objective was to focus on Montella's personal life and his family's future, and they strongly suggested that this was the time to do the right thing and cooperate before it was too late.

At first, Montella ignored the agents' questioning: "I don't know what the fuck you're talking about." He became somewhat hostile. Barrett would have none of that. "We can arrest your ass right now and close your business," he said. "We are not playing games." They explained the details of the investigation that revealed his relationship with Scotto. He became more cooperative as he realized he was also one of the targets of the investigation and had potential criminal liability. The agents persisted in their interview and suggested that if he agreed to cooperate, they would speak on his behalf so he would have an opportunity to avoid imprisonment. They began to leave the meeting, and Montella sat there transfixed and said nothing as Barrett and Freeh walked out the door.

A few days later, Barrett got a call from Montella, who requested they meet again. At this meeting, he committed to cooperate. He admitted paying Scotto and other ILA officials to operate his business successfully. He agreed to wear a body recorder when making future payments to Scotto or his associates. He often met Scotto at predetermined locations, as he would not come to Montella's office.

One day, Montella contacted Barrett and told him he had arranged a meeting with Scotto in the men's room at the Drake Hotel in Manhattan to make an illegal payment. He agreed to wear a body recorder during this meeting. On January 13, 1978, Scotto and Montella met at the Drake, and agents recorded their conversation in the men's room when Montella gave Scotto $10,000. At another subsequent meeting at the Drake on March 13, 1978, he furnished Scotto $5,000. At this meeting, there was an apparent misunderstanding regarding previous payments. We were able to record this conversation and the contents of the discussion established the criminal relationship between Scotto and Montella:

> Montella: "March, I gave you five."
>
> Scotto: "Yeah."
>
> Montella: "June, I gave you five, September, I gave you five. And then December, I gave you ten."
>
> Scotto: "No, I don't know that . . . thought it was earlier, but that's all right."
>
> Montella: "No. All the time, it was like that."
>
> Scotto: "Right."
>
> Montella: "Because I would, you know, when you said."
>
> Scotto: "I got a little screwed up because . . ."
>
> Montella: "Because that was the bonus, you know."
>
> Scotto: "I figured something. I figured it wrong."
>
> Montella: "Yeah."
>
> Scotto: "See, I must have got screwed up when you did a double one at Christmas every year."

Additional meetings were recorded where Montella made payments to Scotto. This evidence was critical in establishing Scotto's criminal culpability. Over three years, Montella paid Scotto $5,000 quarterly and $5,000 extra every Christmas to maintain his business. He also told us that he had built a $15,000 cabana at Scotto's forty-acre summer home in the Catskills as part of the payments he had to make to Scotto.

Scotto's network extended to other Mafia associates, such as Genovese capo Michael Clemente. Clemente's power was particularly pronounced along the Manhattan waterfront, where he held sway over various operations and transactions. New York named Clemente as one of the principal subjects of the investigation. Clemente was a business agent for ILA Local 856, which controlled the piers in Manhattan. He had an extensive criminal record, including a previous conviction for extortion, after which he was removed from his position with the ILA and served five years in prison. Upon his release, he continued his influence with the ILA through intermediaries.

New York instituted surveillance of Clemente to determine his movements and contacts. He regularly frequented the Sheraton Health Club in Brooklyn, where he reportedly met with his associates. How would the agents be able to identify his contacts? Clemente was very conscious of surveillance and we had to use our best people to surveil him daily. He chose the health club, as he felt safe meeting his contacts at this location out of the earshot of FBI agents. Agent Freeh, who was only twenty-five at the time and relatively new on the job, volunteered to take on an undercover assignment to join the health club in an attempt to make observations of Clemente and his associates. This was a sensitive and dangerous assignment, as we could not observe or monitor Freeh's movements inside the club. He would be on his own and, indeed, unarmed.

Reutter gave the idea long and thoughtful consideration before proposing it to Special Agent in Charge Tom Emory. It was agreed to move ahead with certain caveats. Agents would always be stationed in their cars outside the club when Freeh was inside, and his time there would be closely monitored. Freeh joined the club under the cover of being a young attorney needing to get away from the stress of the job and unwind a bit. Freeh was successful in being accepted into the club and befriended Clemente.

At one point, he told Clemente he was unemployed and had lost his position with his law firm. Clemente responded, "Kid, don't worry. I will get you a job with one of the judges who comes to the club." Clemente stayed in the sauna for long periods. Freeh observed men dressed in business suits entering the club, taking their clothes off, walking into the sauna, and handing Clemente an envelope. The surveillance team outside the club would then identify these individuals as they left the club. They were often either officials with the ILA or shipping company executives. These observations later became critical evidence.

The investigation began to pick up steam and sufficient probable cause was obtained to place a court-approved listening device in Anthony Scotto's office. It was the headquarters for the ILA in Brooklyn and numerous incriminating conversations were intercepted. At this point, sufficient evidence had been obtained to establish that the Gambino and Genovese families shared control over the New York ILA locals and had strong ties to the locals in New Jersey. They had control of the entire New York waterfront and influenced every port along the East Coast. Scotto and Clemente were the key Mafia figures in charge of this conspiracy. The investigation identified a significant number of ILA officials and shipping company executives who were also complicit in the conspiracy. These developments far exceeded our initial goals.

McKinney and Maria set up a conference call and proposed that we set up an undercover operation in one of the companies that Teitelbaum controlled. They suggested the port of Savannah, which they believed could be easily penetrated. I was excited about the idea and began preparing a proposal. The use of undercover agents was relatively new and had only been done in a few critical cases. UNIRAC was undoubtedly in that category. I also began to pursue finding the right agent for the assignment.

One Sunday evening, I received a call from an agent who identified himself as Bob Cassidy. I had no idea who he was or how he got my home phone number. This was highly unusual.

He began the conversation by stating, "Sorry for calling you at home, but I heard you are looking for an undercover agent. I want to be considered. I was with the agency for several years."

That rang a bell. The agency could only mean one thing: the Central Intelligence Agency. We talked at length and I was impressed with his credentials and enthusiasm. What a stroke of luck! He had the background and experience to hit the street running. He never did tell me how he got my phone number. I put him in touch with Ray Maria so he could be briefed on the investigation. After further evaluating his background and work record, we selected Cassidy for the undercover assignment.

Teitelbaum also had business interests in additional southeastern waterfronts such as Jacksonville and Mobile. McKinney suggested we also place undercover agents to work with Teitelbaum to develop his relationship with these additional businesses and ILA officials. Cassidy had successfully penetrated the operation in Savannah, so his idea had merit. He prepared a proposal with a recommended budget that would include cash payments to officials without making arrests, which was contrary to Bureau policy. We were going to let the money walk without making an arrest. At this phase of the investigation, we did not want to compromise future developments.

I received the proposal and quickly got Benjamin and McCarthy's approval. Within a relatively short period, we had three undercover agents now working for Teitelbaum at his businesses at the Savannah, Mobile, and Jacksonville seaports. This was the first time the FBI had taken such a step in a criminal investigation. The agents made payoffs on Teitelbaum's behalf to additional ILA officials and shipping executives. All the conversations were recorded and would be critical evidence in future court proceedings. The undercover agents would be able to testify directly as well.

The investigation had reached a point when Miami and New York agreed it was time to take the case down. All the evidence gathered was being presented to grand juries in both districts, and appropriate indictments would be forthcoming. Officials at headquarters and the DOJ agreed and I briefed Associate Director Adams. We were ready to go.

Anthony Scotto was indicted on thirty-three racketeering charges under the RICO statute. Among the counts in the indictment, he was accused of accepting $300,000 in bribes over five years from various businesses connected with the shipping industry and ILA union officials. Scotto was convicted of all charges before United States District Judge Charles E. Stewart, Jr. Just before sentencing, Judge Stewart acknowledged in open court that he had "received letters of support for Mr. Scotto from former New York City Mayor Robert F. Wagner and John Lindsay."

Judge Stewart, ignoring the maximum sentence of twenty years in federal prison, sentenced Scotto to serve only five years and fined him $75,000. His rationale for such a light sentence was inexplicable. After serving only thirty-nine months at a cozy correctional institution, the highest-ranking capo in the Gambino family was released for good behavior. A miscarriage of justice, to be sure.

Anthony Anastasio, Scotto's brother-in-law, and Genovese capo Michael Clemente were indicted and convicted. Both were sentenced to twenty years in prison. Genovese members Tino Fiumara, his associate Michael Coppola, and three ILA local presidents from the New Jersey waterfront were convicted and received lengthy prison sentences. These convictions had a significant impact on the ILA and severely diminished the Mafia's control over the union.

In the Miami phase of this investigation, twenty-two significant players were indicted for violating the RICO statute. Included in the indictment were George Barone of the Genovese family and ILA official William Boyle. Additional ILA officials in Mobile, Savannah, Charleston, Jacksonville, New York, and sixteen shipping industry executives were included in the indictment. They were all convicted and received lengthy prison sentences.

Over 100 agents worked on the UNIRAC investigation simultaneously. Court-ordered electronic surveillance was conducted in ten cities, stretching from the Gulf Coast in New Orleans to New York City. More than 100 individuals were eventually indicted and convicted. The systemic corruption in the International Longshoreman's Association was publicly exposed.

Louis J. Freeh eventually left the FBI after a distinguished career. Freeh subsequently served as a US district judge in New York and in 1993 was nominated by President Clinton and unanimously confirmed by Congress as director of the FBI. On December 12, 2008, former Director Freeh was interviewed on an *Inside the FBI* podcast and made these remarks about the UNIRAC investigation.

"The ramifications of the case were very significant. It was the first major labor racketeering case that the FBI had made. In those days, particularly in New York, the organized crime problem was dealt with by the FBI on a one-on-one basis. The notion of UNIRAC was that we would look at the entire enterprise—in other words, the ILA juxtaposed with the Cosa Nostra groups that were controlling them. So, the result was that Director Webster in Washington established a labor racketeering desk for the first time in the organized crime unit. The Bureau went on to look at cases not just on the East Coast but the central states Teamsters cases and started to look at organized crime as an enterprise target. That was, I think, responsible for the substantial weakening of the Mafia over the next twenty years."

In October 1978, the career board advised me that I was being considered for a supervisory position in Las Vegas to manage the organized crime squad. I had taken a day off to catch up on painting the hallway to make the house more sales-worthy when Benjamin called. He asked me if I would be interested in a transfer to Philadelphia since one of the organized crime supervisors had been transferred. What good fortune. I had not liked the idea of being assigned to Las Vegas. I told George, "Let's go for it." Within days, the official transfer letter came in and I was returning to Philly, where my journey had begun.

CHAPTER 6
The Bruno Family

The Philadelphia office had moved since I left in 1965 to attend the new agents class. They were now located in a new federal building opposite Independence Hall. It was a beautiful and historic section of the city. Upon my arrival, I met with SAC Neil Welch, regarded as one of the most effective field bosses in the country. He was a tall man, impressive in appearance, but had a gruff manner. He did not say much during our introduction other than, "I am giving you the desk of the top squad in the office with one mission: Take down this damn Bruno family. You got that?"

I replied, "Yes, sir," and quickly left his office.

The Mafia in Philadelphia had ruled organized crime activities in the city for half a century. Angelo Bruno took control of the family in 1959 and was appointed by the Commission. He adopted the same style of running the family as his friend Carlo Gambino in New York. He believed in settling disputes peacefully and did not resort to violence unless he had to. He was known as the Gentle Don. He lived what appeared to be an everyday life with his wife Susan and two children in a modest row house in a typical inner-city neighborhood in South Philadelphia.

Previous investigations had determined that the family ran all illegal gambling operations in the city and also focused on traditional crimes such as labor racketeering, loan-sharking, and extortion. They had been under investigation for many years with minimal success regarding prosecution. The squad had several experienced agents and high-level informants who furnished quality intelligence continuously, which was essential. There was an ongoing investigation of the family entitled Operation Gangplank. I just loved the hidden meaning in that title.

Despite appearing to live the lifestyle of a middle-income wage earner, Bruno was a wealthy man. He owned a share of a hotel in Havana, an extermination company in New Jersey, and had investments in another company in Florida. Bruno received much of his income illegally by controlling all organized crime operations in and around Philadelphia. He vacationed regularly in Florida, but avoided traveling to areas where he would draw attention. He occasionally traveled to New York for meetings with Mafia representatives, which the FBI closely monitored.

Soon after moving to Philadelphia, Doris and I separated and eventually divorced. I moved to an apartment near the children's home and tried to adjust to being a bachelor again. It was a complex issue to deal with, particularly for the children. They were too young to understand this sudden change in their lives. Despite the demands of my job, I made a concerted effort to be with them as often as possible. Several months later, my sister introduced me to Susan McCabe at her office picnic. We hit it off immediately, started dating, and fell in love. Marriage followed and we moved to Haddonfield, New Jersey, a short distance from Philadelphia. Life was good again.

On March 21, 1980, Bruno had a prearranged dinner at Cous's Little Italy Restaurant at Eleventh and Christian Streets in South Philly. He loved the Italian cuisine they served and the establishment was usually frequented by customers from the area. His attorney and Raymond "Long John" Martorano, a significant family member, joined him. The restaurant provided a discreet location to conduct business, as the presence of any FBI surveillance was remote. Bruno did not drive, so John Stanfa, a family associate, was designated as his driver and bodyguard. There had been some unrest in the family, as Bruno had an established policy that no member could engage in drug trafficking. Several capos had pushed back on this policy and their voices were getting louder. He was sure he could settle the issue peacefully. After dinner, Stanfa drove Bruno to his home at 934 Snyder Avenue, a few blocks from the restaurant.

As Stanfa pulled up to the front of his home, he rolled down the right front window. Bruno was sitting in the front seat. An individual stepped out of the shadows and fired several shotgun blasts, which struck Bruno in the head, instantly killing him. Stanfa had a glancing wound, but was not seriously injured and was obviously not a target of the assassin. Bruno's wife, Susan, heard the shotgun blast and burst through the front door of their home. She screamed as she saw the bloody carnage: Her husband's head had almost been decapitated.

A neighbor across the street saw two men running to a waiting car on Snyder Avenue. They both disappeared into the night. The neighbor called the police, who in turn contacted our office. Agents assigned to the squad quickly responded, along with detectives from the Philadelphia police department's homicide squad. The entire area was swarming with curious neighbors and bystanders. The press had arrived simultaneously with the police and rudely began taking photographs of the gory murder scene. The Gentle Don was gone.

We had no clue that a contract had been issued on Bruno. This was the first significant murder of any member of the Bruno family in years. Informants were swiftly canvassed; however, they had no foreknowledge that a plot was afoot. This had to be an inside move coming from the underboss or a capo, and if so, the hit had to be approved by the Mafia bosses in New York. The boss of a family is not randomly murdered on a whim or sudden desire by a rival member to take over control of the family. That was just not done. The New York FBI office had no intelligence to offer concerning Bruno's murder.

I assembled the squad and declared, "Let's focus on John

Stanfa. Number one, who is he?" There was no information about Stanfa in our files. We were unaware if he was a member or associate of the family. He was listed in the city directory as a painter. He must have been trusted, otherwise he never would have been Bruno's driver. One of my agents remarked, "Nothing makes sense at this point." Our informants had never heard of Stanfa. We determined that he had recently arrived in Philadelphia from New York. Agent Jim Maher contacted our New York office and they forwarded him helpful but limited information on Stanfa. He was born in Sicily, arrived in New York in the early sixties, and listed his occupation as a bricklayer on his immigration certificate. He married, settled in the city, and later moved to Philadelphia. He had relatives in New York who were reportedly members of the Gambino family. Through these connections, he was able to hook up with the Bruno family in Philadelphia. He had no arrest record.

Full-time surveillance of Stanfa was initiated to determine his contacts. Within a few days, the surveillance paid off. One day, Stanfa hit the New Jersey Turnpike and headed north. He was alone. We assumed he was going to New York, so we notified the office's surveillance squad to have a team on standby to assist, as we were unfamiliar with the area or the players he might be meeting. Stanfa drove to a park in Lower Manhattan and waited on a bench, reading a newspaper. The agents had a clear line of sight to observe his every move, along with their trusted cameras.

Within fifteen minutes, two men approached. Stanfa got up and walked to a nearby picnic table and the two men followed. It appeared they wanted more privacy. They sat down and talked for about thirty minutes. Stanfa seemed to lead the discussion, was fairly animated, and appeared annoyed. He kept flailing his arms back and forth to make a point. One of the New York surveillance agents recognized a participant as a member of the Genovese family, one of the five Mafia families in New York. He identified Frank Tieri, a capo who appeared to be the main focus of Stanfa's attention. After the meeting, they returned to their cars and left the area. We followed Stanfa back to his home in South Philly and attempted to put the pieces together. Who was this guy? Within a short time, we would find out.

One of our highly placed member informants believed that Antonio "Tony Bananas" Caponigro, the consigliere of the Bruno family, was responsible for planning Bruno's murder. His son-in-law Alfred Salerno was the actual triggerman. Caponigro and a few capos were frustrated that they could not convince Bruno to allow them to engage in drug trafficking, which was quite a lucrative opportunity. None of the discussions between Caponigro and Bruno resulted in any policy change, and he decided to kill Bruno and take over the family. Caponigro enlisted the support of Johnny "Keys" Simone and Frank "the Barracuda" Sindone, who were senior members of the family. Before making his move, Caponigro traveled to New York. He met with a highly placed member of the Genovese family, Frank Tieri, and understood from their conversation that he had the go-ahead to kill Bruno and take over the family. As it turned out, Caponigro was mistaken. This information was significant, as Tieri appeared to be a key in this plot to kill Bruno. Why did Stanfa meet with him after Bruno was murdered and appear upset during their discussion?

Caponigro probably did not realize it at the time, but seeking permission to kill Bruno from a representative of the Genovese family was a big mistake. He had gone to the wrong family representative. Bruno had an extremely close relationship with Carlo Gambino, a senior member of the Commission, for many years before Gambino died. The Gambino family was still considered the most powerful family in New York and the current boss, Paul Castellano, was Gambino's brother-in-law. We did not believe that the Gambino family would have approved the murder of Bruno without some compelling reason, which Caponigro did not have.

Caponigro's motive was strictly greed and ambition. He sealed his fate when he contacted Tieri, who was not even the boss of the Genovese family and was not authorized to speak for the

Commission. No tension with the Commission existed to warrant such a drastic act as the assassination of Angelo Bruno.

Only twenty-eight days after Bruno's murder, Caponigro and Salerno were called to New York for a meeting with representatives of the Genovese and Gambino families. Caponigro was expecting to be officially named as the new boss of the Bruno family. Salerno drove Caponigro to New York but did not attend the meeting; he waited in a nearby bar. Caponigro was accused of ordering the hit on Bruno without authorization from the Commission. When he referred to a meeting with Genovese capo Tieri, they did not believe him, as Tieri did not confirm his story. The meeting ended on that note, and Caponigro must have known he was in deep trouble.

Later that day, Caponigro's naked body was found in the trunk of a car in the Bronx. He had been shot several times and twenty-dollar bills were scattered over his corpse. The significance of the bills was a message that the Commission bosses were sending to fellow members of the Mafia. Caponigro's greed resulted in his execution. Salerno's body was found in the trunk of another car and it was obvious that he had been tortured before he had been killed. These two murders were only the beginning. Within days, Johnny "Keys" Simone's wife called our office and reported her husband missing. Agents from our New York office subsequently discovered Simone's body in a field in Staten Island. He had been shot several times in the head. Oddly, Simone did not have his shoes on when he was killed. We eventually would find out why.

The hit on Simone was given to Sammy "the Bull" Gravano, a member of John Gotti's crew. Many years after the murder of Simone, Gravano was arrested and agreed to become a cooperative witness. At his debriefing, he related the following story: Gravano was given the contract to kill Simone by Paul Castellano, the boss of the Gambino family. He had known Simone for years and they were close friends. He did not want to kill him. He told the agents, "I felt terrible that a man with such balls had to be hit.

He was a man's man. But this was La Cosa Nostra. The boss of the family had ordered it. There was nothing I could do."

Simone was snatched in the parking lot of the SkyView Country Club in Washington Township, New Jersey, and driven to a deserted wooded area in Staten Island. Gravano wanted to show Simone some respect even though he had received orders to kill him. En route to the site, Simone had a heart seizure and wanted to take one of his pills. He tried to reason with Gravano, "so I can die like a mobster, by the gun." When they arrived at the site where they planned to commit the murder, Simone requested that he be allowed to take his shoes off. He had told his wife that when he died, "it would be with my shoes off. She always worried that something like this would occur." Gravano granted Simone's wish, and as Gravano's associates grabbed Simone to get him out of the vehicle, he responded, "I will walk out of the van on my own. Let me die like a man." Gravano continued, "He took several steps, lowered his head, and I shot him three times. He died without pain. He died La Cosa Nostra."

In reading this account by Gravano, I couldn't help but wonder how a man such as he, who later admitted killing over twenty individuals on orders from Castellano, could show such remorse for his role in the murder of Simone. We later determined that Gravano had a strong allegiance to Simone's wife and children, eventually motivating him to cooperate and become a critical witness in the Commission case. Hidden behind his life of violence, there appeared to be another side to the man, although his actions as a member of the Mafia were abhorrent.

Frank Sindone, another coconspirator in the plot to kill Bruno, was murdered a short time later. His body was found by the local police inside two plastic bags in the parking lot of a shopping center a few blocks from his home in South Philly. His hands were tied behind him and it appeared he had been tortured. The retribution for Caponigro's betrayal was complete, but the killings within the family would continue for the next two years. It would become the bloodiest period in the history of the Philadelphia Mafia, and it seemed that the agents assigned to the squad never had a day off.

The district attorney convened a local grand jury to look into all the homicides that were taking place. Stanfa was subpoenaed to testify, but did not volunteer any information. He soon disappeared and subsequently turned up in Baltimore. A local warrant had been issued charging him with perjury during his testimony, and he was arrested and sent to prison. We still did not know the extent of his involvement in the Bruno murder, but we now believed he was complicit in setting up the hit. His involvement may not have been apparent to the Commission; thus, he was not the target of retribution.

During the aftermath of Bruno's murder, there was a period of uncertainty and lack of discipline within the family, as a new boss had not yet been officially appointed. Philip "the Chicken Man" Testa, the underboss, kept a low profile after the killings of Caponigro, Salerno, Simone, and Sindone. Many of Bruno's established contacts with union bosses in the city were in a precarious situation after Bruno's murder.

John McCullough, head of the powerful Roofers Union, had a solid and lasting relationship with Bruno, who was now gone. McCullough had been under investigation by our labor racketeering squad for some time, but no prosecution had been forthcoming. Our intelligence revealed that with Bruno's blessing, McCullough had been attempting to organize the Bartenders Union in Atlantic City, controlled by "Little Nicky" Scarfo, a capo in the family. After Bruno's death, McCullough continued interfering with Scarfo's turf and resumed organizing activities with the Bartenders Union.

On the morning of December 16, 1980, Willard Moran, a reputed hit man, appeared at the front door of McCullough's modest home in Philadelphia carrying two poinsettia plants and armed with an automatic pistol. McCullough's wife answered the door, and he muttered, "I have a delivery of flowers for you." Mrs. McCullough allowed Moran into the house. He walked directly to the dining room and placed the plants on a table. Moran observed McCullough on the phone in the kitchen. He walked straight into the kitchen, shot McCullough several times, and quickly left the residence. McCullough lay dead on the kitchen floor with the phone still in his hand. Moran walked right past a hysterical Mrs. McCullough without harming her and escaped undetected by neighbors.

The killing of McCullough came on the heels of Bruno's murder. It significantly impacted the labor community, as he was considered the most powerful union leader in the city. The manner and ruthlessness of steps the Mob would take to address internal grievances had reached a level we had not witnessed before.

Our labor racketeering squad investigated McCullough's murder in coordination with squad one. Agent John Louden, a former Maryland state trooper, was assigned to the case. After an extensive investigation, Louden developed sufficient evidence that identified Moran as McCullough's killer. Upon his arrest, Moran agreed to cooperate and identified Albert Daidone, an official of the Atlantic City Bartenders Union, as the individual who hired him to kill McCullough. Daidone was the brother-in-law of Raymond "Long John" Martorano, a member of the Bruno family and confidant of Scarfo. Martarano and Daidone had been unable to convince McCullough to stay out of Atlantic City, so they ordered his murder without the approval of family leadership. All of the conspirators involved in the murder, except Scarfo, were eventually convicted and received lengthy prison sentences.

After his release from prison, Martorano was driving his car one night near the intersection of Eighth and Walnut Streets in Philadelphia. According to an eyewitness, another vehicle suddenly cut him off, and a shooter on the passenger side unleashed a hail of bullets, killing him. Martorano had been out of prison for only a few months. The reason for his murder was not immediately apparent, but in all likelihood, this was retribution for the McCullough hit. The Mafia had a long memory.

Philip "the Chicken Man" Testa was finally appointed by the

Commission to succeed Bruno. He received the nickname "the Chicken Man" because he had worked in the poultry business as a young man. He was now the main target of the Gangplank investigation, which was winding to a close. Strike Force Chief Joel Friedman had agreed to pursue a RICO indictment, and Peter Vaira, the US attorney, joined Freedman in this effort. Testa and several Bruno family leaders were subsequently indicted in February 1981 for violating the RICO statute. Squad one had accomplished its mission. It was the first time the DOJ had charged a Mafia family as a continuing criminal enterprise. All arrested family members soon quickly posted bail and would now await trial in federal court.

On Sunday morning, March 15, 1981, I received a phone call at home at approximately 2:00 a.m. Sue and I were sound asleep. I quickly answered so Sue would not be disturbed. The agent on duty at the office immediately told me that "Testa has just been blown up at his home." He had been taken to St. Agnes Hospital on Broad Street. I told the agent, "I am on my way."

Sue woke up as I began getting dressed and asked, "What are you doing?" I told her what had happened, and she asked, "Why can't someone else go?"

I kissed her goodbye and told her, "I love you. Don't worry, I will be in touch." I had no idea when I would return home.

As I drove over the Benjamin Franklin Bridge heading into Philly, not quite awake, I contacted the dispatcher at the FBI office. I instructed her to "contact every squad member and have them report to Testa's home immediately." It had only been eight months since Bruno's death. My first thought was, *Who ordered the hit?* When I arrived at Testa's home, the police were already setting up a crime scene, and I met with Inspector Richard Strom of the homicide unit. He told me, "Testa was on the front porch about to enter his home when the bomb exploded."

Testa was pronounced dead at the hospital as a result of his wounds. This was a planned hit. The bomb that killed him was a crudely made device comprised of nails, which had the same effect that shrapnel would have in an ordinary explosive device. The entrance and first floor of the home were destroyed. A shattered staircase remained, leading to the second floor. At this point, they had not done any forensic examination of the crime scene. I offered to assist by having our FBI bomb experts do the examination. The inspector reluctantly agreed to my suggestion, but seemed concerned I would take over his crime scene. That thought had entered my mind.

Testa's home was across from a beautiful park that comprised a complete city block. Homes surrounded the park, so one could visually observe the front of his house from any of the adjoining streets on the park's perimeter. The killer must have been observing the front porch from a vantage point on the perimeter, and when he observed Testa on the porch, he activated a detonator that triggered the bomb. We would have to do a thorough neighborhood inquiry in the morning to determine if anyone saw anything suspicious moments before the killing. In addition, after the bombing, the killer would have quickly left the scene and possibly had been spotted by a police officer on routine patrol.

I went next door to Testa's home after a report that two elderly sisters had been injured. I noted that the living room was in shambles as I entered their home. The stairway to their bedroom on the second floor was unsteady, so I proceeded cautiously. I met with both ladies and although they were frightened and visibly shaken, they appeared to be physically okay. One of them reminded me of my grandmother. I tried to comfort them the best I could and medical assistance was being provided. At the time of the explosion, they were asleep, and the force of the bomb threw both of them from their beds to the floor.

They could not provide any helpful information, but remarked, "He was such a nice man." They needed to rest and I quickly left their bedroom. There was always collateral damage in incidents such as this. Innocent bystanders are often seriously injured or mentally scarred. I hoped, in this case, these two lovely sisters would not suffer mental anxiety from their experience.

Outside the home, a disruptive incident ensued. Testa's son, Salvatore, arrived and had to be forcibly restrained by police from entering the crime scene. He kept shouting, "Who killed my father?" Neighbors began to gather and the scene was starting to become chaotic. The police did a great job maintaining order. Media representatives wanted to have on-the-scene interviews, which was discouraged. There would be time for that later, but not now, as we had a lot of work to do.

We searched Testa's home for any evidence that might shed light on the motive for his murder. Agent Bob Brown approached me. "Hey, boss, look at this." One of the chests of drawers in the bedroom contained over $250,000 in cash stuffed in brown paper bags with no documents connected to the money. In all likelihood, receipts from his illegal activities. The search uncovered no evidence that revealed any leads. A lot would depend on our follow-up investigation.

A limited canvass of the neighborhood developed one lead. Around midnight, a neighbor who lived on a street adjacent to the park had just arrived home from a night out and observed a parked vehicle with a male driver sitting alone in the car. He did not recognize the vehicle and was concerned. "I thought he might be a burglar, so I kept an eye on him for a while and then went to bed." At least we had a potential lead, as someone would have had a clear line of sight of Testa's front porch from that vantage point.

We were done for the day and would pick it up tomorrow. I did not realize it was so late. Everyone headed home. Sue was waiting patiently for me when I arrived. I was too late for dinner, but I could smell the aroma of a meal warming up in the oven. I briefly told her what had occurred without going into gory details. After dinner, we turned on the TV, snuggled on the couch, and watched a comedy. It was good to be home.

First thing Monday morning, I got a call from Inspector Strom, and he informed me that "an officer on patrol in the area of the bombing had noticed a car run a stop sign a few blocks from

Testa's home shortly after the murder." He continued that the officer issued the driver a ticket upon making a traffic stop. "The driver was Rocco Marinucci, a resident of South Philly." There was nothing in our files regarding Marinucci. We had no clue about his background and could not locate him at his residence.

Due to our excellent informant coverage of the Bruno family, we soon put together a scenario of what had occurred. Marinucci was a driver for Peter Casella, the underboss of what was now referred to as the Testa family. Casella was unhappy with Testa's lack of control over the family business and that no one was making enough money. Members still could not engage in drug trafficking. Casella conspired with capo Frank "Chickie" Narducci to kill Testa. He planned to take over the family and make Narducci his underboss.

The Commission had not approved of this plot. Casella and Narducci had not learned any lesson from the Caponigro experience. After the Testa hit, the Commission ordered Casella and Narducci to a sit-down meeting in New York. After listening to their explanations, they banned Casella from the family and he was exiled to Florida. Several weeks later, Narducci was hit and his body was found on a vacant lot in South Philly. Marinucci was shot on March 15, 1982, exactly one year to the day of Testa's murder. His body was found on a vacant lot in South Philly with firecrackers stuffed in his mouth, a reference I assumed to the bomb he planted that killed Testa.

Nicodemo "Little Nicky" Scarfo was appointed by the Commission to succeed Testa. The organization was in a tailspin, and this period was unprecedented in the history of the Philadelphia Mafia. The family had three bosses in less than a year: Bruno, Testa, and Scarfo. Scarfo had been a member since 1954, so he had a long history with the family. He was known for his violent temper and impulsive behavior. He was short and there was speculation that he always felt he had to prove himself because of his stature. Bruno banished him to Atlantic City for his unpredictable behavior. Now, he was returning as boss. His father was a former member of the Lucchese family in New York, which may have influenced the Commission to appoint him as the new boss to succeed Testa.

His first act was to appoint Salvatore Merlino as his underboss and Frank Monte as his consigliere. Scarfo quickly established a "street tax." The head of every organized crime group in the city would have to pay a monthly fee to operate. This unexpected edict met with much pushback from the organized crime community. Scarfo did not relent and targeted Stevie Bouras, a Greek organized crime community leader, to make his point.

On the evening of May 27, 1981, Chelsais "Steve" Bouras decided to take his girlfriend Jannette Curro out to dinner at Meletis Greek Restaurant in South Philadelphia. He invited his good friend Raymond "Long John" Martorano to attend. Radio host and well-known personality Jerry Blavat joined them. Martorano had just been accepted as a capo of the Scarfo family for his assistance in setting up the hit on John McCullough, so the dinner engagement was meant to be a celebration. The party ordered drinks and toasted Martorano's new position with the family. They began reviewing the menu to select their dinner entrées.

Suddenly, a lone masked gunman appeared at their table. He aimed his gun at Martorano and Blavat and ordered them to "step aside." He then shot multiple rounds into the bodies of Bouras and Curro, killing them instantly. There was mass hysteria among the other guests and many ran toward the back of the restaurant, fearing for their lives. The gunman immediately fled. This horrible incident was on the front page of the morning newspaper, and there was a public outcry over all the killings that were taking place in the ongoing saga of the Philadelphia Mafia.

Bouras had been under investigation for drug trafficking and was the head of what had been referred to as the Greek Mob. He had refused to pay the street tax and resented Scarfo taking over the family. Scarfo thus considered him a threat. The killings generated considerable publicity and were just the beginning of what would become known as the Scarfo reign of terror in the city.

Scarfo brought with him one of the bloodiest periods in the

family's history. Within eighteen months, no fewer than twenty family members or associates were murdered. We were finding bodies everywhere. Scarfo suffered from paranoia and his violent nature would emerge time and time again. Harry Riccobene, a former consigliere for Bruno, formed an independent faction to challenge Scarfo, and an all-out war ensued. It was known as the Scarfo-Riccobene War. He enlisted the help of Phil Testa's son, Salvatore, to help him. Scarfo, after learning of this, put out a hit on Salvatore. His murder created a backlash; Scarfo became more resented within the family after the hit on Salvatore, and the Commission in New York was not happy.

Critical informant coverage of what was happening in the family enabled the squad to monitor developments daily. Riccobene was now one of Scarfo's targets; Scarfo ordered Frank Monte to have his crew kill Riccobene. After learning that a contract had been issued, Riccobene assembled his hit team to take Monte out, and they promptly obliged. Riccobene was subsequently charged with this murder along with the shooters, and he received a life sentence. Several family members, including Mario Riccobene, Harry's brother, stepped forward during this period and would later testify as witnesses during future court proceedings involving Scarfo and his underboss, Joey Merlino.

Michael Leyden and Jim Maher, who had extensive knowledge of Scarfo's past activities, were now supervising the investigation of the Scarfo family. They soon got a big break regarding Scarfo. Willard Rouse and his deputy, Peter Balitsaris, contacted the office regarding an extortion scheme. Rouse was a real estate developer responsible for constructing several significant properties in Philadelphia. He was developing Penn's Landing, a multimillion-dollar project in the Old City section of the city. A meeting was scheduled and both men sat down with Leyden and Maher to relate the facts of the ongoing extortion.

Robert Rego, the administrative assistant to city councilman Leland Beloff, had recently contacted Balitsaris to inform him that "Beloff had a problem with supporting the proposal for the

Penn's Landing project." Bellof was a member of the city council and represented the district where the project would be built. For the proposal to move forward, the council and Beloff, in particular, had to support the project. Rego suggested, "We meet to discuss the problem regarding the approval of the proposal." Balitsaris, assuming this was a legitimate issue on the table, agreed to meet with Rego to settle the matter. Rego set up the meeting at a local downtown bar, which seemed odd.

When Balitsaris met Rego, he was introduced to another individual sitting at the table. Rego identified him as "Nick," a representative of Beloff who would be the individual he had to deal with directly. With that introduction, Rego got up and left the bar. Nick threatened Balitsaris: "There will be no project without a substantial payment for Beloff's support." He was taken aback by this threat, particularly after Nick said it would cost the company "one million dollars." Balitsaris did not commit and stated he would have to discuss this issue with Rouse. After discussing the situation, he and Rouse pursued this overture to obtain more information.

A second meeting was held with Nick and Rego. Nick told Balitsaris in no uncertain terms, "Without the payment, the proposal will be dead in the water." Leyden and Maher speculated that Nick could only be none other than Nick Caramandi, a member of the Scarfo family who had been suspected of being involved in several hits ordered by Scarfo. They decided to introduce an undercover agent into this scenario as the future representative of Rouse. Both Rouse and Balitsaris agreed to this plan. They needed to resolve this matter so they could proceed with the project.

Before proceeding, Maher needed to know more about Leland Beloff. He was a member of the city council and his district included Old City, a section of Philadelphia experiencing a building renaissance. The city council had to have Beloff's approval to permit the development of any new building project in his district. Rouse could not build Penn's Landing without Beloff's approval. It was that simple, but where did Caramandi and Scarfo come in? That was the question. Maybe Rego was the connection.

Balitsaris contacted Rego for a third meeting, but on this occasion, he would be accompanied by an undercover agent wearing a transmitter, and all conversations would be monitored and recorded. This would place the agent in a potentially dangerous situation, so we planned to station two agents in the bar to observe the meeting. Caramandi again was present along with Rego. He reviewed their plan's details and demanded a payment of $100,000 up-front before proceeding.

The undercover agent gave Caramandi $10,000 as a reasonable down payment. At this point, Caramandi became hostile and threatening, but the agent assured him, "Do not worry, more money will follow." The additional payments never came. Within days, Caramandi, Rego, Beloff, and Scarfo were arrested and subsequently indicted by a federal grand jury for the extortion of the Rouse Corporation. Caramandi somehow learned that Scarfo had ordered his murder, as he blamed him for the Rouse arrest. Scarfo was also afraid he might cooperate. That was Scarfo's way—he did not trust anyone. Caramandi then contacted Agent Maher and decided to cooperate. He directly implicated Scarfo in the extortion conspiracy and indicated it was initially Rego's idea. Scarfo and his coconspirators were soon brought to trial in federal court.

Caramandi testified to being a hit man for Scarfo, implicating him in the extortion scheme and fingered Rego as a Scarfo associate who set up Rouse. He also pleaded guilty to several murders and attempted extortions. Although he was cooperating with the government, Caramandi realized that he would have to serve time in prison for his past crimes. He was a compelling witness and the jurors were focused on his account of the plot to extort Rouse out of a million dollars. He also described how Scarfo intended to split the money with Beloff and Rego.

All the defendants were convicted. Scarfo received a fourteen-year sentence in federal prison, while Bellof and Rego received an eight-year sentence. Caramandi would testify in eleven additional trials, leading to convictions of family members in all the cases. He became the most essential cooperative witness the Philadelphia FBI office ever developed. Organized Crime Strike Force Chief Joel Friedman said publicly, "Caramandi's cooperation decimated the Philadelphia La Cosa Nostra and its associates." The Bruno-Testa-Scarfo family never rebounded, and one succeeding boss after another was indicted and convicted of RICO violations. After approximately sixty-five years, the Philadelphia Mafia family would never regain the power and influence it once held.

CHAPTER 7
The Irishman

During this period, an investigation was initiated involving Teamsters official Frank Sheeran, the president of Local 326 in Wilmington, Delaware, as informant information and previous inquiries indicated the Mafia controlled him. Sheeran was born and raised in Philadelphia and enlisted in the Army during World War II. He served honorably in the war and engaged in several major European battles involving intense combat and eventual Allied victories. Upon returning home, he worked as a truck driver and joined Teamsters Local 107, the largest Teamsters local in Philadelphia. Sheeran thus began his career with a union that would change his life forever.

Possibly from his war experiences, Sheeran had a propensity for violence. Local 107 was known for intimidating businesses and other unions to obtain lucrative contracts for their members. When they failed, they would resort to whatever means necessary to enforce their demands. Sheeran initially became an enforcer for the union, and officials would turn to him and his associates to do whatever was required to accomplish their objectives.

In 1972, Sheeran was charged with the murder of union representative Robert DeGeorge, which occurred in broad daylight in front of the Local 107 headquarters on Spring Garden Street. As DeGeorge exited his car, witnesses observed Sheeran walking up to him and, without warning, shoot him several times. DeGeorge was killed instantly. After being charged, the case was dismissed on a questionable decision by an appeals court that ruled the case had not been brought to trial within the prescribed time frame. Sheeran was later arrested for the murder of union official Frederick Gawronski in New Castle, Delaware, but he was acquitted. He soon developed a reputation among his Teamsters associates—do not get on the wrong side of "the Irishman."

During this same period, Sheeran met Russell Bufalino, who was a capo in the Genovese family and had influence over the Teamsters locals in Pennsylvania and Delaware. Bufalino was an unknown figure to the FBI in Philadelphia. He lived in Pittston, Pennsylvania, in the state's northeastern section, miles from the city. The Genovese family in New York had directed him to set up a satellite group to control criminal activities. Agent John Tamm was assigned to the Sheeran investigation. He was a very aggressive investigator with a unique instinct that enabled him to develop successful conclusions regarding a complex problem. The Sheeran case would be such a challenge.

We had limited intelligence regarding the history and structure of the Mafia in New York or Bufalino's relationship with the Genovese family. Our New York office was contacted and they summarized an event that answered many of our questions. In 1957, Vito Genovese, the boss of the family, called a meeting with all the Mafia leaders throughout the country. The purpose of the meeting was to solidify his position as the new head of the Commission, which would have absolute control over all disputes nationally. He elicited the support of Bufalino to make arrangements with Mafia leader Joseph Barbara to hold the meeting at Barbara's estate in Apalachin, New York. This location was away from the city and would be discreet enough to avoid detection by law enforcement. As it would turn out, they were mistaken. The meeting was set for November 14, and over 100 Mafia bosses and capos from throughout the country were invited. A select number of Mafia members from Italy also were expected.

Genovese had recently ordered the murder of a family boss, Albert Anastasia, and installed Carlo Gambino to take over the family. He also had his protégé Vincent "Chin" Gigante shoot Frank Costello in the head, pushing him into retirement to make way for Genovese's own ascension as family boss. He wanted to reassure all the bosses that nothing would change now that he was in charge. Items such as drug trafficking, union racketeering, and control over legitimate businesses were on the table. This meeting was unprecedented in the history of the Mafia. Unfortunately for the attendees, the meeting was suddenly interrupted.

A local state trooper became suspicious when he saw the number of Cadillacs and chauffeur-driven limousines suddenly showing up in the small town of Apalachin. He knew of Barbara's presence in the community and the location of his estate a few miles from town. In an unmarked car, the officer discreetly surveilled one of the limos driven directly to Barbara's home. What he observed shocked him. There were at least forty vehicles parked at various locations on the perimeter of the house. He recorded several license plate tags, some from out of state. He determined that many of the cars were registered to convicted felons. The trooper obtained a local search warrant, assembled a group of officers, and raided Barbara's home.

The attendees at the meeting were tipped off by a caretaker who spotted a state police vehicle entering the driveway. They all quickly scrambled to the nearest exits. Some ran for their cars and others mistakenly fled into the surrounding woods, stumbling as they fled. They were like children running away from the wicked witch. Over sixty were arrested, charged in local court, and received a minimal fine. The state police later estimated over 100 mobsters were attending the meeting. They were all booked and photographed by the state police, which became the source of an intelligence windfall for the FBI. Joe Ida, who preceded Angelo Bruno as boss of the Philadelphia family, was arrested along with Gambino boss Carlo Gambino and his capo Paul Castellano. Carlos Marcello, the boss of the New Orleans family, was present but successfully escaped through the woods. He was one of the few who managed to escape. Bufalino was arrested, attempting to drive away from the home. Vito Genovese himself was in Bufalino's car and was also arrested. Bufalino's involvement in this event drew the attention of the FBI in New York, and he was recognized as a critical player in the Genovese network.

Another positive result of the Apalachin meeting related to an issue the FBI now had to recognize. Director Hoover could no longer deny the existence of the Mafia, as the event generated national publicity, and the press and public wanted answers. Within a relatively short period, Hoover announced the creation of a new program the FBI would initiate to develop intelligence information regarding the Mafia. As only a few federal statutes were in place that could be the basis for conducting criminal investigations, the new program focused primarily on collecting intelligence regarding the Mafia. Unfortunately, as I discovered, it would take years to develop an investigative approach the FBI could successfully implement to take down the Mafia as a criminal enterprise.

Agents Jimmy Maher and Henry Handy approached me and stated they had an opportunity to operate a confidential witness named Charlie Allen, who was a drug dealer and hit man. Allen had recently been arrested by the Drug Enforcement Agency (DEA) for manufacturing amphetamines, and he was willing to make a deal if he could receive favorable treatment. During an initial debriefing, Allen admitted to having a close relationship with Frank Sheeran and bluntly stated, "I have done a lot of work for him." Allen agreed to wear a body recorder in future meetings with Sheeran.

I believed we should pursue this opportunity, so I contacted Joel Friedman, head of the Organized Crime Strike Force. Friedman initially hesitated in his assessment and commented, "I am not sure of this one, Frank—it sounds risky." He was right, but I assured him, "We will keep him under wraps." Friedman did agree we could work with Allen as a potential cooperative witness, but "he would have to plead guilty to the existing drug charge, and the DEA would have to agree."

I then met with the DEA agents assigned to the Allen case, who were not happy to see me. Entering their office, one of the agents commented, "Oh, here comes the FBI to steal our case." I ignored the remark. After twisting some arms, they agreed to our participation in working with Allen as long as he would continue to work with them on drug investigations.

Maher and Handy would be the lead agents handling Allen and Tamm would be directly involved as the case agent. Allen had a scheduled meeting with Sheeran in a local bar. He was unsure what Sheeran wanted, but we requested that he wear a body recorder. Maher and Handy were stationed in a car close by, monitoring the conversation. Tamm and his partner Bob Brown were in a backup car in the event a problem developed so they could quickly intervene. I monitored the meeting from our command center, as I had concerns about this one. We assumed Sheeran would be armed and being overly cautious, he might pat Allen down to see if he was wired. That could present a severe problem, particularly in a public place.

When Allen entered, Sheeran was sitting alone at the bar. Two additional agents were already sitting at the other end of the bar within proximity. Allen and Sheeran met for about forty minutes and then Sheeran abruptly left after paying the bill.

After the meeting, Maher contacted me over the radio and said, "We have a problem." When they returned to the office, we sat in the conference room and listened to the tape recording of the conversation between Sheeran and Allen. Sheeran referred to a local Teamsters union official named Bobby Marino, who had been murdered a few years ago. He thanked Allen "for handling Bobby—it meant a lot to me." This revelation presented a complicated issue for us to navigate. Allen had never even hinted to us that he knew about the murder of Marino. I told Maher and Handy to pick up Allen and take him to a secure location to get the details of the Marino hit and his criminal history. They were to emphasize that "the deal is off if he does not tell us everything."

Allen had been affiliated with the Bruno family his entire life. When confronted by the agents, Allen freely admitted to killing Marino and described to us how he had murdered him at Sheeran's request. He was not paid for killing Marino and nonchalantly stated, "I did it as a favor. Marino had always been on the outskirts of the family, and nobody trusted him." Sheeran had a serious dispute with Marino over a union contract he was attempting to obtain and could not resolve the issue, so he requested that Allen kill him. Allen denied responsibility for any additional Mafia-ordered hits. The agents had to take Allen at his word. At this point, we were unsure of his truthfulness, but these were the cards we had to play. This development necessitated another visit with DOJ attorneys to get authorization to continue working with Allen. Trafficking in drugs is one thing, but murder is a whole different ball game. I also had to get the okay from FBI headquarters and notify the DEA.

Upon getting the authority to operate Allen as a cooperative witness, we set up several meetings with Sheeran to develop additional evidence. The investigation progressed and we uncovered enough evidence to indict Sheeran and another union official for the murder of Marino. We did not have enough evidence to indict Bufalino, whom we believed had to okay the hit on Marino. A warrant was issued for Sheeran's arrest. Several agents and I went to his apartment in the city's northeast section early one Sunday morning. We did not anticipate he would resist arrest; however, we had to be cautious, as he had a violent nature and had previously been charged but not convicted of two homicides. As we banged on the door to his apartment, we announced, "FBI, open up! We have a warrant for your arrest." We knew he was in the apartment, as we had made a pretext call to him shortly before we arrived. He did not respond to our demands.

I wouldn't say I liked this situation—a forced entry was not always a good idea. I was sure Sheeran had a gun inside his apartment. We went ahead, however, and made a forced entry. As it turned out, he was physically unable to answer the door when we arrived, as he was showering. After he was officially arrested, I spoke to Sheeran briefly, and he seemed somewhat understanding and cooperative. I handed him my card with my home phone number and told him to call me to discuss his situation. That turned out to be a mistake on my part. After appearing before a federal magistrate for arraignment, he quickly made bail and was released.

A few weeks later, my son and daughter were over for dinner and a board game. We tried to do this at least once a week; it was a great way to unwind and pay attention to my two prized possessions.

The phone rang and a woman said hello without referring to me by name. She had a serious tone and said, "I know who you are," and indicated she knew me from the past. She said something to the effect of, "We used to fight a lot and I am not your friend." I asked her who was calling and she said "you will soon find out." She wanted to know if I was alone and I said no. With that, she hung up.

I was alarmed by that call and told the children it was time to head home. I drove to their house, hugged them, and said good night. They were now safe with their mother. I was still determining my next move. I returned to our house and Sue asked, "Who was that on the phone?" I was truthful and told her I did not know, but did not go further. We eventually went to bed and I tried to analyze what happened.

Who was this woman who called and why did she emphasize, "I am not your friend"? No one from my past would do such a thing. I was more than concerned and placed my gun on the night table beside our bed. Sheeran must have passed my home phone number along to one of his associates. How else would the woman know my number? I had a restless night.

It appeared that they were attempting to intimidate me, as that was Sheeran's style. I did not want to make a big deal out of this, as there was no direct threat, but at the same time, I could not ignore what had occurred. In the morning, I spoke to a few experienced agents on the squad to get their thoughts. They responded, "We will pay Mr. Sheeran a visit." I thought this would be a good idea as long as they did not discuss the case. We did not want to taint the prosecution. They understood what they had to do. The agents reported later, "We got our point across in no uncertain terms. We told Sheeran there is a line you do not want to cross with us." Things settled down and we moved on.

Sheeran subsequently went on trial and a jury was selected. The trial lasted about two weeks and he was defended by Emmett Fitzpatrick, a former Philadelphia district attorney who was an excellent defense counsel. His flamboyant personality tended to overshadow that of the prosecuting attorneys. Allen was our key witness and struggled to stay coherent under Fitzpatrick's relentless cross-examination. In addition, Allen was an admitted killer and drug dealer, and we knew the jury might question his reliability and truthfulness. Sheeran also had a couple of his goons in the courtroom daily, mingling with the attendees and staring down the jury, attempting to intimidate them.

In a surprise move, Fitzpatrick called Sheeran to the stand, and of course he denied all the allegations in the indictment. We did not expect this move and the prosecuting attorneys, less experienced than Fitzpatrick, should have prepared for this development. The lead attorney called for a recess and we all huddled in the corridor outside the courtroom. They had no planned outline of a possible cross-examination and I sensed uncertainty in their discussions. I looked over at Tamm and he also had a concerned look. He raised his eyebrows as if to say, "I don't believe this." The cross-examination of Sheeran did not go well. The lead prosecutor then replayed the taped conversation between Sheeran and Allen, but it did not appear the jury was paying attention. Sheeran was found not guilty and all charges were dismissed.

Tamm and the prosecutors were naturally disappointed at the verdict. Although they understood Allen would have credibility problems due to his background, they still felt they had a strong case. The tape depicted the critical conversation between Sheeran and Allen regarding the Marino hit, but it was not enough to convince the jury of his guilt. Did Sheeran's goons in the courtroom intimidate the jury? It was a real possibility. Philadelphia was a strong labor union community and it was tough to convict corrupt officials. The prosecutive team did an outstanding job presenting the evidence, which was not the issue. We had to put this setback behind us and keep our eye on Mr. Sheeran.

There is always another day. Years later, Sheeran was indicted in a labor racketeering case, convicted, and sentenced to thirty-two years in federal prison. He was paroled after serving thirteen years and released. He died on December 14, 2003, at the age of eighty-three. Bufalino was subsequently indicted, convicted, and received a lengthy prison sentence. His Mafia group in upstate Pennsylvania, which formerly had ties to the Genovese family, was no longer a functioning body capable of engaging in serious criminal activity. Mission accomplished.

CHAPTER 8
The Final Solution

In September 1981, I had been in contact with Special Agent Jim Kossler in New York, the coordinating supervisor of the organized crime program. Jim was highly regarded by the Bureau and had earned the reputation of being an outstanding supervisor. He advised me that New York was reevaluating the division's management structure, which might affect the organized crime program's overall direction. He commented, "I am not sure what they have in mind, but things are a mess up here."

Several weeks had passed when SAC John Hogan summoned me to his office. Hogan said, "Frank, I just got off the phone with headquarters. You have been promoted to a new position in New York as assistant special agent in charge of the organized crime program for the entire division." I sat there and just took in the words without any reaction. I was unaware that I was being considered for this position, nor was I familiar with the specifics of the management reorganization in New York other than what Jim had told me.

In the FBI, we were always subject to being assigned to wherever headquarters decided you were needed. We were made aware of this policy on day one. Due to the nature of the Bureau's challenges, you can understand this is how it has to work. Still, adjusting to suddenly being transferred is challenging. It is easier for the agent to adapt to a new assignment, as the FBI universally functions in the same way. It is much more difficult for the agent's family. That night, I broke the news to Sue, who was four months pregnant. She was not too upset, as New York would still be close to her family. We decided not to sell our home due to the high cost of living in New York. Our baby was expected in the spring. I would find temporary housing in New York until things settled down.

I contacted New York and advised the SAC of the criminal division of my travel plans. I took the Amtrak to New York. The trip to the city was short, but gave me some time to think about what was ahead of me. I had a pad of paper, which I always relied upon to write down my thoughts when focusing on issues. As the train rumbled on, I began making notes relating to what I already knew about the organized crime problem in New York. If we were going to win the battle against the Mafia, it had to begin in New York, where the American Cosa Nostra was born.

I began to envision, as our objective, the ultimate takedown of the Commission and the key leaders of the Five Families simultaneously. It was a tall order that many in the FBI would not believe attainable, but that thinking differed from the FBI I had recently witnessed. The UNIRAC and Bruno family investigations had taught me a lot. Could we develop a similar approach in New York? We were up against an enemy that had been entrenched in the fabric of New York for over seventy-five years. In addition to their long-standing involvement in traditional organized crime activities, the Five Families controlled several significant unions and legitimate businesses crucial to the city and the nation's economy. I began to sense that now was the moment we had to act and move boldly.

The New York division was the largest field office in the country, with 1,200 agents assigned. The organized crime program had ten squads of agents located in three separate offices: Manhattan, Brooklyn, and New Rochelle. Approximately 140 agents, many of whom were inexperienced, were assigned to the program. There were five families, not one as you would find in cities where the Mafia was prevalent. In addition, the boss of each family was a member of a formal group that oversaw the activities of the Five Families. This group, called the Commission, had enormous power nationwide. I learned this firsthand in the aftermath of the murder of Philadelphia bosses Angelo Bruno and Philip Testa. The Mafia had existed in the United States since the 1920s and had never been penetrated. The family names of Gambino, Colombo, Lucchese, Genovese, and Bonanno were references to previous bosses who had since died. There were at least 1,200 made members scattered throughout the Five Families. They controlled five times as many associates as part of their criminal enterprises.

Through control of the unions, they could extort payment from the owners of various companies in the garment district, the construction and trucking industry, and, of course, the shipping industry, as we had learned through the UNIRAC investigation. The New York office had several successes in the past with prosecutions of individual members of the Mafia; however, the Five Families still operated as usual without relinquishing their control and influence throughout the city. It was almost as if they were a separate governmental entity that was part of the infrastructure and lure of New York. The final notation on my notepad as the train pulled into Madison Square Garden was to take it one step at a time and see where this road would lead. I also had my friend RICO to help me along the way.

The New York office was in the federal building at 26 Federal Plaza, five blocks north of the World Trade Center. It was an enormous building and the FBI had offices on the twenty-sixth and twenty-seventh floors. When I arrived at the office, I reported to SAC Richard Bretzing. He oversaw three investigative branches in the division, which were white-collar crime, general property, and organized crime. We had an excellent initial discussion about what he expected and why I was chosen for this new position. He laid the cards on the table and said, "The task before you will be difficult, and I am not looking for quick fixes. The program is floundering and there is a total lack of a coordinated effort. I want you to fix it." Wow, that was a mouthful and right away I realized, *Okay, this is the big leagues, and it is your turn at bat.* With those clear marching orders, I told Bretzing, "I'll do my best." It was obvious that Bretzing cared very much about the program's future success. I made a personal commitment to myself that I would not disappoint him.

After our meeting, I walked to where I thought my office would be located, but I only found a secretary sitting outside a cubicle that appeared to have been quickly assembled. There was a desk and phone present and what seemed to be a couch, but there was an immediate problem. The couch was a bright orange. I burst out laughing and thought this was a joke. I was partly right. It turned out that since my position had just been created, they did not know where to put me and they were still working on logistics. *Okay*, I thought, *welcome to the neighborhood.* An assistant chief clerk soon arrived and began to straighten everything out. Susan called later that afternoon, and we both had a good laugh when I recounted my first day in the Big Apple.

A week or so after I arrived, a conference sponsored by US Attorney Thomas Puccio of the Eastern District of New York was scheduled in Brooklyn. Puccio was a renowned prosecutor and considered one of the few officials serious about pursuing prosecutions of Mafia members. The subject of the meeting was the organized crime problem that New York faced, and the heads of various law enforcement agencies and their assistants would be in attendance. Bretzing had made arrangements to introduce me and have me present my views on how to address this issue. I approached this assignment with concern, as I had not prepared for such a moment after just arriving in the city. What would I say to get their attention and help establish my bona fides?

We traveled together across the bridge to Brooklyn and on the way, Bretzing remarked, "I need you to do a good job, or I will have your buttons." What the hell did that mean? Was I in the army, and would I be discharged if I failed to impress the attendees at the conference? This was not the first time I'd had to give a presentation. I would focus on the new approach and solution we planned to introduce to our investigations of the five Mafia families.

I was nervous as I began to speak; there must have been at least fifty officials in the room. I began by referring to my experience with the UNIRAC investigation, much of which was based in New York. I also referred to the Bruno investigation, which had involved members of the Genovese and Gambino families. I strongly emphasized that provisions of the RICO statute made those investigations successful, and we intended to utilize the same approach to take down the Five Families simultaneously. The attendees did not take notes, but paid attention to every word I said, and I saw some nodding their heads in agreement, including Puccio. I finished by emphasizing, "We will all have to work together to accomplish the task ahead of us, which is formidable." I spoke for about thirty minutes. On returning to the office, Bretzing did not refer to "taking my buttons."

I soon sat down with Kossler, who gave me a sense of each squad's organizational structure and mission. He believed "our approach has to be better coordinated, with defined objectives." I agreed and asked Jim to call each supervisor to tell them we would meet to discuss the program and that "they should bring lunch, as it would last all day." The New York office had the reputation of doing things independently and had a baked-in culture developed over the years. It was also a challenging assignment for many agents due to the cost of living and the long commute to work every day. Many were in a bad mood before they even started the day. Introducing a new solution to our investigative approach in that atmosphere would be challenging, particularly when I was the new guy in town and not a New Yorker.

I said very little at the start of the meeting other than, "I want to get a sense of where we stand in our investigative effort to take down the Mafia." It may have been their first time hearing that expression, but I wanted them to think about our primary objective as we moved forward. I asked each supervisor to give a brief presentation regarding the makeup of his squad and its mission. I was not impressed with the majority of responses. “We arrest wise guys,” or “We just work cases and see where it takes us.” One supervisor had very little to put forward.

The meeting lasted several hours. Kossler did an excellent job of laying out the extent of control the Five Families had established over the years. He discussed the provisions of the RICO statute and the goal of using this relatively new law as the basis for looking at each family as a criminal enterprise. The supervisors were attentive during his presentation; some even took notes.

I closed the meeting by explaining that I strongly believed in using court-authorized electronic surveillance as an investigative tool. None of the squads had an active case where this investigative technique had been used. I jokingly said, “I want you to think of each family as a Christmas tree. I am hoping we light up each tree with wiretaps and microphones. If we do that, we will have the solution to this problem.” This got a few laughs and nods of the head. The scope of our proposal may have taken them back a bit, but they seemed committed to the plan.

Steve Carbone was a native New Yorker and had recently supervised the Lufthansa heist, which occurred at JFK International Airport. The case involved the burglary and armed robbery of the Lufthansa facility that contained millions of dollars in cash. Steve’s organized crime squad solved the theft committed by a group associated with the Lucchese crime family. He had an excellent reputation as a very competent supervisor. An experienced group of agents were assigned to the squad, but they had no specific objective and worked cases as they appeared on the radar screen. Steve contacted me the next day and we had a follow-up discussion.

Steve needed clarification on the new approach we had outlined. He candidly told me, “I disagree with what you want us to adopt. Based on my experience, agents do not want to work on long-term investigations. They like to turn over cases and move on to the next one. They will lose interest if they follow your idea."

I responded, "How long did the Lufthansa investigation last? Well over a year, right? We are not playing cops and robbers here—we aim to dismantle five Mafia criminal enterprises. I would project that may take us not one year, but more than likely two."

His response was weak and he did not attempt to soften his position. I thought he had some of the New York attitude prevalent in the office's personality: "We will do it our way." I admired that he spoke candidly; that is precisely what I was looking for in my supervisors. I thanked him for his opinion and left it at that.

The next day, I knew I had to make a move. I gave up Carbone's supervisory position and transferred his squad to the general property crimes program. Steve, not surprisingly, was happy with this decision. There was one catch, though. A few of his best agents would stay in my program and be filtered out to the other organized crime squads. It was a win-win move and caught the attention of all the other supervisors.

Kossler and I then met to discuss how reorganizing priorities and approaches might help us reach our objectives. This was a collaborative effort and Kossler, being very familiar with the provisions of the RICO statute, was a key player. The path New York had taken all these years had failed to work through no fault of Jim's. He had a great deal of experience in organized crime investigations and had been grappling with this problem for quite some time. He did not have the support of the front office to make necessary adjustments to the program. That would soon change.

The approach I laid out to Jim was relatively simple. We would select one squad to investigate a particular family and thus have all five families under simultaneous investigation. Each squad would develop sufficient evidence to establish that the family was a criminal enterprise. "The RICO statute will be our lantern to guide the way. We will aim to establish that the Commission is a separate criminal enterprise, but directly controlled the Five

Families. If successful, we will indict the Commission bosses and the key players in each family."

Jim looked at me with a smile, leaned back, and lit up his pipe. He was not a smoker, but when he was focusing on an issue, he had a habit of turning to his pipe so he could reflect on the moment. He did so in this case and commented, "Are you sure we are not attempting too much at one time?" This was a good point.

I replied, "No, I am unsure, but let's give it a shot."

Jim concluded, "Okay, I'm all in." I had the good fortune to have Jim by my side.

I placed a conference call to Section Chief Sean McWeeney, chief of the organized crime at headquarters and his deputy, Jules Bonavolonta. Both had previously been organized crime supervisors in New York and were now responsible for monitoring the program nationally. They needed to support our new approach, as I anticipated I would need future agent resources and increases in our budget as we moved forward. The scope of our proposal came to them as a surprise, but they quickly committed to the idea. They had years of experience fighting organized crime and their counsel in the future would be a valuable asset. Things were falling into place; Jim and I now had to find the right mix of five supervisors to accomplish our established goal.

My first choice, Bruce Mouw in Brooklyn, was an easy one. His squad was already focused on the Gambino family, making it a natural fit for his new objective. Two agents, Joe O'Brien and Andy Kurins, were the principal case agents, focusing on Paul Castellano, the family's boss. Their knowledge of the family's inner workings was quite remarkable. Mouw's laser focus and calm demeanor, honed from his tour in the Navy, made him an ideal choice for this assignment.

Lew Schiliro, an inexperienced supervisor, was also assigned to the Brooklyn office. He had a low-key approach, but an excellent feel for conducting and supervising investigations and—more importantly—the respect of the agents assigned to his squad. He had an air of independence, which was a good quality. At times, his team had not focused on one particular target. They were developing cases and locking up wise guys. He knew Brooklyn, the headquarters for the Bonanno family, so it now would be his baby.

Anthony "Fat Tony" Salerno's headquarters in the Bronx presented a strategic location for the Genovese family, with interests scattered across the city. Supervisor Don Richards, newly appointed to the program, may have had little experience, but his determined approach and refusal to accept no for an answer convinced me of his potential. With the support of the right agents, I felt confident he would excel. He got the Genovese ticket.

Damon Taylor, a veteran supervisor assigned to the Manhattan office, would be the perfect choice to lead his squad in pursuing the Colombo family. Dennis Maduro, one of his agents, would emerge as the team's star, as we would later determine. Damon lived in Manhattan, so he knew the city's pulse. He also had experience as an intelligence analyst and knew the inner workings of the Mafia very well. He would target Carmine "the Snake" Persico, the boss of the Colombo family.

We assigned Supervisor Dave Binney to direct the investigation of the Lucchese family. Dave, a graduate of West Point, had been a supervisor for a few years and knew the Lucchese Mob well. As with all the squads, his agents were mostly under thirty and inexperienced, but were willing to go through a wall to reach their objective. Agent Tommy French, one of the more experienced agents assigned to the program, would also be available. They now had the Lucchese family in their sights.

Jim and I discussed the quality of the available informants, furnishing information relating to the criminal activities of the Five Families. He felt we had excellent coverage of four families, but the Gambino group had not been penetrated. Agent Lin DeVecchio had been very successful at developing highly placed informants. He had sources who were made members or associates in each family except the Gambino enterprise. Quality informants would be critical to the success of our efforts. We could surveil wise guys' meetings forever, but we had to know what they discussed. The information our informants could provide would help establish the probable cause for an affidavit to present to a federal judge to authorize interceptions of Mafia conversations. My confidence began to grow as we proceeded on our ambitious journey.

More changes were taking place in the management of the office. SAC Bretzing had been promoted to the Los Angeles division. Headquarters announced that Thomas Sheer, an experienced manager and former supervisor in New York, would succeed Bretzing. He had supervised the resolution of a major bank robbery and hostage situation, which later had been depicted in the movie *Dog Day Afternoon*. He also had been a Marine Corps captain and a Vietnam veteran.

Shortly after Sheer arrived, I briefed him on our new proposals for reorganization of the program, and he supported the concept. Tom suggested that after he settled in, he would like to meet with John Martin, the US Attorney for the Southern District of New York, and US Attorney Raymond Dearie, whose office oversaw federal prosecutions in the Eastern District. Tom contacted both officials and they agreed to the meeting. He believed they both needed to agree to coordinate our investigations in anticipation of future indictments that would cross district lines. Neither Tom nor I were acquainted with either official.

We subsequently met in Tom's office and discussed our plans and the need for close cooperation between both districts due to the nature of the Mafia's activities, which occurred in all five city boroughs. Dearie immediately recognized the significance of a coordinated effort, and his manner and responses were enthusiastic and not guarded: "It's about time we take a new approach." Martin seemed reluctant to commit. His demeanor was more skeptical. He explained, "I do not believe a cooperative effort between the two offices would work based on past experiences." We emphasized that our investigations would cross their jurisdictional boundaries and require the assistance of both offices almost simultaneously with ongoing developments. Again, Dearie agreed, but Martin did not concur and became reluctant to engage. We ended the meeting at this point and thanked them for coming. Both districts had special sections assigned to handle organized crime matters, and we would have our agents deal directly with the attorneys assigned to those units. Tom's idea of working together did not appear to work, so we would do what we had to do.

I needed to touch one more base. Ronald Goldstock was head of the New York State Organized Crime Task Force and was in charge of an investigation into Anthony "Tony Ducks" Corallo, the boss of the Lucchese family. He had an experienced group of detectives assigned to the case, and according to Kossler, they were making progress. He was familiar with the RICO statute. They also could use authorized electronic surveillance as part of their investigation. The FBI had not sat down with Ron or offered assistance to date. That would stop. I called Ron and he knew about my recent arrival in New York. We set up a meeting and I drove to his office in New Rochelle. I briefed Ron on the details of our new approach, and he agreed that "You are finally on the right path." He would focus on the Corallo matter and the family's control over various businesses and labor unions. That was their principal target.

Ron said, "Corallo holds many meetings in a Jaguar owned by his bodyguard, Salvatore Avellino. He is constantly on the move." The task force was attempting to get enough probable cause to place a wire in the vehicle to record their conversations, and they were well on their way to doing so. I suggested we join forces regarding this investigation, and I would have my supervisor contact his office to establish a mutual working relationship. I also offered any technical or surveillance assistance he might need from our special operations branch. We shook hands on this agreement, which would be one of the best moves we had ever made.

It became apparent that we would burn many man-hours during this project. We usually had sufficient agents to fulfill our responsibilities, but our new investigative approach might need reinforcement. If we successfully installed authorized electronic surveillance of the targets in each family, that would require many agents to monitor and analyze the conversations. In addition, there would be necessary follow-up work due to new information continuously coming over the wires. I knew the New York police department had an elite group of detectives assigned to an organized crime unit. Would they entertain an invitation to form a joint effort with our teams? The department had already committed a sizable number of detectives to the Joint Terrorism Task Force, and they were officed in our space and integrated with our three squads assigned to this program. I approached Sheer with this idea and he loved it. He contacted Deputy Chief of Operations Patrick Murphy and set up a meeting. The commitment of the NYPD to this joint effort was clear, and it reassured us of the strength of our partnership.

We met with Deputy Chief Murphy and outlined our idea about forming a joint task force. He was very supportive, but somewhat taken aback by the scope of our project: "Are you sure we can do this?" However, he committed to assigning some of his finest detectives to join us. He also volunteered to assign an inspector to supervise his group, who would work with Kossler to coordinate the transition of his detectives and identify their specific assignments.

When we returned to the office, I met with Kossler and informed him, "The cavalry is on its way." We then briefed the supervisors and identified space in the office for what would become the police department's Organized Crime Task Force. The detectives would be available to carry out investigative assignments and had a wealth of experience and knowledge about the Mafia's activities in the five boroughs. In addition, they were older and seasoned veterans, which would be a good balance for our younger agents, a majority of whom were getting their feet wet. I felt confident that we had all our planning and reorganizing behind us and were ready to play hardball.

Just before Easter in 1982, Susan called me at the office and said, "Honey, you have to come home. I need to go to the hospital soon—our baby is on the way." I left the office right away and headed home. I arrived home within two hours and as I entered the house, Sue was lying on the sofa dealing with labor pains. We rushed to the hospital, but our baby was not ready to arrive yet. We returned to the hospital two days later and our son David was born on Good Friday morning. The proud parents had Easter dinner in the hospital with our son watching from his bassinet. Several days later, I had to return to New York. The only thought I had when I again drove north on the dreaded turnpike heading back to New York was that this arrangement was not working, and we had to move. It was too much of a strain on Susan. Now we had a new family member to take care of, our son David.

A new development occurred that would directly affect our investigative effort. US Attorney John Martin resigned and Rudolph Giuliani was appointed to oversee the Southern District. He was a former assistant attorney general and a native of Brooklyn. After his arrival, Tom and I met with him and his staff regarding our plans. He had never prosecuted a RICO case, but was aware of the new statute. He appeared enthusiastic about supporting our effort. "I am all in and will assign my best people to this investigation project" were his closing comments. His approach was much different than we had experienced with former US Attorney Martin. He also agreed to contact Ray Dearie in the Eastern District and set up a coordination plan with his office.

Sheer and I had one more candle to light. We wanted to do a press release and let the Mafia know we were in town and ready to do business. We aimed to stir the pot a little and put the families on the defensive and in a position where they would start mistrusting one another and make tactical mistakes. We sat down with Selwyn Raab, who had been reporting on the Mafia for several years and was an outstanding journalist who would go on to write the seminal *Five Families*. We outlined the approach we would adopt using the RICO statute to conduct simultaneous investigations of the Five Families. Raab listened intently and asked perceptive questions, as he had more knowledge of the inner workings of the families than any other reporter in New York.

On August 31, 1983, *The New York Times* carried a front-page story by Mr. Raab regarding the facts discussed in our interviews captioned FBI ATTACKS ORGANIZED CRIME IN NEW YORK AREA. The most pointed reference to our effort was Sheer's quote: "We are going after enterprises rather than individuals. In the past, when we took out one person, even a boss, he was too easy to replace. This time, we intend to knock out the enterprise and make it difficult to re-establish these criminal networks." A dynamite summary and just what we needed.

Sheer's management style was different than that of most SACs. He "managed by walking around" and talking to his supervisors and agents. He wanted to know what issues they were dealing with and offer his help if needed. You got the feeling that we were all on the same team and had one objective: to solve the problem in front of us. He would often walk into my office to chat and, on several occasions, ask, "Frank, have you seen my glasses?"

I would respond, "Tom, they are on your forehead." It seemed to relieve some of the tension that was always present in New York.

There is a universal saying among agents when someone would ask, "What do you think of your SAC?" If the agent thinks highly of the SAC, they would respond, "He is an agent's SAC."

That, in my opinion, is how they would describe Tom Sheer.

CHAPTER 9
The Gambino Family

I spent several days reviewing information accumulated over the years regarding the history of the Gambino family. It had a long and storied past and came into existence in 1931. Initially, Vincent Mangano controlled the family and Albert Anastasia served as his underboss. The family primarily engaged in labor racketeering and illegal gambling operations; however, Anastasia had other ideas. He formed a group of hit men that performed contract murders nationwide, which became known as Murder, Inc. Anastasia also had close ties with officials of the ILA. His brother Anthony "Tough Tony" Anastasio became president of an ILA local. The family controlled the entire Brooklyn waterfront. Mangano appointed Carlo Gambino to the position of capo and he soon became a man of considerable influence. Paul Castellano, a reasonably new member, married Gambino's sister, Nina, which would benefit his future status in the family hierarchy. He became a member of Gambino's crew.

One day, Mangano suddenly disappeared, but his body was never found. The Commission met and confronted Anastasia, who had assumed family control. He denied killing Mangano and they accepted his denial and approved his official elevation as boss of the family. Information developed by local law enforcement indicated that Anastasia, indeed, had ordered the hit on

Mangano with instructions that his body should never be found. Gambino became consigliere and would become Anastasia's top adviser on family issues. Anastasia was a ruthless murderer and this created concern with the other four Commission bosses. He was unpredictable. One particular senseless act eventually led to his demise.

Willie Sutton, a notorious bank robber, had escaped from prison and became the subject of a manhunt throughout the East Coast. He was placed on the FBI's ten most wanted fugitive list but, over a two-year span, had been evasive and continued to rob banks. He had contacts with a few New York Mafia members who admired his exploits. A private citizen, Arnold Schuster, spotted Sutton on a New York subway and followed him as he got off the train. Schuster kept up with Sutton as he walked along a Manhattan street and had time to call the police from a nearby pay phone. The police quickly arrived and Sutton was arrested.

The event received extensive media coverage. Schuster became an overnight celebrity and appeared on local media outlets recounting how he helped apprehend Sutton. He was becoming somewhat of a celebrity. Anastasia became outraged over Schuster's cooperation with the police and, according to a police source, shouted to one of his associates, "Kill this son of a bitch!" Schuster was subsequently murdered while walking toward his home in Brooklyn. The murder of Schuster was never solved. His killing created a public furor. Anastasia took credit within Mob circles for ordering the murder and bragged about it to his confederates. The Commission was outraged at the heat this senseless act generated once the media suspected that Anastasia might be responsible.

In researching the events involving Anastasia, I recalled a conversation I had with Special Agent Dick Armstrong when I worked in the Philadelphia office as an administrative assistant. One of my duties was to prepare the mail to be sent out to FBI headquarters and other field offices each evening. On many occasions, Dick would walk over to the mail desk with a communication that had to be mailed to the fugitive section at headquarters in Washington, DC. It summarized his work that day to locate Fred Tenuto, who was on the top ten fugitive list. Tenuto, a convicted felon, had ties to the Mafia in Philadelphia and New York. He had been serving a sentence for armed robbery at Holmesburg Prison, located in the Tioga section of the city. His cellmate was Willie Sutton and they naturally developed a close relationship. Armstrong's investigation led him to believe that a representative of Anastasia contacted Tenuto and gave him the contract to kill Schuster.

Dick speculated that Tenuto was then murdered to prevent him from testifying against those who had ordered the hit. He could not convince headquarters of this conclusion; thus, Tenuto remained on the top ten list. I could hear the frustration in Dick's voice when he told me this story. Little did I realize at the time of this conversation that I would analyze this event fifteen years later. The FBI eventually removed Tenuto from the list.

Anastasia continued to run the family for some time, but his antics reached a point where the Commission decided they had had enough. On October 25, 1957, he was shot and killed while sitting in a barber's chair at the Park Sheraton Hotel in Manhattan. A dozen customers and several barbers witnessed the shooting, but of course, they saw nothing. It was suspected that Gambino had set up the hit at the direction of the Commission. Gambino was then appointed boss and Paul Castellano became his underboss. The family's illegal enterprises thrived under the leadership of Gambino and Castellano, and they became the most powerful Mafia family on the East Coast. When Gambino died of natural causes, Castellano succeeded him, and his reign as boss had begun. He appointed Aniello "Neil" Dellacroce as underboss.

I sat down with Bruce Mouw to discuss the status and direction of the investigation into the Gambino family. Mouw began the meeting by saying, "Frank, I totally buy into your approach." Bruce had a very thoughtful and deliberate manner, and I got the sense that he was persistent and patient at the same time. He knew the path forward would not be easy. I believed he was up to the challenge. He asked Joe O'Brien and Andy Kurins, the case agents assigned to the investigation, to join us in our discussion.

Their main focus was Castellano, who lived with his wife, Nina, in a mansion he built in Todt Hill on Staten Island. O'Brien remarked, "He does not move around much and when he leaves the house, is always escorted by his driver, Tom Bilotti." They had conducted physical observations of the home without detection; however, continuous surveillance was difficult due to its location. Several family members, including capos and the underboss, Neil Dellacroce, constantly came and went. Mouw's objective was to develop sufficient probable cause to establish that there was reason to believe criminal conversations were occurring in Castellano's home. They would need good intelligence from a highly placed informant to confirm the obvious. Informants already available to us had been tasked to provide more information regarding the nature of the meetings.

Another primary target was John Gotti, a capo in charge of his own crew. He reported to Castellano, but friction constantly existed between them. Dellacroce was Gotti's mentor and attempted to keep him under control. O'Brien believed, "Gotti envisioned himself as the future boss someday and was a persistent threat to Castellano. He had a propensity for violence when he needed to settle a dispute. His temper sometimes got the best of him, and he made reckless decisions and was unpredictable." The agents believed that would work against him and they were right—a Mafia boss who reacts in that manner is never successful for long.

The Gambino family was the wealthiest and most prominent of the Five Families, with over 400 members and a dozen separate crews, each run by a capo. This would be a difficult task for Mouw and his relatively small group of twelve agents, many of whom had limited experience. Mouw closed the meeting with some reassurance, "Boss, we got this." I loved his confidence, but it occurred to me: Was Kossler right? Had I set the goalposts too high by simultaneously going after all five families? Then again, if we were successful in our initial assault and I needed more troops, headquarters would have to send me reinforcements. I would cross that bridge when I came to it.

There were two factions of the Gambino family. One held allegiance to Castellano and the other faction favored Dellacroce. Several members believed Dellacroce should have been appointed boss of the family when Carlo Gambino died. Castellano's group focused on white-collar crime and labor racketeering. The capos that reported to Dellacroce concentrated on traditional illegal activities such as loan-sharking, illegal gambling operations, and extortion. Castellano had the ultimate authority over the entire family. This split of interests and control was a constant source of divisiveness within the family.

Agent Jim Abbot, who was assigned to the Brooklyn office, had a highly placed informant who was a member of the Gambino family and could furnish information that family business was discussed in the boss's house in Staten Island. Additional informants also began to corroborate that the home was a meeting place for family members. O'Brien and Kurins began putting together an affidavit requesting a federal district judge to authorize the FBI to intercept illegal conversations at the Castellano home. Mouw called and notified me, "We got the authorization, but now we have a bigger problem. Tell me how the hell we are going to make the installation."

Fortunately, the office had agents with the technical expertise and training to install listening devices without being detected by the subjects under investigation. This group was the special operations branch, supervised by Jim Kallstrom. Castellano's home, however, would be a difficult challenge. Kurins and O'Brien had determined that the home was never empty. Castellano and his wife did not travel far from home and had a live-in maid who was always present. Electronic sensors monitored the perimeter and outside signage indicated that a private security company monitored an alarm system.

It was concluded that some surreptitious entry would have to be made to gain entry. We had one advantage: An informant had attended meetings in the home and knew the exact location where Castellano held court. It was agreed that we would have to develop a ruse allowing us to enter the home with their knowledge, but in a way that would allow our real intentions to go unnoticed. Knowing where to install the bug was no longer an issue.

The den off the kitchen area would be our target. Castellano did not discuss business over his telephone, as he assumed we were listening. If a capo called and needed an audience, he was instructed to "come to the house on the hill." With this information in hand, Mouw and Jim Kallstrom sat down and devised a plan of entry. It was decided to create an electrical malfunction in the home that needed attention.

A repairman would show up almost simultaneously under the pretext of being notified by the electric company that they had detected a problem. The repairman would be FBI Agent Joe Cantamessa, who would be prepared to install a microphone in the presence of the occupants. The plan worked and a device was installed while Castellano was at home. He was grateful that Cantamessa had solved the problem and offered to tip him for his services, which was quite a twist. Agents had rented an apartment nearby and had set up their monitoring equipment, waiting to listen to criminal conversations. It was not permissible to listen to conversations that did not contain illegal content. After some technical adjustments, they began picking up criminal discussions in Castellano's home. We were in business.

We knew that representatives from the Gambino, Genovese, and Colombo families were allegedly extorting numerous owners of concrete companies who were awarded building contracts in the city. They controlled the unions, as Colombo capo Ralph Scopo was president of Local 6A of the Cement and Concrete Workers Union. He had been an official of the union's district council for many years, representing over 4,000 workers. The Gambino family was in control of Teamsters Local 282, whose members worked for the companies that supplied drivers for the concrete companies. With that much power over union workers in the industry, the Mafia ensured building contracts were awarded to specific companies as long as they paid 2 percent off the top of a bid over $2 million. This conspiracy was called the Concrete Club, referring to the victim companies participating in this scheme.

The agents began intercepting conversations in which Castellano confirmed the Gambino family's involvement in this conspiracy. The electronic surveillance continued for months and critical evidence was developed regarding illegal activities involving the Gambino family and pertinent evidence and intelligence about the other four families. As evidence was developed, Mouw would confer with the prosecuting attorneys and appropriate reports were submitted. Grand juries were convened and the evidence was presented along with the testimony of cooperative witnesses. The case was coming together.

Castellano and the bosses of the other Five Families were indicted on the morning of February 25, 1985. Warrants were issued the same day and simultaneous arrests were planned for the following morning. At 6:00 p.m., Mouw received an unexpected call from Kossler. Sheer had ordered the men to move immediately, as there had been a leak to the press.

Mouw contacted Agents O'Brien and Kurins: "Okay, guys, let's roll." O'Brien quickly led a team to the house on the hill with a warrant to arrest Castellano. He was caught up in the moment as he maneuvered the car up the long driveway. After all these years of chasing this guy, he thought, *Damn it, we finally got him.*

O'Brien knocked on the door, and a male voice responded, "Who is it?" O'Brien immediately knew it was Castellano.

He announced, "This is the FBI and I have a warrant for your arrest." Castellano opened the door and demanded, "What is this all about?" His wife, Nina, and maid, Gloria, were in the living room.

As he and Kurins entered, O'Brien explained, "You have been

indicted for a RICO violation and will have to appear before a magistrate, who will outline the charges that have been filed."

Gloria became emotionally upset and must have called Castellano's daughter, who lived just two houses away. She and her husband suddenly appeared at the front door. It was getting tricky and O'Brien wanted to get Castellano out of the house as quickly as possible without family interference. Castellano then, out of a natural concern for the family, reassured them that "This is all a mistake. I will be home shortly." Nina slowly placed a coat over her husband's shoulders, and they marched him out of the house and placed him in the back seat of their car with Kurins by his side. They did not handcuff him out of respect for his family.

The ride into Manhattan was long and slow due to rush hour traffic. Castellano spoke first, wanting to know, "What am I specifically charged with?" He knew O'Brien, having spoken to him and his partner previously. O'Brien felt this was an opportunity to break the ice and told him that all the bosses were being arrested after a three-year investigation and that his home had been the object of electronic surveillance.

Castellano appeared stunned when he heard this news. He seemed offended that the FBI would bug his home. "How could you violate a man's home?" He could not believe they were able to compromise the security precautions he had taken. He shook his head in disbelief. He thanked O'Brien for giving him this information. Joe knew they would have to advise his attorney of the same facts. He was not divulging any secrets. His objective was to get Castellano to trust him, as he planned to contact him in the future if possible. Castellano was taken to the federal lockup to await a bail hearing. The "boss of bosses" was now in federal custody.

When Gotti learned of the indictment, he saw an opening. He assumed Castellano was now a weak leader and family members would be concerned about his future viability as boss. He discussed his feelings with his trusted associate, Sammy "the Bull"

Gravano. Gotti began planning to take over the family by killing Castellano.

Gravano told him, "Don't be hasty. We have to think about the ramifications of such a bold move and have the support of our people." Gotti told Gravano that he would make his final decision on his own and not consult representatives of the Commission. "It's risky—I don't give a damn. We are ready to move. Let's wait a few months until things settle down."

Castellano had been aware of unrest in the family, as the issue of getting involved in drug trafficking was still on the table. It had been months since his arrest and he still could not resolve this issue. He knew Gotti was unpredictable and could make a move on him. He needed to hold a private meeting with a trusted capo, Frankie DeCicco, who was close with Gotti, and look for options to settle the existing dispute. Little did he know at the time, Gotti had already contacted DeCicco to enlist his cooperation in setting up Castellano for the hit. Castellano eventually contacted DeCicco and asked him to set up a private meeting. DeCicco immediately notified Gotti that they were ready to make their move. He would arrange to meet Castellano at a familiar spot, Sparks Steak House on East Forty-sixth Street in Manhattan.

On December 16, 1985, Castellano kissed his wife, Nina, and left his home for the last time to attend the meeting with DeCicco. He was accompanied by his bodyguard and driver, Tom Bilotti. Sparks was one of his favorite restaurants and he felt safe there, out of earshot of the FBI. At approximately 5:30 p.m., Bilotti parked in front of the restaurant, courtesy of the management. As Castellano stepped out of the car, he was hit by a hail of bullets fired from the guns of three masked assassins lying in wait. Bilotti suffered the same fate. Both men were killed instantly, with a crowd of commuters and Christmas shoppers watching. It was a bold and daring act.

We would later determine that on the afternoon of the murder, Gotti and Gravano had driven to Manhattan and arrived at the corner of Forty-sixth Street and Third Avenue at approximately

5:00 p.m. Gotti was driving and parked the car near the corner with a clear line of sight to the front of Sparks Steak House. Castellano and Bilotti arrived and drove right past their vehicle. Gravano was concerned that Bilotti might have observed them, but apparently, he hadn't, as he continued to drive up the street and parked just outside the front entrance to Sparks. Frankie DeCicco was waiting patiently inside.

Three of his shooters were stationed outside, anticipating Castellano's arrival. Gotti and Gravano heard the burst of gunfire, waited a few seconds, and then drove by the bodies to ensure that both Castellano and Bilotti were dead. The three shooters made their escape. DeCicco quietly got up from his table, left the restaurant, and walked up Forty-sixth Street. The shooters quickly walked away and disappeared into the crowd of onlookers. Gotti and Gravano returned to the Bergin Hunt and Fish Club in Queens, toasting Castellano's demise.

Agents and homicide detectives immediately responded to the scene. The press was everywhere, taking photographs, and large crowds gathered. The bodies of Castellano and Bilotti were visible to the general public from the sidewalk and motorists passing by the restaurant. The site resembled a scene out of *The Godfather*. No witnesses came forth with any information regarding the shooters.

The Commission questioned Gotti regarding the murder of Castellano. He denied, of course, any complicity and assumed he would be appointed boss. Neil Dellacroce, Castellano's underboss, had died in early December. The Commission did not buy Gotti's assertion that he had nothing to do with the murder and refused to appoint him as Castellano's successor. Nonetheless, Gotti began assuming the role of boss and named Gravano his underboss. Again, he disregarded the authority of the Commission, which did not sit well with key bosses of the other families, particularly Anthony "Tony Ducks" Corallo, the boss of the Lucchese family. After several months had passed, Corallo and Vincent "Chin" Gigante, the boss of the Genovese family, decided to act.

Weeks later, Gotti was scheduled to be driven by DeCicco to a social club to meet with capo James "Jimmy Brown" Failla and his crew. Failla had been very close to Castellano and Gotti was hoping to mend fences, as there were hard feelings after Castellano's murder. At the last minute, Gotti changed his mind and sent DeCicco as his representative. This decision may have saved his life. Upon learning of Gotti's intentions, Failla had contacted Corallo of the Lucchese family, who, in turn, put together a hit team comprised of two of his trusted capos, Vittorio "Little Vic" Amuso and Anthony "Gaspipe" Casso.

DeCicco went to the club alone. Soon after DeCicco arrived, the hit team showed up, planted a bomb underneath his car, and kept the vehicle under surveillance. They observed DeCicco leaving the club after the meeting, accompanied by an individual who resembled Gotti. As both men entered the car, the hit team triggered the bomb and DeCicco was killed instantly. His associate was Frank Bellino, ironically a member of the Lucchese family who survived the bombing. Gotti quickly realized his life might be endangered and temporarily assumed a low-key profile.

After the assassination of Castellano and the Commission's failed attempt to murder Gotti, they decided to avoid any future conflicts. They did not want an all-out war. Gotti officially became the boss of the family. Gotti and his crew had a big celebration at the Ravenite Social Club, which the agents had under surveillance. He did not realize it then, but he had a big problem. His new status made him the FBI's number one target moving forward.

Gotti had a different persona than Castellano: He was flamboyant, outspoken in public, and loved the media attention. He dressed like the type of gangster portrayed in the movies. For this, he was called the Dapper Don. The press gave all his moves constant coverage and also began to refer to him as the Teflon Don, as he had recently been acquitted of several serious charges. Well, we were intent on changing that headline. Mouw assigned one of his best agents, George Gabriel, to direct the investigation of Gotti. Gabriel was young, like many of the agents assigned to our investigations, but he was a hard charger and very determined. Mouw made the right choice.

Amid our focus on Gotti, I got a call from Mouw, who stated that US Attorney Diane Giacalone of the Eastern District was potentially exposing one of our top Gambino informants, Wilfred "Willie Boy" Johnson. Johnson was a close associate of Gotti and had been indicted along with Gotti and other crew members in a separate investigation she had directed. Giacalone had become aware that Johnson was our informant and wanted him to testify against Gotti. She threatened to expose him publicly in court if he did not do so.

I told Mouw, "This is outrageous."

Mouw said, "Johnson's agent handler had spoken to Johnson, but he refused to testify and go into the witness protection program." He then remarked, "Giacalone might issue a subpoena for you to testify in a closed court hearing regarding our long-standing relationship with Johnson."

Johnson had been an informant for over fifteen years and furnished quality information about the Gambino family. He was one of our best informants. He was not a made member, because he was of Native American descent. He was known as an enforcer for the family. Giacalone contacted me and I informed her it was against Bureau regulations to discuss any possible relationships with individuals who provide us with confidential information. This did not deter her from pursuing this issue. I assumed she must have called the DOJ about her position. I contacted FBI headquarters and was subsequently advised that the Justice Department had determined I had to testify. The fact that Johnson had been indicted for committing federal crimes must have influenced the department's decision.

A hearing was scheduled before a federal district judge and I appeared as ordered. I was furious at this development and the situation I was being placed in, which I could not control. It was a closed hearing. Johnson sat with his attorney at the counsel's table, and his wife sat behind him. No reporters were allowed in the courtroom. Giacalone addressed the court and acknowledged that she would represent the government. I was sworn in and forced to admit that Johnson had been an informant for the FBI for over fifteen years without going into detail about the information he had provided.

Johnson glared at me as I spoke and I had difficulty making eye contact. The trial of Gotti and Johnson subsequently proceeded and they were both acquitted. Several months after this trial, Johnson was murdered by two hit men as he left his home. The shooters were never identified, nor was the reason for his murder made clear. I realized that Attorney Giacalone was doing her job and could not control all the circumstances that were presented. She had an excellent reputation and was highly regarded by her superiors. The Johnson matter was a tough call.

Initial attempts to identify a frequent meeting place for Gotti were difficult as he moved around frequently and, on many occasions, walked the streets of Brooklyn with associates discussing business. He was usually accompanied by Gravano. He spent considerable time at the Ravenite Social Club, which we already had under constant surveillance. Still, intercepting intelligible conversations would have been impossible due to the number of associates and members who frequented the club. Gotti also held frequent meetings outside the club entrance, making intercepting discussions unlikely.

Agents determined, however, that he and Gravano were frequently observed walking up a stairway leading to floors above the club. An informant corroborated that Gotti met with Gravano and other members periodically in an apartment on the third floor of the building rented by Nettie Cirelli, the widow of a deceased former member. Through the informant, we confirmed Gotti's movements through surveillance, put all our findings into a new affidavit, and obtained authorization to place listening devices in the apartment. Making entry successfully could be complicated and dangerous for our agents. One afternoon, Cirelli was observed leaving the apartment and surveillance of her was initiated. Kallstrom and his team made their move and quickly installed the listening devices. They were just magicians—what more can I say!

For over a week, agents monitoring the listening devices heard no conversations involving Gotti or Gravano. Frustration started to build over the lack of meetings in the apartment. But then the floodgates opened. We finally hit the jackpot. On November 30, 1989, the monitoring agents could hear Gotti, Gravano, and capo Frank LoCascio distinctly as they entered the apartment. Gotti openly reminisced about his poor relationship with Castellano and his fear that "Big Paul planned to hit me." He denounced Castellano as a "rat motherfucker who was tearing the family apart." Gotti continued to ramble on about how respected he was as the new boss and his plans for the family. We now had Gotti in our crosshairs and were ready to pull the trigger.

A week later, Gotti was in the apartment with LoCascio. He referred to himself as the boss of the family and went on to say he had to authorize three murders. He quickly identified Robert DiBernardo, a soldier on the Castellano hit team. He commented that DiBernardo had to go when he found out he was disrespecting him to other members.

He then jumped to Louie DiBono. "Louie DiBono, you know why he's dying. He's gonna die because he refused to come in when I called. He didn't do nothing else wrong." He then went on and discussed a third murder, that of Liborio Milito, a Gambino soldier who was a member of the Castellano faction.

A trove of incriminating discussions followed over an extended period between Gotti, Gravano, and other key family members. Sufficient evidence had been uncovered to present to a federal grand jury in the Eastern District. The grand jury voted to charge Gotti, Gravano, and Frank LoCascio with violating the RICO statute. The indictment included charging Gotti with the three murders he had admitted to during the taping of his conversations, and warrants were issued for their arrests.

Gotti had anticipated that he might be indicted. He knew a

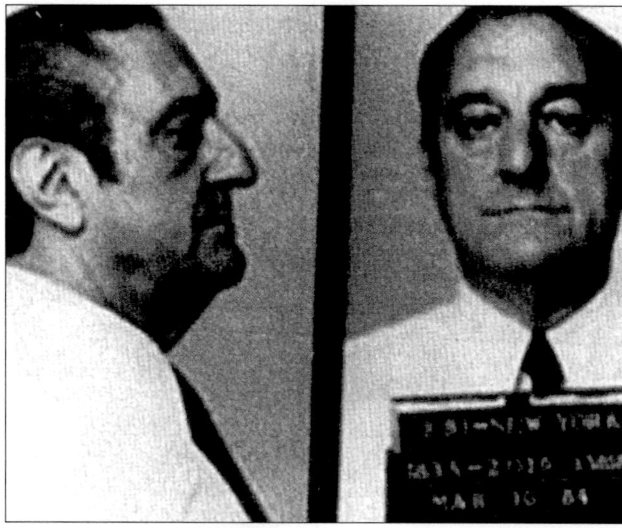

Paul Castellano,
Gambino family boss.
FBI.

Anthony "Fat Tony" Salerno,
Genovese family front boss.
FBI.

Philip "Rusty" Rastelli,
Bonanno family boss.
FBI.

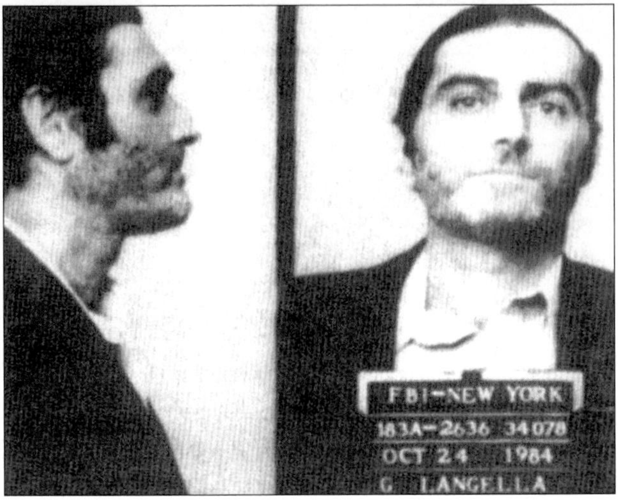

Gennaro "Gerry Lang" Langella, Colombo family acting boss.
FBI.

Anthony "Tony Ducks" Corallo, Lucchese family boss.
FBI.

Vincent "Chin" Gigante, Genovese family boss, at the time of his arrest by the FBI on May 30, 1990, for violation of the RICO statute.
FBI.

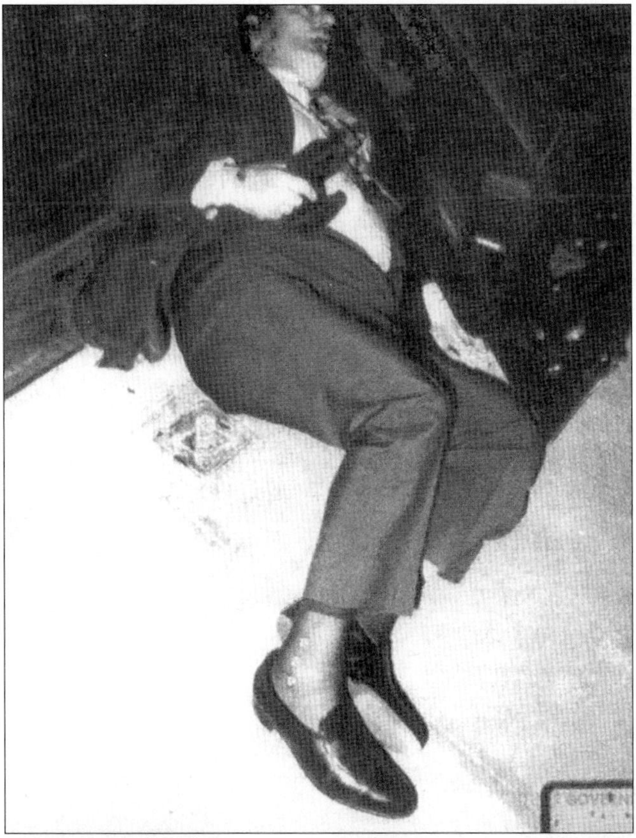

Paul Castellano moments after being shot and killed outside Sparks Steak House in Manhattan on December 16, 1985. *FBI.*

Fat Tony and his capo, Vincent "Fish" Cafaro (standing), meeting outside the Palma Boys Social Club in East Harlem, New York. *FBI.*

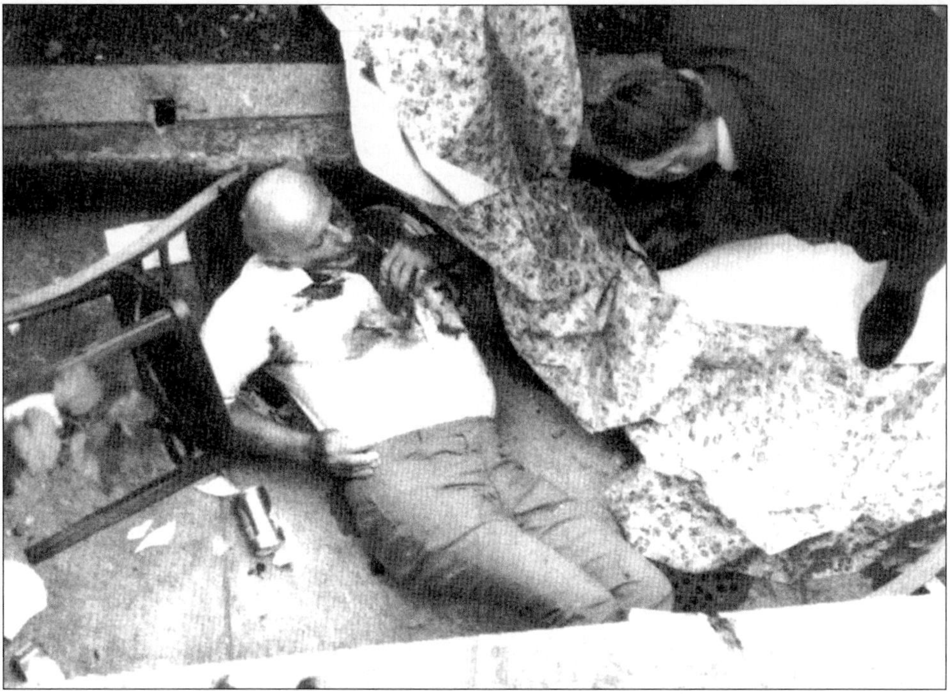

On July 12, 1979, Carmine "Lilo" Galante lies dead on the patio of Joe and Mary's Restaurant in Brooklyn. He had attempted to assume control of the Sicilian Mafia drug enterprise. *Hal Goldberg, New York Post.*

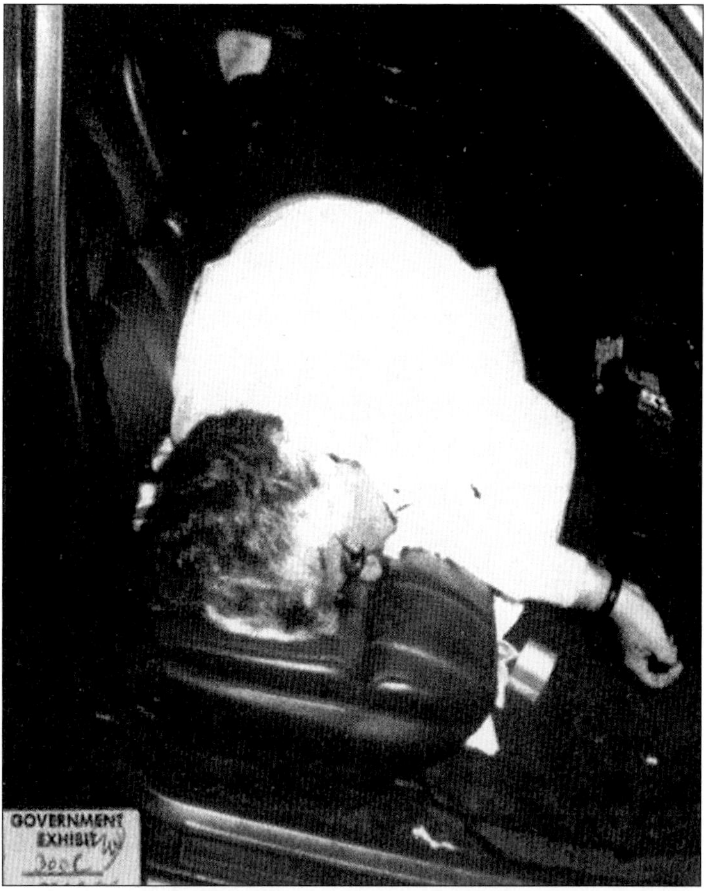

Gambino soldier Louis DiBono lies dead in his car. John Gotti ordered his murder simply because DiBono refused to meet with him after he became the boss of the family. *FBI.*

Gerry Lang, Gambino underboss Thomas Bilotti, and Colombo capo Ralph Scopo leaving the Commission meeting in Staten Island, New York. *FBI.*

John Gotti meeting with his trusted capo Angelo Ruggiero outside the Ravenite Social Club. Gotti often met with family members on the street to avoid FBI wiretaps. *FBI.*

Victor Orena, Colombo family boss, called a meeting to obtain permission to kill Thomas Ocera, a soldier in the family. John Gotti and Frank LoCascio, his underboss, attended the meeting.
FBI.

FBI agents digging up the body of Thomas Ocera. His murder was ordered by Victor Orena, as he was concerned Ocera would become an FBI informant.
FBI.

Mug shot of John Gotti, who had succeeded Paul Castellano as boss of the Gambino family, after his arrest by the FBI on December 11, 1990, for violation of the RICO statute.
FBI.

Mug shot of hit man and Gambino family underboss Sammy "The Bull" Gravano after being arrested by the FBI on December 11, 1990, for violation of the RICO statute.
FBI.

Collage of newspaper articles depicting the arrests of various bosses and members of the five Mafia families assembled by the author and given to each one of the "game changers" assigned to the investigation.
Author's collection.

Home of Philadelphia Mafia boss Phil Testa in the aftermath of a bomb exploding on his front porch, killing him. The author, wearing a trench coat, approaches the porch to participate in a crime scene investigation.
Vicki Valerio, The Philadelphia Inquirer.

grand jury in Brooklyn was investigating him and the family. No public announcement was made that he had been indicted, so he and his crew conducted business as usual. One night, Mouw's team learned he and the entire crew were at the Ravenite. How fortunate we had them all together. Mouw and his agents immediately raided the club and arrested Gotti, Gravano, and LoCascio. The door had to be taken down and a forced entry was made. This was a concern, as they assumed everyone inside was armed. The agents acted quickly and were well-armed with shotguns at the ready. They made it clear as they entered that this was not a drill as the lead agent shouted, "This is the FBI! Do not move!"

At least twenty-five members stood by in disbelief. All three subjects were cuffed and dragged out of the club. Gotti, in particular, did not go gently—he was defiant as usual. Gravano was not. He must have realized that he was now in deep jeopardy. All three men were denied bail and confined to the federal lockup to await trial. Based on their documented propensity for violence, confinement was an easy decision for the judge to make. The arrests caused quite a stir and received an incredible amount of publicity.

Gravano now felt alone, desperate, and worried that he would never see his family again. He knew his life as a mobster was over. Members of his family began encouraging him to cooperate, but he knew that would be a death sentence. Despite his fears, he eventually reached out to the two agents who had arrested him and said, "We need to talk."

Arrangements were made to set up a safe house and transport Gravano to that location to be debriefed. He spent a week supplying us with detailed information about his life in the Gambino family and all the illegal acts he had committed. To begin with, he admitted to being a hit man who was responsible for killing at least twenty individuals at the request of Castellano or Gotti. He provided the specific details of the Castellano murder and the reason Gotti ordered the hit. Gravano was now considered a cooperative government witness who would testify at Gotti's forthcoming trial.

Thomas Gambino, the son of Carlo Gambino, was a man of importance in the family and was now the focus of our attention. When Frank DeCicco scheduled the meeting with Castellano at Sparks, Gambino and capo James Failla were invited. Gambino arrived at Sparks seconds before the hit, but DeCicco quickly ushered him away, knowing what would soon happen. Failla arrived at the restaurant late. After observing the carnage, he quickly left the scene. Neither Gambino nor Failla were aware of the planned hit. We were unaware of these facts until the Gravano debriefing occurred.

Gambino, by all appearances, seemed to be a legitimate businessman. Upon graduating from Manhattan College, he married Tommy Lucchese's daughter. At the time, the Gambinos and Luccheses worked closely together and controlled several legitimate businesses. When Lucchese died, he passed control of the garment district to his son-in-law, Thomas Gambino. By virtue of Castellano's marriage to Nina Gambino, Carlo's daughter, Thomas Gambino was now related to Castellano through marriage.

Thomas Gambino became very successful through the influence he could exert over the trucking companies that had contracts with businesses in the garment district. The drivers of trucks delivering clothes to the center had to join the Teamsters Union, whose officials were controlled by the family. Gambino would shut them down if the manufacturers did not make labor peace payoffs by calling a workers' walkout. Through this scheme, he acquired millions of dollars for himself and the family, and Castellano awarded his efforts by making him a capo of his crew. So, you now had a Gambino capo running the garment district. How sweet was that for the Mafia?

Over time, the family acquired ownership of several trucking companies and began charging excessive shipping rates. Our investigation stepped up and a federal grand jury was convened to investigate corruption allegations in the garment district. Gambino was indicted for obstruction of justice and extortion. He accepted a plea deal, resulting in $12 million in fines. Subsequent charges resulted in a five-year prison sentence.

There was one more critical issue to resolve: Angelo Ruggiero's status. He had survived all this turmoil within the family and was one of the most powerful capos still standing. He was close to Gotti and Gravano—they had grown up together in Brooklyn. He and Gotti were arrested several times for local violations, and both were inducted into the family during the same period. We had excellent informant coverage of the family and were well aware of Ruggiero's activities and habits. He had a reputation within the family as a prolific talker who would discuss his illegal activities in almost a braggadocio way. Family members jokingly referred to him as "quack quack." Ruggiero had significant standing in the family, as he was the nephew of the former underboss Neil Dellacroce.

Surveillance determined that Ruggiero spent considerable time at his residence in Cedarhurst, Long Island during the day. Several known crew members would meet with him at his home, and he had previously been observed visiting Castellano at his house on the hill. Our informant also confirmed that he used his home telephone to conduct family business. An agent assigned to Mouw's squad prepared an affidavit for a court order to tap his phone and place a listening device in the den, where he held meetings.

The electronic surveillance was very successful in developing enough evidence to demonstrate that he was involved in a multimillion-dollar drug trafficking conspiracy along with Gotti's brother, Gene. He had been engaged in drug trafficking even though Castellano had previously forbidden this activity. Castellano had not been aware of Ruggiero ignoring his policy; otherwise, he would have had him killed. Ruggiero, Gene Gotti, and three members of his crew were indicted for heroin importation and trafficking. Ruggiero was subsequently diagnosed with terminal lung cancer. He died at the age of forty-nine, waiting to be tried on the drug trafficking case. Gene Gotti and the other coconspirators were convicted.

Mouw's squad had now conducted unprecedented investigations that led to the indictments of the four top leaders of the Gambino family: Castellano, Gotti, Thomas Gambino, and Angelo Ruggiero. Their understanding of what techniques to employ in investigating the Mafia would be a lasting part of their squad's legacy and a road map for future investigations involving major criminal enterprises.

CHAPTER 10
CBS Murders

On April 12, 1982, Margaret Barbera had just left work and walked to a rooftop parking garage on the Upper West Side of the Manhattan waterfront. She attempted to unlock her car, but the key would not turn and it appeared jammed. Confused, she paused for a moment and tried again. A van was parked adjacent to her vehicle, but she paid no mind as she tried to open the car door. Donald Nash, a hit man and member of the Westies, a West Side Irish organized crime group, waited for her in the van. Nash suddenly bolted from the van and shot her in the head with a .22-caliber revolver. She fell dead to the garage floor. Nash began to pick up her body to place it in the van.

At that moment, three employees of CBS were entering the same garage floor to retrieve their cars. Leo Kuranuki, Robert Schulze, and Edward Benford saw Nash lifting Barbera's body. They moved in his direction to lend assistance, not realizing that he had just shot her. Nash observed them and quickly confronted all three men. They saw the gun in his hand and began running for their lives. They did not make it.

Nash instantly shot and killed all three men. He returned to the van and placed Barbera's body inside. A fourth employee of CBS had arrived at the garage and witnessed the shootings. He quickly turned away and ran down the exit ramp to safety. He was able to call 911 from a nearby phone booth. Nash, not noticing him, fled in his vehicle at a high rate of speed, according to the garage attendant. It was a horrible scene.

When Kossler entered my office, I knew something was wrong. "We just lost a key witness in the Irwin Margolies case. Margaret Barbera has just been murdered in a parking garage on the West Side." Barbera was involved in a multimillion-dollar fraud investigation with organized crime implications. The case was in the trial stages—now everything would be turned upside down. Barbera was not just a key witness, but the principal player, a former employee who could directly implicate Margolies, the CEO of Candor Diamond Corporation.

"Damn it, get a team of agents out there immediately." I quickly realized this was not just another homicide case; someone had hired a hit man to kill Barbera. The first order of business was to locate the killer as soon as possible and find Barbera's body.

Within a short period, we got a tremendous break. An anonymous caller notified the police that they had seen an individual dump what appeared to be a body in a landfill just south of the city. He gave a detailed description of a van along with a license number. Detectives and agents rushed to the scene of the landfill, and Barbera's body was soon found. The vehicle was registered to Donald Nash, who lived in the city. A quick check of our files identified Nash as a member of the Westies. We now knew at least who we were hunting.

This was the second witness in this case that had been murdered. Jenny Soo Chin, a former bookkeeper at Candor, was kidnapped in January while leaving her home by a man wearing a mask who forced her into her car and left the scene. Chin's body was never found. Her vehicle was located several days later and her bloodstains were discovered in the interior. A .22-caliber spent cartridge was also found in her car. Forensics would later determine that the bullets recovered from both crime scenes were fired from the same gun. We were looking for a hit man for hire.

Several days after the murders, the New Jersey state police reported that Nash's vehicle had been spotted on the New Jersey Turnpike heading south, not far from the city. A surveillance team was dispatched to intercept him. Our vehicles had similar speed capabilities as state police cruisers and by the time they reached Philadelphia, they had Nash under observation. We monitored the surveillance from our command center. I had ordered the agents not to arrest Nash in his vehicle, as he was extremely dangerous. He continued heading south and then detoured toward Kentucky and began heading southwest. The tension was building and the voices of the agents betrayed their weariness.

We notified the Kentucky state police of the events and asked them to have units available if we needed backup. A transmission came over the wire: "Nash is pulling over into a rest area." The agents followed cautiously and after several minutes, the Kentucky state solice arrived in unmarked cars and would assist in the arrest.

Approximately thirty minutes passed, when an agent casually approached Nash's car. He positioned himself away from the vehicle, but had a clear line of sight. The area where his car was parked was isolated for drivers who intended to rest for more extended periods. Visibility was somewhat impaired due to the subdued lighting. He reported that "Nash has fallen asleep." The team was prepared to make the apprehension, but had to be extremely careful. This was a tense moment.

The state police discreetly cleared the parking lot. Within minutes, the arrest team cautiously and quietly approached his vehicle with guns drawn. They assumed Nash would have weapons in the car and might shoot it out if directly confronted. We received a message from the group leader: "We are about to make our move." They smashed the driver's window, yanked open the front door, and took Nash into custody before he knew what hit him. Nash still had the .22-caliber revolver in the van, along with other weapons. He was taken to the nearest lockup until arrangements could be made for a removal hearing in the morning to transport him back to New York. There was no need for an interview—the agents had their man.

Nash was convicted of the murders and sentenced to serve 100 years. He had been a member of the Westies for some time. The gang had direct ties to the Gambino and Genovese families. Our follow-up investigation and subsequent court testimony determined that Margolies had paid Nash $16,000 for killing Chin and Barbera and an additional $5,000 for killing the CBS employees. Nash thus killed five innocent citizens for a measly $21,000. Margolies later entered a guilty plea to the federal fraud charges and received a twenty-eight-year sentence. In state court, he was charged with the murders of Chin and Barbera and sentenced to serve fifty years. Neither Nash nor Margolies would ever again see the light of day.

Although we had limited manpower, we could not ignore what had just occurred. I asked Kossler to "assemble a group of agents and initiate a RICO investigation directed at the hierarchy of the Westies. Let's take these bastards down." We already had a few highly placed informants who could produce critical background information regarding the group and their current criminal activities.

According to our files, the Westies were a crime organization responsible for extorting bars and restaurants on the West Side of Manhattan. They also were involved in drug trafficking and operating illegal gambling outlets and reportedly performed contract murders for the Mafia, particularly the Gambino family. They were centered in the Hell's Kitchen area on the Upper West Side. They were a very close-knit organization with a limited number of members, most of whom grew up in the same neighborhood.

Mickey Spillane had been their leader for the past twenty years. He was not only an intelligent criminal, but also had political connections. He was married to the daughter of a prominent member of the city administration. Through Spillane's leadership, the Westies began to exert control over local unions handling building contracts on the West Side, including the New York Coliseum and the Javits Center, which had yet to be completed. The Javits Center was to be built in the Hell's Kitchen neighborhood, and the Westies saw a tremendous moneymaking opportunity in their backyard. The Gambino and Genovese families had other ideas.

Roy DeMeo, a capo in the Gambino family, ran a group of hit men called the DeMeo crew. Bruce Mouw's squad had already developed significant information regarding DeMeo. Paul Castellano was interested in the opportunity that presented itself with the proposed Javits Center. The Gambino and Genovese families had primary control over the Teamsters and trade union locals whose members would be hired for this project. Castellano was concerned that Spillane was causing delays in construction and attempting to extort union bosses on his own. The Genovese family's boss, Anthony Salerno, was also invested in the Javits Center construction site and had agreed to share whatever profits they could generate with the Gambino family.

After several attempts, it was apparent they could not reach an accommodation with Spillane, so Castellano ordered DeMeo to kill him. As in most Mafia hits, no one is ever charged. Although the murder was never officially solved, available intelligence confirmed that the reason for the hit was obvious. It was believed DeMeo committed the murder in concert with Spillane's top assistant, Jimmy Coonan, who wanted to take over the gang and was willing to compromise with Castellano and Salerno.

Castellano then ordered DeMeo to contact Coonan to form an alliance. Coonan agreed to meet with Castellano and Salerno, and the Westies decided to become an adjunct partner. The Westies and both families would share all profits through their labor racketeering scheme at the Javits Center. Coonan agreed to have his people handle murder contracts for both the Gambino and Genovese families. Salerno, however, felt threatened by three of Spillane's top enforcers who were still on board and would resent Coonan taking over as the new boss. Salerno issued contracts on

Tom Devaney, Tom "Tommy the Greek" Kapatos, and Edward "Eddie the Butcher" Cummiskey, formerly Spillane's top lieutenants. The murders were committed by Joseph "Mad Dog" Sullivan, a notorious hit man for hire. Coonan could now run the gang as he saw fit without interference from Spillane's former supporters.

Roy DeMeo was never charged with the Spillane murder, nor any of the other murders he committed for the Gambino family over an extended period. DeMeo began to engage in various criminal enterprises that the family did not approve of, and he was acquiring a reputation of being out of control. He ignored warnings from underboss Neil Dellacroce and other members to no avail. Castellano had had enough and a contract was issued. It is believed that members of his crew murdered DeMeo. Our agents last observed him attending a meeting at the home of Patty Testa, a member of his crew. His body was found days later in the trunk of his car with a chandelier on top of it. The chandelier's significance is unknown, but you might surmise it was a signal that he had "fallen from the grace of Castellano." The Mafia frequently would leave calling cards on the bodies of victims to send a message to other members of the family.

"Mad Dog" Sullivan was also never charged with the contract hits he committed for Salerno. However, his luck ran out in Rochester, New York. He had received a contract to kill a Teamsters boss, John Fiorino, who was caught between two factions of the Mob in Rochester that were in the middle of a gang war. After studying Fiorino's habits, Sullivan traveled to Rochester and cornered him in a restaurant parking lot one day. He shot Fiorino in the head with a shotgun blast and fled the scene. The FBI in Rochester responded and opened an investigation. Months later, Sullivan returned to Rochester to pick up money still owed to him for the hit. The FBI in Rochester got a tip that he was in town and spotted his car at a local motel. He was subsequently arrested without incident, convicted of Fiorino's murder, and sentenced to prison for life.

The agents working with the prosecutors assigned to the strike force now focused on Coonan and his associates Richard "Muggsy" Ritter and James McElroy for possible violations of the RICO statute. Enough evidence was collected after an extensive investigation and they were all indicted. The crimes alleged included murder, extortion, loan-sharking, and drug trafficking. Mickey Featherstone, who was second-in-command to Coonan and a hit man for the gang, agreed to testify in the hope of gaining leniency from the judge. His testimony was crucial in convicting Coonan.

Featherstone gave us a complete history of how the Gambino and Genovese families took over the Westies. He provided the details concerning the murders ordered by Castellano and Salerno. Coonan received a seventy-five-year prison sentence, Ritter forty years, and McElroy, who was a notorious enforcer for the Mob, received a sentence of sixty years. The Westies organization was in total disarray and leaderless. Over time, there would be others who would step forward as the new boss, but the Westies never held the power they once held. They suffered the same fate as the other Five Families from the relentless attack that the FBI had initiated. We were not going away.

Fast-moving developments were coming at us, one after the other. It was like we had cracked open Pandora's box. I was starting to feel the stress of it all. Living alone in an apartment on the East Side was not my cup of tea. I took the two-hour drive home on a Wednesday night, but I had to drive back to New York on Thursday morning, leaving Sue and a four-month-old baby boy, David. Sue naturally was upset with the whole arrangement.

I came home one Friday night and before we sat down to dinner, Sue said, "I have an announcement to make: We are moving." She had traveled that day to North Brunswick, New Jersey to find our new home and located a two-bedroom garden apartment less than an hour from New York. The lease had been signed and Sue said, "You are invited to come along if you wish."

I laughed and gave her a big hug. My mother told me long ago, "A happy wife makes a happy life." Sue seemed delighted and I sure as hell felt the same way. We rented our home in Haddonfield, called the moving company, and were on our way to a more normal lifestyle.

It became apparent to me that due to the pace of our investigations and the manpower we were expending, we might be moving toward agent burnout. We now had over twenty electronic surveillances ongoing of Mafia members and related businesses that required considerable agent time to monitor. As many of our investigations would lead to further opportunities to conduct electronic surveillance, I feared we would reach a point where we could not adequately respond to fast-breaking developments. I sat down with Sheer and gave him a detailed overview of where we were and where we intended to go. I emphasized to Tom that I needed at least fifty more agents.

Before responding, he lifted his glasses to his forehead and paused momentarily. "Let's get our butts down to headquarters and go for a hundred agents." He picked up the phone and called Assistant Director of the Criminal Division Floyd Clarke and requested a meeting.

I prepared an outline of the presentation we would make to Clarke and had the exhibits section assemble a couple of small charts so our plan could be visualized. It was a bit dramatic, but I wanted to get their attention. We met with Organized Crime Chief McWeeney, Clarke, and the associate director, Buck Revell. They knew what we had accomplished, but needed to be briefed on the significant work still ahead of us.

Sheer pleaded his case. "We have come a long way, but need reinforcements to finish the job." He requested that a hundred agents be transferred to New York on a temporary duty assignment. This had to be an unprecedented request. Our hosts ended the meeting by politely saying they would get back to us. They had always supported us in the past, so I was hopeful. Driving back to New York, we were not sure which way they would go. The success of our project depended on their decision. Clarke called Sheer the next day and partially honored our request.

Sheer entered my office and proclaimed, "We got fifty agents. That should do it." Sheer pointed out that asking for more than you need is always a good idea when requesting additional manpower. This was another reason why he was the SAC; the man knew what he was doing.

CHAPTER 11
The Lucchese Family

In developing a plan of attack on a Mafia family from an investigative perspective, it is essential to understand its origins and to analyze the type of criminal activities the family focuses on. We found that each family differed and the bosses did not govern similarly. The Lucchese family dates back to the early 1920s. Tommy Gagliano was the boss and Tommy "Three-Finger Brown" Lucchese the underboss. At that time, the organization was referred to as the Gagliano family. Initially, the family became involved in traditional Mob activities such as illegal gambling, loan-sharking, and extortion, but they kept a low profile. They mainly operated in the Bronx and New Jersey. Gagliano died in 1951 and Lucchese succeeded him. The organization was then known as the Lucchese *borgata*. In the Sicilian language, *borgata* means "close-knit community." This was the only family in New York that referred to itself as a *borgata*.

Lucchese had big ideas for generating more revenue for the family. He focused on infiltrating legitimate businesses by controlling unions. He teamed up with Carlo Gambino and eventually, his family became one of the most powerful in New York. He supported Gambino in his efforts to take over the Commission. His relationship with Gambino grew even closer when Gambino's son married his daughter. Their relationship allowed them to have the last word when arbitrating family disputes. When Lucchese died in 1967, his family had over 250 members and controlled all illegal activities in the Bronx. He was never the subject of a successful investigation by law enforcement, nor convicted of any crime. He was, after a string of intermittent leaders, succeeded by Anthony "Tony Ducks" Corallo, who would now be the subject of our attention.

Corallo was nicknamed "Tony Ducks" for his reputation of constantly ducking prosecutors' subpoenas and never serving a lengthy prison sentence. He always avoided confrontations with law enforcement. We were determined to put an end to his luck. Corallo had a profile unlike that of John Gotti. He had grown up in the Italian neighborhood of East Harlem. He was married, had a son and daughter, and reportedly had an unassuming personality. Surveillance had determined he spent more time at his Oyster Bay Cove residence in Long Island than in the city. He was an avid gardener and neighbors perceived him as a decent family man who never bothered anyone. We often heard similar comments from neighbors of other Mafia members during our investigations.

Corallo grew up in the same neighborhood as Anthony "Fat Tony" Salerno. At a young age, Tony Ducks was involved in petty street crimes and joined the Gagliano family in 1935. He worked himself up from a foot soldier to capo and eventually boss. We knew Corallo had developed extensive contacts with many construction and waste management industries and unions. Our focus would be establishing enough evidence to expose his corrupt influence and status as a member of the Commission. He was concerned about being recorded by authorities while discussing criminal activities. He did not frequent one particular social club or restaurant like many Mob figures, and he was constantly on the move.

Upon taking over the family, Corallo expanded his influence to Newark, New Jersey and established a crew to control illegal activities. They took over all the major illicit bookmaking and loan-sharking operations in North Jersey, enabling him to solidify his position with the Commission.

I arranged to meet with New York State Organized Crime Task Force chief Goldstock regarding the status of their investigation of Corallo. He revealed the task force had determined that Corallo spent most of his days in an XJ6 Jaguar driven by his bodyguard and one of his capos, Salvatore Avellino. They had informant information indicating the conversations concerned family business. His investigators had prepared an affidavit and obtained court authorization to place a mic in the Jaguar. I offered any assistance we could provide, including surveillance from our special operations branch. Goldstock's group would directly target Corallo's control over the specific carting companies in Nassau and Suffolk Counties, and we would focus on his other business interests and involvement with the Commission.

This was a fantastic development, as we now had an ongoing investigation by a separate agency that might develop evidence on the Lucchese family that ordinarily we would have to obtain on our own. Dave Binney was the supervisor of the Lucchese investigation. I gave Dave an update on what I had learned from Goldstock and told him to "contact Ron and develop a close working relationship with his group—it's critical." We knew Corallo's people already had a scheme monopolizing refuse removal on Long Island. They could extort waste removal company owners because they controlled the Teamsters locals who supplied the trucks' drivers. Each family used similar methods to extort various business and construction companies in New York. It had been ongoing for decades and was the basis for their great wealth, power, and influence.

The microphone placed in the Jaguar recorded many discussions between Corallo and Avellino. Conversations were intercepted that established the family-controlled waste-hauling businesses on Long Island. Avellino told Corallo he had read a newspaper article that the authorities suspected he controlled the toxic waste disposal industry.

Avellino: "It said in that, in that article, it says about Tony, 'Tony Ducks,' about how he controls the garment center, he controls waste foliage, disposal business, and the construction."

Corallo: "Yeah, sure, didn't you know that?"

Avellino: "Course I know that. I know it because I'm with you, but not everybody knows that."

Corallo: "Yeah, well, they ain't supposed to know."

Corallo's responses during this conversation would return to haunt him.

Corallo often visited Salerno at the Palma Boys Social Club. We had previously obtained court authorization to install a microphone in Salerno's headquarters. On one occasion, they were discussing an article that appeared in the paper concerning allegations that the Lucchese family was involved in drug trafficking. Corallo had a standing rule that none of his members could engage in this activity, and he was livid at the suggestion that he would allow it. Corallo had a simple and direct policy that he had conveyed to his family members.

Corallo told Salerno, "If you fuck around with drugs, you will be killed." Castellano had already established this policy, but not all the families had complied. Several members of the Bonanno and Colombo families, according to our informants, were engaging in drug trafficking. Philip "Rusty" Rastelli and Carmine "the Snake" Persico, the bosses of those families, ignored their activities in the hope that Castellano would not find out.

On another occasion, Salerno and Corallo were conversing over a dispute about the best way to recruit new soldiers into the families, and our agents recorded that conversation. Salerno complained to Corallo about a serious problem he had with a made member that he could not resolve. Corallo's answer was simple: "Kill him." We could not identify the individual they referred to, but the conversation displayed how utterly ruthless the Mafia could be. One fact we took away from our investigations was that the leaders were not very good at peacefully settling disputes. When somebody they thought was acting out of line or a threat to them, they were killed without remorse and or consequences. The Mafia had no moral compass.

One of the critical conversations that occurred between Salerno and Corallo at the Palma Boys Social Club, which helped establish their roles in the Commission, came about unexpectedly one day:

> Corallo: "I come to see you, and then I am going."
>
> Salerno: "How you feeling?"
>
> Corallo: "All right, much better, getting along. Did you reason with him?"
>
> Salerno: "This kid is with Walsh in a dispute with 'Matty the Horse,' told that kid to sell his business, and never go near the fish market again."
>
> Corallo: "Did you reason with him?"
>
> Salerno: "I don't know what to do. I swear I don't. I know you'll retire."
>
> Corallo: "And you have to run downtown when you want something done."
>
> Salerno: "No, I'll retire, I don't need that."
>
> Corallo: "I know you'll retire, I know you'll retire."
>
> Salerno: "Listen, Tony, if it wasn't for me, there would be no Mob left. I made all the guys. And everybody is a good guy. This guy don't realize that. I worked myself. Jeez, how could a man be like that, huh? He even called me Fat Tony to my face. Here's to your health."
>
> Corallo: "No, I know the way he talks. Shoot him; get rid of them; shoot them; kill them. You can't go on, it's disgusting."

Corallo and Salerno were sharing a drink. Corallo then stated, "Well, here's to your health."

Salerno replied, "I gotta make a decision I hate to make."

The conversation then turns to Corallo settling a $500,000 loan-sharking deal with an associate for $275,000. Corallo said, "You want two-seventy-five, then you get two-seventy-five, I'll settle. I don't want to get involved with these shylocking loans back and forth, and I made him give them the two-seventy-five."

An analysis of these conversations indicated that Salerno's dispute was with an individual attempting to interfere with their control over the Fulton Fish Market. Matty the Horse was Matty Ianniello, a capo in the Genovese family. He had tried to resolve the dispute unsuccessfully and Salerno was now contemplating killing this individual, which he appeared reluctant to do. Corallo was encouraging him to "kill them." We never identified the individual they referred to. When Corallo mentioned, "And you have to run downtown when you want something done," he referred to the Commission.

Corallo's comments about the loan-sharking debt confirmed that he was directly involved in this type of criminal activity, which we had already suspected.

Corallo and the other Commission members were indicted on February 25, 1985 for violating the RICO statute. Corallo was not arrested because he was hospitalized at the time. We notified his attorney of the indictment, and he surrendered upon his release from the hospital a few days later. Corallo's underboss, Salvatore "Tom Mix" Santoro and consigliere Christopher "Christie Tick" Furnari were also indicted. Corallo was convicted in the Commission trial and received a sentence of 100 years in federal prison.

Before going to prison, our informants advised that Corallo had appointed Anthony "Buddy" Luongo as acting boss. However, his reign only lasted several months. Luongo suddenly disappeared. We believed he had been murdered, but his body was never found. We suspected that Vittorio "Little Vic" Amuso, his underboss at the time, killed Luongo. Amuso then named himself acting boss until the Commission formally approved him. He then appointed his close friend and associate, Anthony "Gaspipe" Casso, underboss. A whole new approach to running the Lucchese family was adopted. Amuso and Casso would bring violence to the family, rivaling John Gotti's exploits.

The FBI would assume the lead in investigating the remnants of the family. Due to how Amuso and Casso ran the family, we would have to adopt a purely "cops and robbers" approach. The Lucchese squad was now dealing with two Mafia leaders who did not rule by conventional means—they ruled by the gun. Amuso and Casso had a long history of violence and had been suspected of committing numerous murders of their rivals in the past. Amuso had been a member since 1970 and belonged to the "Christie Tick" Furnari crew. He and Casso were suspected of being involved in the Frank DeCicco hit when a bomb intended for him and Gotti was placed under DeCicco's car.

The investigation now focused full-time on the activities of Amuso and Casso, and we could not let them pick up where Corallo had left off. Our informants were in place, and electronic surveillance was an option if a particular location was identified where they held meetings. Peter "Fat Pete" Chiodo, a capo in the family, had just been indicted in a scam possibly involving Amuso and Casso. They were concerned that Chiodo would cooperate with the FBI as he had pled guilty to the charges, which usually indicated that a plea deal had been made with the government. They thus ordered a hit on Chiodo and assigned it to Alfonso "Little Al" D'Arco.

On May 8, 1991, "Fat Pete" Chiodo was confronted and shot twelve times. However, he survived the shooting, due to the obesity that gave him his moniker. While recuperating in the hospital, Amuso then threatened Chiodo's family. Chiodo had initially rejected attempts by us to flip him, but after the threats to his family, he called the FBI agent in charge of the case and agreed to cooperate. Meanwhile, D'Arco became concerned that he had failed to kill Chiodo and that Amuso might kill him out of spite. He also contacted the FBI and offered full cooperation. It was difficult for the agents to keep up with these fast-moving events. The collaboration between Chiodo and D'Arco now provided an excellent opportunity for Amuso and Casso to be taken down.

D'Arco told the agents he was so concerned about his family's safety that "we had to hide in my mother's house on Long Island." Amuso was violating the code of the Mafia; family members were not to be the victims of any act of violence. D'Arco believed "Amuso and Casso were out of control." A team of agents was quickly dispatched to rescue his family from harm, and he and the entire family entered the witness protection program. Within a short period, the FBI had two made Lucchese members ready to blow the lid off the family. It would eventually lead to the indictments of Amuso and Casso, but not before more lives were lost.

Casso took another avenue and went after Chiodo's sister, Patricia Capozzallo, who was shot several times but somehow survived. A capo they wrongly suspected of cooperating with the FBI, Steven Crea, was then targeted and murdered. After sufficient evidence was developed implicating Casso in Crea's murder, a warrant was issued for his arrest, but his whereabouts were unknown.

Information was developed that he might be hiding out in the home of his mistress, Rosemarie Billotti, in New Jersey. A surveillance of the home was initiated. A plan had to be developed to safely make entry, as there was great concern that Casso would not surrender peacefully. The house was a small ranch home on a sizable lot, not closely adjacent to surrounding homes. The SWAT team was called to the site to make a quick, forcible entry so Casso would not have a chance to react. The agents had Billotti's phone number and made a pretext call to confirm that she was in the house. This was a hazardous situation; they would have to make a flawless entry, or else, in all probability, they would soon be engaging Casso in a shoot-out. They were ready and confident to go in. Within a few seconds, the door came off the hinges. The agents were lucky—Casso was taking a shower. Rosemarie screamed as she sat on the sofa watching a soap opera.

Agents searched Billotti's home and recovered a rifle, $340,000 in cash, and records Casso kept concerning the inner workings of the Lucchese family. The records contained a concise accounting of Casso and Amuso's profits from their illegal enterprise. They also included a list of the members of the family and the tribute that each member had to pay Amuso and Casso. It was a windfall. Casso was placed in a federal lockup to await an appearance in court. During his period of incarceration, he had a lot to think about.

After several days, Casso, through his attorney, reached out to us and agreed to a meeting. He volunteered to cooperate and enter the witness protection program. We could not agree to that request up-front, but indicated that after a thorough debriefing, we would evaluate the truthfulness of this information and its accuracy. If he furnished credible information, we would discuss his position with the federal prosecutors, but he also would have to agree to testify in court to the evidence he supplied. He agreed to these conditions and our debriefing sessions began. They would last an entire week.

Casso gave our agents a detailed account of his life and activities in the Lucchese family. In particular, he shed light on the events surrounding the murder of Gambino boss Paul Castellano. In early December 1985, Casso met with Frank DeCicco at his request. He had previously worked with DeCicco and knew his capo, John Gotti. As a member of the Lucchese family, DeCicco wanted Casso to support a plan that he and Gotti were working on to kill Castellano so Gotti could take over the family.

Casso refused and told DeCicco, "You have to get permission from the Commission." After Castellano was murdered, Casso went to Anthony Corallo, his boss at the time, and informed him of the meeting he had with DeCicco.

Casso told Corallo that he strongly admonished DeCicco and warned him, "You cannot assume that the Lucchese family will support the hit on Castellano."

DeCicco ignored his warnings and commented, "We will do what we must do." Casso was tempted to kill DeCicco right then and there. After listening to Casso's revelations, Corallo met with Anthony "Fat Tony" Salerno and Vincent "Chin" Gigante, and they put out a contract on Gotti and all those who participated in the killing of Castellano.

Casso and Amuso were given the Gotti contract and planted a bomb under DeCicco's car when he and whom they thought was Gotti left a planned meeting at the Ravenite Social Club. The bomb's blast killed DeCicco, but the passenger was only injured. This confession by Casso officially identified the perpetrators of this particular incident. Still, the motive for the killing of DeCicco had already been surmised by us from the information we had received from informants. We confirmed, however, two points: 1) who was responsible for the actual murder of DeCicco, and 2) the Commission had put the contract out to kill Gotti. This evidence would help substantiate our theory that the Commission controlled the Five Families.

The debriefing of Casso continued and the number of murders he had committed in the name of the family was staggering. The agents and prosecutors could not imagine offering him leniency in return for this future testimony. They also felt his actions were beyond the norm and a jury would not believe his account. For this reason, he was rejected for consideration of entering the witness protection program. He eventually pled guilty to several murders and was sentenced to life in prison—455 years in total.

Vic Amuso was indicted and charged with multiple counts of the RICO statute. Alfonso "Little Al" D'Arco became a key witness at the trial. The investigative approach the agents had adopted to take down the Mafia was working. Another Mob boss in jail. The more they penetrated each family and began convicting significant leaders, the more opportunities developed for members to flip and become informants or cooperative witnesses. The Mafia code of omertà no longer existed. This whole image that the Mafia had projected all these years was just a sham. They were nothing but low-level street criminals hiding behind the façade of being an invincible, well-oiled machine. That now, in our eyes, was a myth. The FBI had them in their sights and were determined to destroy this menace once and for all.

CHAPTER 12
The Colombo Family

Joseph Profaci became the boss of a family in 1928 when it was known as the "Profaci gang." It was the smallest and newest of the five organized crime groups at that time. He named his brother Salvatore consigliere. His brother-in-law Joseph Magliocco became his underboss. He surrounded himself with his closest relatives to serve as his counselors, as he had a reputation for trusting no one. By the early 1930s, the organization prospered by controlling all illegal activities in Brooklyn. Profaci, also known as "Olive Oil King" due to his olive oil import business, was close to Joseph Bonanno, the oldest Commission member, and the Profaci-Bonanno alliance was born.

Profaci died in 1962 and Magliocco succeeded him as boss. The Commission acknowledged that he was the new boss, but would not appoint him to the Commission. They were unsure of his ability to run the family. Magliocco resented this snub and asked Bonanno to intervene, but Bonanno could not resolve the dispute. Bonanno believed the Commission had disrespected him, particularly as he was the senior member, and his request should have been honored. He began devising a plan, along with the help of Magliocco, to kill their rivals on the Commission: Tommy Lucchese and Carlo Gambino.

Magliocco gave the contract to Joseph Colombo, one of his

trusted capos. Colombo, realizing he was in a no-win situation, went to Gambino and revealed the plot. The Commission summoned Bonanno and Magliocco and demanded an explanation. Bonanno fled to Arizona and retired, albeit reluctantly after staging his own kidnapping and losing the Banana War of the mid-sixties. Magliocco admitted to being involved and pleaded for his life. The Commission spared him, but banished him from the family and appointed Colombo the new boss. He was only forty-one and the youngest of the five bosses.

Joseph Colombo was a bit different from the traditional Mafia boss. His father was a former member of the Profaci family, so although he grew up in a Mafia environment, he also had other interests. He grew angry and frustrated when the media and public would equate Italian heritage with the Mafia. He felt it had gotten out of hand and the stigma of the Mafia was damaging the sense of pride in the Italian community. In 1970, he had an idea. He founded the Italian-American Civil Rights League in New York, which organized rallies supported by the Italian-American Organization. Prominent Italian businessmen and entertainers appeared at the rallies and spoke of their heritage. The movement grew in popularity and received widespread media coverage. Colombo himself made TV appearances emphasizing his concern about this issue.

On June 28, 1971, an Italian Unity Day rally was scheduled at Columbus Circle in Manhattan. The Commission had ordered Colombo to develop a lower profile with this organization because the publicity it received cast unwanted scrutiny on the existence of the Mafia. Colombo ignored their warnings, even though Carlo Gambino had ordered him to back off. Thousands of Italian Americans attended the rally. It was a festive and enthusiastic occasion.

As Colombo was addressing the crowd, shots rang out and he fell, seriously wounded. He was hit in the head by three bullets and was initially feared dead. The shooter, Jerome Johnson, was immediately killed by Colombo's bodyguards. Johnson was a member of a black group of criminals who reportedly had allegiance to "Crazy Joe" Gallo, an ambitious capo in the family. Gallo became an immediate suspect, especially after his reckless war with the previous family boss, Joe Profaci, in the decade prior. It was speculated that he had hired Johnson to kill Colombo because he wanted to take over the family. The police, however, could not link Gallo to Johnson, but within Mafia circles, everyone believed Gallo was responsible.

Colombo survived the shooting, but was paralyzed and unable to resume his role as the boss. A more likely scenario for the attempted hit was the simple fact that Colombo was causing too much attention to be paid to the Mafia. He ignored the directive of the Commission to back off. When he refused, his fate was sealed, and the Commission thus ordered Gallo to kill Colombo. After months of infighting, the Commission appointed Carmine "the Snake" Persico as the new boss. Persico was a capo and a top moneymaker who had the support of key family members. He had been in the family for approximately twenty years. One of his first acts was to issue an open contract on Gallo's life. He was basically calling upon any Mafia member to kill Gallo on sight.

On April 7, 1972, Joey Gallo and his family celebrated his birthday at Umberto's Clam House in Little Italy, owned by Matthew "Matty the Horse" Ianniello, a capo in the Genovese family. His wife and sister joined him, along with his bodyguard. A Colombo associate, Joseph Luparelli, was sitting at the bar, but Gallo did not recognize him. Ianniello was in his upstairs apartment. What happened next is uncertain, but either Ianniello or Luparelli notified someone in the Colombo family that Gallo was in the restaurant. Within what seemed like minutes, three masked shooters entered the restaurant. Witnesses say Gallo recognized what was happening and drew his gun, but it was too late. The shooters fired over twenty shots, mortally wounding Gallo. He staggered to a side door and fell to the pavement. He was dead. The shooters fled the scene. An FBI cooperative witness, Joseph Luparelli, a member of the Colombo family, later identified fellow members Carmine DiBiase and Philip Gambino as two of the shooters. They were never charged due to a lack of corroborative evidence. Persico then appointed Gennaro Langella as his underboss and designated him to oversee their involvement in the Concrete Club scam. Langella's street name was Gerry Lang. Each family, except for the Bonannos, had a piece of the extortion scheme that the Mafia had enforced on the unions and contractors constructing high-rise buildings in Manhattan. Ralph Scopo, a high-ranking union official in the building trades local, reported directly to Langella. Persico was in and out of prison, so there were often long stretches when Langella was the acting boss controlling the family. He would report to Persico from time to time, but that was difficult when Carmine was in prison.

We had designated FBI supervisor Damon Taylor to manage the Colombo investigation. He had previously been an intelligence analyst monitoring the Five Families. He and his wife lived in the city, so he knew the pulse of New York as well as anyone. He was independent and often worked outside the margins in his approach to running the squad. I wanted people in these positions who could think for themselves and solve investigative problems independently. I was impressed that he had brought his own leather chair into his office. This showed me that he had an independent streak and was unafraid to cross the line. Taylor's squad was a short distance from my office and I often joined him for a cup of coffee in the morning. His squad had several young and inexperienced agents assigned, but they were focused on their objective. Dennis Maduro, a recent law school graduate, was designated as the case agent for the Colombo investigation. As it turned out, this was a great choice. Maduro was enthusiastic and intelligent and had a cheerful attitude.

Taylor's initial objective was to develop sufficient probable cause to intercept conversations between Langella and members of the Colombo family. Kallstrom assigned an experienced team of agents to surveil Langella. They soon established a pattern. Langella frequently met with identified members, including Ralph

Scopo, at the Casa Storta Restaurant in Brooklyn. Under the guise of two lovers out on a date, Taylor sent two agents into the restaurant when Langella was present. One of the agents told the headwaiter, "My mother was born in Sicily and she loved Italian food." They immediately accepted our two lovers.

The agents were able to frequent the restaurant on several occasions. The waiter would fuss when they did not show up for a few days. He would comment, "Where have you been? We missed you." Little did he know! They observed Langella and Scopo meeting frequently in a room off the back of the restaurant. Other family members would join them and their discussions were always intense. It was apparent to the agents that they were not there to enjoy the food. The observations and intelligence gathered enabled Maduro to prepare an affidavit requesting court authorization to install listening devices in the back room of the restaurant. The installation was going to be a challenge.

Kallstrom assigned his best men to enter the restaurant early one morning. Their target was a lamp hanging over the table where Langella and his associates gathered. They intended to install a listening device in the lamp, allowing Taylor's agents to record conversations at an off-site location. This installation would require many technically trained agents and a substantial backup team on the perimeter. The group inside making the installation needed to be promptly alerted if the police arrived at the location for any reason. They also had to be concerned about any wise guys in the area.

Back at headquarters, I waited in the command center with bated breath as I monitored what was happening in Brooklyn over the radio. Kallstrom was on the scene, personally supervising this one. As the agents entered, the lead agent radioed Kallstrom, "Jim, we have a problem!" There was a watchdog on duty, an aggressive German shepherd. We always anticipated this type of possibility; it was quickly handled by spraying the shepherd with a harmless solution that got his attention away from the agents.

An hour or so passed and I was getting nervous back at the command center. Kallstrom soon got on the radio: "Boss, mission accomplished." I breathed a sigh of relief. Another job well done by our special operations branch.

Many critical conversations at the Casa Storta were recorded, but one in particular demonstrated how the Commission would intervene in disputes involving more than one family. Langella was meeting with one of his capos, Dominic "Donnie Shacks" Montemarano. Langella complained about the Commission's decision relating to a financial dispute he had with Lucchese's boss, Anthony "Tony Ducks" Corallo. Langella, an acting boss, was outvoted by Corallo, Castellano, and Salerno, and he felt disrespected, but he knew better than to protest the decision. It was unacceptable to disagree with a directive issued by the Commission, but he was resentful at how he was being treated. This type of evidence was critical in establishing that the Commission monitored and controlled the affairs of each Mafia family.

Due to his position with the union, Scopo was a key player in managing the extortion conspiracy involving awarding building contracts to the seven contractors who were members of the Concrete Club. Surveillance of Scopo uncovered that he was meeting contractors in his car and at his union office. We were now able to observe his meetings and document them. It was becoming clear that Scopo might be the most essential player in the Colombo family. Developing sufficient evidence and understanding the workings of the Concrete Club became the squad's priority. Scopo was a mere soldier, but his status and importance were elevated as he was the president of Local 6A of the Cement and Concrete Workers Union and the district council, which had at least 4,000 members.

Contractors hired the local union members to construct buildings all over Manhattan. Scopo had the power to cause a work slowdown for any minor infraction that might occur, or he would manufacture a union issue if it suited his purpose. The Gambino family–controlled Teamsters Local 282 was comprised of truck drivers who delivered the concrete. The Commission thus controlled the workers who built the buildings and the trucking companies that delivered the concrete. The contractors were hamstrung; they either paid up or would not receive any contracts and would be out of business. The Colombo and Gambino families were the principal players in this criminal conspiracy, but the Genovese and Lucchese families shared in the generated profits.

We placed a court-approved microphone in Scopo's car and instituted continuous surveillance of his activities. During meetings with contractors, he would refer to payments that were due and contracts that were pending and, in some cases, became threatening when he felt he was meeting resistance. The family had direct control over contracts under $2 million and would receive a 1 percent kickback on the gross cost of the project. They also received a kickback on all concrete delivered to a jobsite. If a contract was over $2 million, only contractors who were members of the Concrete Club could bid, and the family would receive a 2 percent kickback on those particular contracts. This arrangement was extremely lucrative for the Mafia families, but very costly for the contractors, who considered it a cost of doing business in New York. Seven specific contractors were members of the Concrete Club.

Our agents contacted James Costigan, president of XLO Concrete Corp., who had been recorded having a conversation with Scopo. He greeted the agents with a warm welcome: "Thank God you're here. I am sick of paying these bastards money under the table." He had been a victim of this extortion plot for a long time. Costigan was an honest man who was attempting to run a legitimate business. When he attempted to obtain a building contract, he received a visit from Scopo, who presented himself in a threatening manner. Scopo told Costigan he would have to kick back 2 percent of every contract he was awarded and also pay him a regular fee to maintain labor peace. He later would testify that Scopo further elaborated, "It's going into a pot and would be divided among the families."

After his release from prison, Persico had been indicted in a separate RICO case in October 1984, fled his home, and became a fugitive. After a few months, due to his position in the Mafia, he became the 390th fugitive to be placed on the FBI's ten most wanted list, the first time a Mafia boss had been so honored. All efforts to locate him had failed. Taylor entered my office on the morning of February 15, 1985. He hurriedly announced, "We just got word that Persico is living with his nephew outside the city."

Fred DeChristopher, the nephew, called Dennis Maduro and informed him that Persico was living in his attic at his Wantagh, Long Island home. DeChristopher was willing to cooperate and just wanted "Persico out of the house." I wouldn't say I liked the sound of him hiding in an attic on the third floor. That presented an immediate problem for safe entry to the property. DeChristopher feared for his family's safety with Persico's continued presence. Persico had members of the family visit from time to time, and this too was a concern.

I told Taylor to assemble an arrest team and we arrived at DeChristopher's home within forty-five minutes. We positioned ourselves a safe distance from the house, a three-story bungalow on a quiet street. Persico's apprehension would not be easy. He had been prone to violence and the target of several murder investigations, and he was desperate. A Mafia boss does not flee after being indicted. We usually call upon the SWAT team to execute an arrest in these situations. That would have been our next step, but I wanted to convince Persico to surrender and leave the house peacefully.

We had DeChristopher's phone number, so I asked agent Tom Brown, who had previously interviewed Persico, to call him and try to convince him to surrender. Brown made contact and a woman who answered the call refused to cooperate and bring Persico to the phone. Brown felt Persico was in the house due to the woman's manner of speaking. Brown discontinued the conversation and we regrouped to consider our next move. They say "Patience is a virtue," which was my next thought. My first responsibility was to ensure that none of my agents would be injured or killed during this apprehension. I still felt a forced entry was too risky unless we used SWAT.

Deputy Assistant Director Ken Walton had accompanied us to the scene. Ken was always very blunt and did not pull punches when he wanted to make a point. He personally made the next phone call and told the party who answered the phone, "He comes out with his hands up, or else we are going to storm the house with a dozen fucking FBI agents." Within three minutes or so, Persico walked out of the house with his hands up and this short-lived drama was over. No harm, no foul. Persico was transported to the federal lockup to await trial on the pending charges. He was subsequently convicted with the other Commission members for violation of the RICO statute and received a life sentence.

Persico now realized he would never be released from prison to head the Colombo family again and he could not accept this fact. After Langella was also convicted of a RICO violation in the Commission case, he wanted to ensure his family still received their share of the profits from Mafia operations. He named his brother Alphonse "Allie Boy" Persico as acting boss, reporting directly to him even though he would still be in prison. He had no intention of stepping down as boss. This assumption on his part was a bit unprecedented; although some bosses had attempted this move in the past, it was never successful. "Allie Boy" did not serve in this position for an extended period. After being indicted and convicted of loan-sharking, he received a lengthy prison sentence. Colombo capo Victor "Little Vic" Orena was then named acting boss under the condition that once "Allie Boy" was released, he would take over. Orena would now receive orders from the imprisoned Persico; however, this arrangement soon created significant conflicts within the family. As all these changes took place, Agent Lin DeVecchio turned a highly placed member of the Colombo family into an informant who provided almost daily intelligence regarding all these new developments.

Vic Orena had risen through the ranks of the Colombo family over a span of years and had developed a close relationship with John Gotti, as they were very much alike. As the new boss of the Gambino family, Gotti sought Orena's assistance in many new enterprises that were profitable for both families. Persico did not support Orena's efforts to act independently and a rift developed between them. Many family members latched onto this conflict and two factions emerged that were now at odds: those who supported Persico and a significant number who wanted to see Orena succeed. The dispute could not be settled peacefully and the family was about to enter one of the bloodiest periods in its history.

In the fall of 1989, DeVecchio's informant advised that Orena contacted Gotti and arranged a meeting with the representatives of all the families over an issue he had with one of his associates, Thomas Ocera. He felt Ocera was a risk to the Gambino and Colombo families, as he was recently arrested by the police and had given up all his loan-sharking records. He wanted consensus from the group to hit Ocera. Agents were able to monitor the meeting and photograph all the participants as they were exiting a home in Brooklyn. Efforts by our agents to locate and warn Ocera of this planned conspiracy to kill him failed. Within days, Ocera disappeared. Many months later, we received information that Ocera was indeed murdered on orders from Orena. Agents determined where he was buried and dug up his body.

Our informant reported that "Orena had developed a natural distrust toward Persico." He seemed too timid since his incarceration, preventing the family from moving forward with new opportunities to make sizable profits. Orena also had learned that Persico had contacted a representative of a news outlet and was involved in negotiations to do a televised series on his life as a Mafia boss. Orena met with the Commission and requested they remove Persico as boss and officially name him the successor. They refused his request. Persico's recently appointed consigliere, Carmine Sessa, alerted him to Orena's efforts. Persico instructed Sessa to put together a hit team to kill Orena.

Sessa recruited fellow members John Pate and Henry "Hank the Bank" Smurra to take out Orena. On June 20, 1991, they were in position near Orena's home on Long Island. They anticipated killing Orena in his car to prevent him from returning fire. However, Orena spotted them lying in wait and quickly made his escape. Persico had thrown the first stone, but there was much more to follow. The family was now officially at war.

- On November 18, 1991, Orena sent a hit team to murder Gregory Scarpa, a Persico loyalist, but Scarpa was able to avoid the killers.
- On the same day, Hank Smurra, a member of the hit team that attempted to kill Orena, did not fare as well. He was shot dead inside a Brooklyn doughnut shop.
- November 29 was the target date in an attempt to kill Carmine Sessa, but somehow, he survived his wounds. Eventually, Sessa agreed to cooperate and became an FBI witness.
- Scarpa and his team retaliated by attempting to kill Joseph Tolino, an Orena loyalist, but instead killed his companion, Genovese member Thomas Amato. This killing caused a significant reaction from the Genovese family.
- Orena countered by ordering the murders of Rosario Nastasi and Vincent Fusaro, two Persico associates.
- It was now Persico's move. He ordered the execution of Nicholas Grancio, a loyal Orena soldier.
- Within a few weeks, Matteo Speranza, an employee of a business owned by a Persico family member, was murdered in his shop.

Over the next year, the killings continued. First, it was Orena's turn, followed by Persico's. Who was going to win? Nobody. It was just back and forth and represented a war the Mafia had not seen in years. The wars inadvertently resulted in the murders of three innocent bystanders. Eighteen family members or associates disappeared and were never seen again. We assumed they were murdered and their bodies buried somewhere on Long Island. The bloodiest Mob war in the history of the Mafia took place right before our eyes, and we could do nothing to stop the bloodshed.

The Third Colombo War eventually ended. Persico resumed control over the family from prison and his son Alphonse (not to be confused with Carmine's brother "Allie Boy") became the acting street boss. "Little Allie Boy" was reckless and not mature enough to run a Mafia family. William Cutolo, a highly placed capo, was running day-to-day operations and had ambitions to become the boss. In a move to appease the Orena faction of the family, Persico named Cutolo acting underboss. Cutolo was well-known to the Colombo squad and they monitored his activities closely. He had risen quickly after becoming aligned with Orena and commanded a crew of several hit men who directly participated in the Colombo War. He led the team that killed Hank Smurra. Our follow-up investigation also determined that he was more than likely responsible for at least three of the eighteen known murders that took place during the wars.

During this period, "Little Allie Boy" was arrested in Florida on a weapons charge. He was observed by the Coast Guard speeding in his boat and when they pulled him over, they found a shotgun in his possession. Persico, fearful that his son would be sent to prison and Cutolo would take over the family, put together a hit team under the direction of his son to kill Cutolo. Persico ordered Cutolo to attend a meeting at the home of Dino Saracino, a highly placed family member. I assume Cutolo thought he would be named acting boss to succeed "Little Allie Boy," who was facing a prison sentence. Instead, he was greeted by Dino Calabro and Thomas Gioeli, who, along with Saracino, murdered Cutolo. They all were eventually arrested and "Little Allie Boy" and the others received life sentences. Persico was now running out of options and decided to oversee the family from prison alone, using intermediaries to deal with issues that would arise.

Taylor's squad conducted an extensive investigation of Cutulo's murder. Through the use of cooperative witnesses and intercepted recorded conversations, agents were able to develop sufficient evidence to indict and convict "Little Allie Boy," Gioeli, Saracino, and Calabro of the Cutolo hit. They all received lengthy prison sentences. Carmine Persico continued attempts to run the family from prison. The family was now decimated with under fifty active members. The Commission no longer recognized Persico as one of them. The influence and control over labor unions and the construction industry the family had enjoyed no longer existed. The family would never regain the footing that it once held. In a way, it became a nonentity compared to its previous position. Remnants remained and Colombo's wise guys would always be out there, but they had to constantly look over their shoulders because the FBI would always be there. Carmine Persico was never released from prison. He died at the age of eighty-five in 2019.

Orena was indicted for violation of the RICO statute and went into hiding at his girlfriend's home in Valley Stream, New York. One of the counts in the indictment related to the murder of Thomas Ocera. An informant gave us the location of the house and agents arrested Orena without incident. Incidental to the arrest, agents recovered shotguns, ammunition, and a considerable amount of cash. He was eventually convicted and received a life sentence in federal prison. The Colombo family was suddenly without a boss and no one was eager to step forward. Another nail in the coffin.

It seemed to me that our new approach was working and the investigative effort was coming together. I decided to call a timeout and get the supervisors and agents together for a social hour after work. We picked Nino's Bar and Restaurant in Brooklyn, one of their favorite haunts to unwind after a tough day on the job. I was surprised at the turnout; the place was packed. I took the opportunity to thank everyone for a job well done at this point on our journey and reminded them that "we still have a long way to go before we score the final touchdown." We had a couple of hearty toasts and headed home, ready to hit the bricks the next day.

CHAPTER 13
The Genovese Family

The Genovese family was the oldest and largest Mafia organization in New York. Its history went back to the 1890s, seeing such bosses as Giuseppe "the Clutch Hand" Morello and Joe "the Boss" Masseria, both of whom were killed in the Castellammarese War of 1930–1931. The family became prominent during the reign of boss Charles "Lucky" Luciano, who together with Meyer Lansky and the other gang leaders across the country first made crime organized via the National Crime Syndicate. It was known as the Luciano family from the early 1930s to the late 1950s, when Vito Genovese took over as boss from Frank Costello. He was dispatched to federal prison in 1959 on drug trafficking charges. However, the organization continued to be referred to as the Genovese family.

Genovese was succeeded by Vincent "Chin" Gigante, a semi-recluse who constantly feigned mental illness. For the most part, Gigante ran the family's business from his apartment in Greenwich Village, and he appointed Anthony "Fat Tony" Salerno as his underboss and the face of the family. For all practical purposes, Salerno was the family's street boss and was treated as such by the members and the FBI. Informant information indicated that Salerno operated from the Palma Boys Social Club in East Harlem, and most of his meetings with family members were held at this location.

Our previous investigations had determined that the extent of influence of the Genovese family had extended beyond the city of New York. They also had interests in the suburbs and the surrounding counties. The family was directly involved in several industries, such as trucking, waste hauling, and construction. Smaller Mafia organizations in Buffalo and Rochester, New York, as well as the Russell Bufalino family in upstate Pennsylvania, all operated under the umbrella of the Genovese family. Since the assassination of Philadelphia boss Angelo Bruno, they also had begun to exert some control over the casino industry in Atlantic City as they supported the elevation of Nicky Scarfo as the new family boss. Through our previous investigation in Philadelphia of the Bruno murder, we determined that the family had ordered the killing of those responsible for Bruno's death.

Several smaller Mafia groups operated throughout New England, the strongest of which was the family in Providence, Rhode Island, under the leadership of Raymond Patriarca. They also controlled illegal activities in the North End of Boston. The Patriarca family had been aligned with the Genovese family since the days of Prohibition. We also learned from the UNIRAC investigation that the Genovese family had been directly involved in controlling various waterfront industries along the East Coast by infiltrating the ILA.

The review of Salerno's background was very revealing. He was raised in East Harlem and initially became involved in loansharking, where he would loan money to individuals without credit. He would then charge them an exorbitant interest rate. If not paid, he would threaten the borrower and sometimes resort to violence to collect the money. This racket was standard in every family. Salerno also controlled a numbers racket for the family. He was a moneymaker, grossing millions of dollars yearly. Over the years, he became quite wealthy. He owned a horse farm in Rhinebeck, New York, spent considerable time in Florida, and had an apartment in Manhattan—not bad for a guy with no legitimate income.

Our focus had consistently been identifying locations where

the bosses would meet with their members to discuss family interests. Through continuous surveillance of Salerno, it was evident that the social club was his location. The club was in a typical New York residential neighborhood, with residents milling about and shopping at a local grocery store. Kids played in the street and a patrolman always seemed nearby. This presented an obstacle for us in conducting discreet surveillance, but we had a solution. We rented an apartment one block from the club and set up a high-powered camera to monitor and photograph those entering and leaving. The club was not open to the general public and there was always a doorman at the front entrance. Upon making an observation, the agent would transmit a radio communication to a surveillance agent, who would swing by the club to pick up the license plate. Within a relatively short period, we had sufficient observations of known Mafia members entering and leaving the club. Coupled with critical intelligence information that Salerno and his associates frequently discussed criminal activities in the club, we obtained court authorization to install electronic surveillance equipment.

Salerno was at the club almost every day. He was a throwback to a bygone era. He could never be called the Dapper Don like John Gotti. He resembled an older man who wore shabby clothes and pants that drooped, supported by suspenders. He always had a cigar in his mouth and a worn-out hat on his head that was tilted toward the side. He was overweight and his beer belly was pronounced; thus, the nickname "Fat Tony" emerged. Salerno would have looked perfect in *The Godfather*. When we had previously interviewed him, his tone was sarcastic, belligerent, and somewhat defiant. Well, hopefully, we were about to change all that. After Kallstrom and his team successfully installed the surveillance equipment, it was time to turn on the recorders.

Salerno met regularly with family members and was a prolific talker, which fit the profile we had developed. Our prior investigation showed that Gigante and Salerno built their empire by extorting legitimate businesses through their ability to control the labor unions that supplied the workers. All five families had a piece of this action. They had learned that this is where the real money could be made. Our objective was to establish that the Commission controlled all Mafia-related criminal activities in New York and other cities nationwide. Monitoring agents were vigilant in intercepting any conversations supporting this fact. On October 8, 1984, we hit pay dirt. Our surveillance team observed John Tronolone and Joe Pieri enter the club. They were members of the Cleveland family headed by Angelo Lonardo.

Tronolone and Pieri were in New York on a mission. Agents began hearing references to a family dispute over who would be the next boss in Cleveland. A highly placed member wanted to take over the family and push Lonardo aside. The majority of the membership was against such a change. Salerno became very annoyed at the suggestion that such an attempt would be made to overthrow an existing boss without permission.

The agents intercepted the following statement by Salerno and could not believe their good fortune in capturing this devastating evidence: "Let the Commission decide. Tell him it's the Commission from New York. Tell him he is dealing with the big boys now."

Shortly after this statement was made, Tronolone and Pieri were observed leaving the club, and one of our surveillance teams followed them out of the city. The agents monitoring the call contacted their supervisor, Don Richards. They were elated at this development. After days of superfluous discussions about family business, they finally got the home run they wanted. Monitoring an electronic surveillance installation is one of the most boring assignments in the FBI. An agent could sit on a wire for days without any noteworthy evidence being developed. This particular conversation would later be introduced at an eventual trial we hoped would materialize involving the Commission. It was a significant accomplishment, but as it turned out, we were only beginning.

Philip "Rusty" Rastelli had become the boss of the Bonanno family and now wanted to be formally made a member of the

Commission. This was the standard procedure. You could not just assume the role of the boss of a family without the approval of the entire membership of the Commission. The membership must then approve your formal acceptance. During a meeting Salerno had at the club with one of his capos, the agents listened as Salerno discussed how he prevented Rastelli from being immediately approved by the Commission: "I told the Commission, 'Ah, hey, listen, he wants to be the boss. He can be the boss as far as I am concerned, but he cannot be on the Commission.' One vote is enough to throw it out. Cause, the Commission thing. It's supposed to be such a sacred thing."

Salerno's concern about Rastelli related to his history in drug trafficking and his relationship with a Sicilian faction that had been operating under the umbrella of the Bonanno family. He had referred to Rastelli's reliance on "junk guys" as a direct reference to drug dealers. Castellano had forbidden drug trafficking and every family was aware of the policy and had to abide by it. One day, out of the blue, the agents observed "Matty the Horse" Ianniello, a family capo of significant rank, and James Ida, another member, enter the club. Within minutes, they were involved in a discussion with Salerno. Ianniello told Salerno that Rastelli wanted to add new members to his family. Salerno responded angrily to this suggestion and the agents were able to record the following conversation: "Listen, we don't recognize him down there. I did not want to meet; Paul did not want to meet. Tony Ducks told Rusty, 'Listen, take care of your family first. Straighten out your family, and when you straighten them out, then we talk about the Commission.'"

We analyzed this conversation and it was clear to us that the Commission was upset with Rastelli for allowing his members to engage in drug trafficking. Salerno, Castellano, and Corallo, the Commission's leaders, would not meet with Rastelli regarding his acceptance as a member until he resolved this issue. This evidence became crucial in establishing the Commission's existence. Our investigation of the Genovese family, however, was not complete. We had additional avenues to pursue.

One of the most critical developments in our investigation related to Vincent "the Fish" Cafaro, a protégé of Salerno's. He was born near Vicenza, Italy and grew up in the same neighborhood as Salerno in East Harlem. Cafaro had been a member since 1974 and was responsible for influencing the Council of Carpenters Union and extorting labor peace payoffs from concrete supply companies. Within a short time, we indicted Cafaro and fourteen other members for violating the RICO statute. He received a lengthy prison sentence.

One day, an agent on the Genovese squad received a telephone call from Cafaro. His only words were, "I have to speak to you right away." We were happy to oblige and two agents were immediately dispatched to debrief Cafaro. It was one of the most extensive and detailed accounts we had ever received of a Mafia family's inner workings and structure. It would blow the lid off the Genovese organization.

At the outset of the meeting, which took place on the prison premises, Cafaro was highly nervous and his hands were trembling. He had known one of the agents, so he felt somewhat comfortable. He was about to break the Mafia code of omertà, and he understood this at the outset. "Listen, you have to understand," he implored. "After we talk, if they reach out for me, I am a dead man."

The term *omertà* originated in southern Italy and denotes that all those who take the oath of allegiance with the Mafia must always remain silent about their membership and family business. At the induction ceremony into a family, the capo of the crew you will be part of holds a small saucer holding a holy picture, often of a saint. As a prospective member raises his right hand, he pledges he will abide by the code of omertà. The capo then burns the holy picture as he mutters those words. If a member violates that oath, he is marked for death. We told Cafaro, "We will protect you and your family; everyone will be placed in the witness protection program."

He nodded. "Okay, I trust you, let's talk."

Cafaro's primary function was to exert influence in the District Council of Carpenters, headed by Theodore Maritas, an associate of Vincent DiNapoli, a family member. The family had total control over the union membership, as one of the Genovese soldiers, Onofrio "Frankie Zip" Armone, was their union representative. Cafaro supplied us with detailed information regarding the hierarchy of the Genovese family and, in particular, their involvement in labor racketeering. We already knew many of these facts, but did not know the specifics that he was able to provide. We saw an opportunity here to request Cafaro to cooperate with us with the understanding that we would bring this to the court's attention and attempt to have him released on bail. His future term in prison would depend on the extent of his cooperation.

Cafaro agreed to this arrangement. We subsequently discussed this opportunity with the prosecutor's office, and they filed a sealed motion with the court to have Cafaro released on bail under our supervision. For the next five months, Cafaro wore a body recorder during all his meetings with the Genovese family members. A team of agents was always standing by in case any problems developed where they would have to intervene. He accumulated many recorded conversations that would be extremely important in future prosecutions of the family.

Just before cooperating with us, Cafaro had been indicted along with thirteen other Mafia and union representatives. Theodore Maritas, head of the Carpenters Union, was one of the individuals indicted. He was considered a high risk and there was concern within the family that he would cooperate. A hit order was sent down and Maritas suddenly disappeared. His body was never found. Cafaro commented during the briefing, "This is how it is done."

In a sworn declaration Cafaro submitted, he revealed specific details regarding the family's control over the Carpenters Union: "The Genovese family controlled the hiring of carpenters at the New York Coliseum and the Jacob Javits Center. Jobs at the Convention Center are very desirable because they involve easy work, overtime, and opportunities to make additional money through various rackets at the Convention Center. Many organized crime associates are given positions with the Carpenters Union at the Convention Center. Several families had influence at the Convention Center, but the Genovese family had primary authority over illegal activities and labor peace payoffs."

Agent Brian Taylor was one of the principal agents investigating the Genovese family's control over the Fulton Fish Market. He had a unique idea. Brian suggested we adopt another approach to neutralize the family's criminal enterprise. We would now go after their business interests both civilly and criminally. The market supplied seafood to companies that employed United Seafood Workers Local 359 members. The Genovese family controlled the union. Why not develop specific evidence to petition the court to file a lawsuit charging the Mafia with running the market? Taylor was very persuasive and said that it might just work. I consulted with Kossler and Richards and we all agreed: "Let's do it."

We were now running into a logistical problem, which I had anticipated. Many balls were in the air and I did not want to drop any, but I was running out of game changers. I spoke to Sheer and suggested we enlist the police department in this effort, as the fish market directly affected the city's economy. Tom called his counterpart in the police department and an agreement was reached that we would conduct a joint investigation. An inspector was assigned to work with Taylor and a team of detectives with experience in organized crime joined the Genovese squad.

The joint investigation was designated Operation Seaprobe. We had a habit of identifying major cases by code names, as they took on an air of added importance, and this particular case, due to its potential, certainly justified a special title. Brian Taylor was now directing a squad of twenty-four agents and detectives, and we had to set up a specific work area for them. Kallstrom and his team would support any unusual surveillance requests. We were ready to go.

The investigation developed the necessary evidence to allege in the suit that the Genovese family had controlled the Fulton

Fish Market and Local 359, which supplied the employees at the market for over fifty years. In the 1970s, Carmine Romano, a family member previously convicted of racketeering, ran the market. His brother, Vincent Romano, succeeded him, and he reported to Thomas "Crazy Tommy" Contaldo, who was a capo in the family. The suit alleged that the Genovese family had handpicked Anthony Cirillo as the president of Local 359, but Vincent Romano was the de facto head of the union.

The extortion scheme that the family had implemented earned them millions of illicit funds over the years. The market was the primary seafood supplier throughout the East Coast and included approximately 100 wholesalers who operated shops and warehouses at the South Street Seaport. The companies had a collective bargaining agreement with Local 359. Agents surveilled the activities of the market for themselves so they could understand how it functioned.

Between 3:00 a.m. and 8:00 a.m., there was total chaos, but uniform efficiency. Trucks continually arrived to unload seafood, which crew members from the union emptied. The cartons of fish were immediately taken to wholesaler stalls, where they were offered for sale. Speed was essential, as the products were perishable if there were undue delays. The union officials could force work stoppages or delays for contrived reasons. Thus, they could demand labor peace payoffs from wholesalers who would lose considerable funds if they did not sell their products on time. This scheme was similar to what we had run into during the UNIRAC investigation.

On October 16, 1987, *The New York Times* headline read MAFIA RUNS FULTON FISH MARKET. U.S. SAYS IN SUIT TO TAKE CONTROL. The headline was in response to federal prosecutors filing a civil RICO lawsuit seeking to seize control of the market, declaring the Mafia dominated it. It was the first time such a lawsuit had been filed in federal court.

The head of the New York office, Tom Sheer, stated in a follow-up press release that this was a major investigative effort and a "blueprint for the future and that the FBI hoped to return the economy to our society and leave the Mafia like a fish out of the water, flopping on the shore." Tom had a way with words. The *Times* article also cited comments made by Police Commissioner Benjamin Ward. He read an article published in *The New York Times* about efforts by law enforcement to clean up the market, published in 1934. "Now," he said, "we will try a new tactic," referencing previous unsuccessful efforts. This remark drew laughter from the reporters in attendance. The success of this current action represented another step forward.

The FBI's probe of the Genovese family also focused on Anthony "Tony Pro" Provenzano, a powerful capo and a high-ranking official in the International Brotherhood of Teamsters. He was president of Local 560 in Union City, New Jersey, thus giving the family control over the union and all the trucking companies where members worked as drivers. The government had a longstanding interest in Provenzano, going back to when he was subpoenaed before the Senate Racketeering Committee by counsel Robert F. Kennedy. He took the Fifth Amendment forty-four times. His brother Sal Provenzano was appointed trustee of the local, and his other brother Nunzio was appointed a business agent. They appeared to be taking this "family thing" a little too seriously.

In the late seventies, Provenzano was convicted of extortion and sent to a federal prison in Lewisburg, Pennsylvania, where he reunited with former Teamsters boss Jimmy Hoffa. He also had been convicted of extorting funds from the union. Provenzano and Hoffa had been close friends and had previously formed a working relationship in controlling union activities on the East Coast. However, hard feelings had developed between them in prison, which continued when both men were released. The FBI had investigated alleged corruption in the union for decades and numerous prosecutions materialized; however, the top leaders, except Hoffa, always seemed to avoid arrest.

Upon his release from prison, Hoffa had hoped to regain his

position as president of the Teamsters. He began encountering resistance from within the union and the Mafia bosses who had direct oversight of the union. Hoffa publicly spoke about being blackballed and mistreated by those he had previously supported. The Mafia families controlling the Teamsters became concerned that Hoffa might turn against them. He reached out to Provenzano for his support.

On July 30, 1975, the FBI's investigation determined that Hoffa was to meet with Provenzano and Anthony Giacalone, the boss of the Detroit Mafia family, at the Machus Red Fox Restaurant. Hoffa's family said the meeting was to occur around 2:00 p.m.; however, he never returned home and they reported that he was missing. At first, they feared he had been kidnapped. His son, James Hoffa, notified the Detroit office of the FBI that he had received an extortion demand by telephone in return for information about his father. As a result of this information, the FBI opened a new case entitled "Hoffex."

Our investigation determined that Provenzano never showed up for the meeting and had an alibi establishing that he was in Union City, New Jersey. Intelligence revealed that Provenzano associates Gabriel Briguglio and Thomas Andretta were observed in the restaurant area that afternoon. When FBI agents caught up with Provenzano, he was belligerent and hostile to their questioning. He only responded, "I was playing cards with Stephen Andretta." Stephen, Thomas's brother, refused to be interviewed to corroborate Provenzano's alibi.

To this day, the FBI and other law enforcement agencies have not been able to solve the mystery of Jimmy Hoffa's disappearance. It was our theory that Hoffa was abducted and murdered on orders from the Commission. For the Mafia to kill such a high-profile union leader as Hoffa, it had to be approved at the highest level. Based on our intelligence, there was a serious concern that if Hoffa did not regain control of the Teamsters, he would become a cooperative government witness. This seemed the most logical answer to this continuing mystery.

Due to my involvement with Frank Sheeran, journalists have periodically contacted me over the years, seeking my opinion. Sheeran and Bufalino's names have been bandied about as setting up the hit on Hoffa due to their close relationship. I never supported that theory and always assumed Giacalone and Provenzano were solely responsible. However, based on my most recent research, I could offer a plausible possibility that both Sheeran and Bufalino were directly involved.

Sheeran and Bufalino were very close to Hoffa, as he constantly visited Philadelphia, given the significant presence of Teamsters in that area. He knew Sheeran had more influence than any other Teamsters official as president of Local 326 and his connections with the largest Teamsters locals in Philadelphia. He needed Sheeran's support in the past, and it would stand to reason that he may have been recently in contact with Sheeran to help him regain control of the union. Bufalino reported to Provenzano, the most powerful Mafia figure in the Teamsters. The FBI had identified him as a prime suspect in the Hoffa disappearance. If Provenzano had ordered Bufalino to participate in setting up Hoffa, he would have had to do so or else be killed. Bufalino logically would have reached out to Sheeran to gain his support, and although Sheeran was close to Hoffa, he was part of Bufalino's crew and could not have refused to participate.

When Hoffa vanished from the Machus Red Fox Restaurant parking lot, we wondered whose car he had gotten into and who the occupants were. It is doubtful he would have entered a vehicle occupied solely by Provenzano or a member of his crew. However, if Frank Sheeran had been in the back seat, Hoffa would have gotten in that car, as he implicitly trusted Sheeran. This is just a what-if scenario. We will probably never know what happened to Jimmy Hoffa that day, but I do not believe you can rule out the above possibility.

Although the Hoffa case was not solved, the FBI looked upon this as a bold criminal act that personified the vast control the Mafia had over the legitimate union movement throughout the country. It fostered a new emphasis on labor racketeering as a national priority that must be investigated vigorously. Along with the UNIRAC investigation, it demonstrated what a stranglehold the Mafia had achieved over many years over the legitimate function of significant labor unions. Provenzano was subsequently convicted in another RICO indictment and sentenced to serve twenty years. In 1988, he died of a heart attack at California's Lompoc Federal Penitentiary at the age of seventy-one. Both of the Andretta brothers were eventually convicted of other federal violations and sent to federal prison. No one has been arrested for the murder of Jimmy Hoffa.

On February 25, 1985, Anthony "Fat Tony" Salerno and the other four bosses were indicted and a warrant was issued for his arrest. Agents continued to watch Salerno, who spent most of his time at the social club. After the apparent leak of the indictments surfaced, we had to assemble a team to raid the club. Based on information from Kallstrom's group, we knew a reinforced door was locked. Agents approached the entry door and yelled, "FBI, we have a warrant!" The lookout, who always watched for strangers approaching the building, opened the door immediately. Salerno was sitting alone in the back next to a table with a telephone nearby, casually smoking his cigar. He was arrested for violating the RICO statute and advised of his Miranda rights. He was immediately confined in handcuffs. When the agent asked if they were too tight, he replied, "Fuck you." His belligerent attitude continued as he was transported to the federal lockup. While being transported, he complained of chest pains and, after being checked by medical personnel, was placed in a cell to await a bail hearing.

Simultaneously with the Salerno investigation, we had been focusing on one of his top moneymakers, "Matty the Horse" Ianniello. He was one of the highest-ranking capos in the family and controlled over fifty topless bars and pornography shops that were prevalent in Times Square during that period. His scheme was simple: The operators of the bars and shops had to pay him protection money to continue to operate. He eventually acquired ownership in several bars and restaurants and had an office above Umberto's Clam House on Mulberry Street in Lower Manhattan. We suspected he was financially invested in this restaurant since his associates constantly met there.

Continuous surveillance of Ianniello's meetings with known Mob associates and informant information furnished to our agents led to obtaining court authorization for electronic surveillance. The recordings directly resulted in his indictment for the extortion scheme, ending in a conviction and significant jail sentence. Ianniello was sentenced to serve twenty years in a federal prison. Many bars and shops he controlled eventually closed after a new official was appointed superintendent of the police department, and existing laws were aggressively enforced. Within a relatively short period, Times Square returned to the entertainment center it was meant to be, and the Genovese influence was over. The top leaders of the family had been indicted and the remaining members were on the defensive, waiting for the FBI to kick the door down. They now would always be looking over their shoulder. We were unsuccessful, however, in pinning down the elusive "Chin" Gigante.

After the Genovese investigation success, I felt a little worn out. The constant give-and-take of all these investigations was starting to wear on me. I talked to Sue about it. She had sensed the same thing and encouraged me to take some time off.

I came into work one Monday and was not feeling myself. I felt lightheaded and a little weak. My secretary Loretta remarked, "Frank, you look pale," and suggested I visit our in-house nurse, Barbara Gormely. I stopped by Barbara's office, and after a brief visit, she called a doctor uptown and made an appointment to see him immediately. As I weaved my way through traffic, I was having a hard time focusing. After a thorough exam, the doctor suspected that I had a bleeding ulcer and contacted Saint Peter's Hospital near my home in New Jersey and told them I was on my way. I called Sheer and told him what was going on and that I needed an agent to drive me to the hospital. I asked Tom to call Sue and let her know. Agent Dennis Maduro soon arrived to pick me up and we were at the hospital within an hour.

Tests confirmed that I had a bleeding ulcer and my blood count was below standard. The doctor said, "You are not leaving until procedures can be done to stop the bleeding and your blood count is normal." This was not good news. My son Trip was scheduled to graduate from high school that Friday night, and I had to attend.

Kossler visited me the next day, which was good. Jim had always been by my side since I arrived in New York. Sue was there every day and I could feel her concern. By Thursday, my condition had improved and I was released from the hospital Friday morning. I made it to Trip's graduation.

This episode taught me a lesson. While I had an important job, I had to focus on taking the time to smell the roses and ensure that I stayed healthy. I had a family to take care of. On Monday, I returned to work with a new attitude, and the bounce had returned to my step.

CHAPTER 14
Vincent "Chin" Gigante

In our initial debriefing, Vincent "the Fish" Cafaro stated that the true boss of the Genovese family was Vincent "Chin" Gigante, not Anthony Salerno. Everyone assumed Salerno was the actual boss until Cafaro confirmed it was Gigante. He had created a ruse to fool the government and divert attention away from himself. Gigante became a recluse and hid behind the walls of his home in Greenwich Village. In public, he would appear wearing a bathrobe and pajamas and talk to himself as if he had hallucinations. We had suspected this was a ruse for some time. Still, we were not sure of Gigante's mental health. Our files contained many details about Gigante's life. He began his crime career as an enforcer for the Luciano family and before that, he was a professional boxer.

A New York grand jury indicted Luciano for operating a large-scale prostitution ring, a successful prosecution by District Attorney Thomas E. Dewey. After Lucky's conviction, he was deported to Sicily, and Frank Costello succeeded him as boss. Vito Genovese was named underboss and Gigante was a soldier at this time. Genovese and Gigante were very close, having served in prison together for drug trafficking. Upon his release from prison, Genovese and Costello did not get along, and there was constant friction in their relationship. Genovese was ambitious, became frustrated, and decided to make a move and ordered Gigante to kill Costello. This was not going to be easy. Costello was cautious and always had bodyguards accompany him to meetings. He lived on the Upper East Side in an upscale apartment complex and routinely had dinner alone at a nearby Italian restaurant within walking distance.

Gigante decided that he alone would carry out this hit to prevent any leaks within the family. On May 2, 1957, he went to Costello's neighborhood and stood in the shadows adjacent to the entrance to the apartment building. As Costello exited the building, Gigante fired several times and wounded Costello, but he survived. Follow-up investigation by the local police did not result in Gigante being charged. Costello got the message that it was time to move on and stepped down as boss of the family. He was even thanked by Gigante for not ratting him out in court.

Genovese succeeded Costello and took over as boss. The family was now referred to as the Genovese family. Gigante's status in the family grew under the leadership of Genovese and he was appointed a capo with his own crew. He became a prominent moneymaker for the family. With the help of Anthony Salerno, he developed a vast network of illegal gambling and companion loan-sharking operations. He began focusing on influencing several labor unions and legitimate businesses. Genovese eventually ended up in prison after a drug conviction in 1959 and died ten years later, and Philip "Benny Squint" Lombardo became boss, but had to relinquish the title when he became ill in 1981. The Commission then apparently appointed Gigante boss, and Salerno became the underboss. It was at this point when Gigante became a recluse and assumed the role of a demented old man who had mental difficulties.

The FBI assumed Salerno was the boss and Gigante was almost invincible. Agents continued to surveil Gigante's apartment periodically; he seldom had visitors, however. At times, he would stroll through the neighborhood in his robe and pajamas with an old hat on his head. Cafaro had told us this was all an act to give law enforcement and the press the impression that he was mentally impaired and no longer an active member of the Mafia. We eventually determined that nothing could be further from the truth.

We had a key informant begin to focus on Gigante's current movements. He reportedly still attended Commission meetings as long as they were held at discreet locations. If he left his apartment, he would have one of his soldiers stand guard, as he was concerned that the FBI would enter while he was gone and install a listening device. Cafaro told us that Gigante's ruse started many years ago, and key family members were aware of Gigante's motives. The investigation of Gigante became more focused on his role, as it now appeared he was the actual boss of the family. After several months, the investigation did not progress. Gigante was unlike any boss we had encountered. He was so elusive and cautious that we could not make any headway. Supervisor John Pritchard took a fresh look at the case. This was John's first supervisory assignment, but he had successfully investigated several cases. He assigned the investigation to Agent Richard Rudolph, whose goal was to finally break through this impenetrable wall of deceit that Gigante had created.

Lew Schiliro was directing his squad in a critical drug investigation. They were focusing on a lower-level drug trafficker, Barclay Farenga, a member of the Genovese family who was involved with a significant drug trafficking network that was their real target. They hoped to flip Farenga. They had an undercover agent make a drug buy from him and shortly thereafter, he was arrested. Facing a lengthy jail sentence if convicted, he agreed to cooperate. Farenga began offering information regarding an ongoing scam involving both families. He did not have specific details, but was aware it was related to the New York Housing Authority and the rigging of bids for millions of dollars. Farenga also supplied Schiliro with information regarding two hits he participated in with Genovese soldiers Gerard Pappa and Peter Savino. They had killed Richard Scarcella and Thomas

"Shorty" Spero, a capo in the Colombo family, but it was not clear who ordered the hits. He assumed the Commission approved the killings, as Spero was a capo. Farenga also mentioned that Savino was directly involved in the scam involving the housing authority.

Schiliro, realizing this information might be valuable, picked up the phone and told Rudolph, "We have a breakthrough on the Genovese family. Peter Savino is running a scam involving the New York Housing Authority." Rudolph had already been aware that there was talk about some profitable scheme underway with the housing authority, but had no specific information. He needed to develop information regarding Savino, how he fit into the scam, and whether he was now vulnerable to cooperating. His implication in two Mafia hits might have been the incentive Savino would need to cooperate.

Farenga's information was sketchy, but he mentioned that Savino had a window manufacturing business and devised a plan to rig bids for installing windows in housing projects. Searching available business records, Rudolph determined that Savino owned two companies that manufactured and distributed windows. The windows had to be installed by members of Local 580 of the Iron Workers Union, which the Genovese and Lucchese families controlled.

We had been down this road before with the Concrete Club scam, the Fulton Fish Market, the Teamsters, and the garment district. Now we were talking windows. What did the Mafia not control? I told Kossler, "If we continued with all our investigations, we may shut down the economy of New York."

He laughed and said, "We will save the economy of New York." Looking back on it now, Jimmy was right on.

Rudolph thought the best approach was to go right after Savino. With the information that Farenga had supplied, agents were able to locate and dig up the bodies of Scarcella and Spero in a warehouse owned by Savino. They had been buried beneath a concrete slab. Rudolph discussed his plan with the strike force attorneys in the Eastern District. He would offer Savino a deal: If he agreed to cooperate, the government would consider entering him into the witness protection program. Rudolph and Strike Force Attorney Charlie Rose then secretly met with Savino in a remote location and offered him their terms. Not only did they want him to agree to testify in court, but he would have to wear a body transmitter during all future conversations with everyone involved in the "windows case." He agreed and from that point on, Savino was under Rudolph's control.

Rudolph and an agent from the Genovese squad debriefed Savino for three days. Savino described in detail the windows scam. His company was one of several involved. All the families participated, but he reported directly to the boss of the Genovese family, "Chin" Gigante. Several of the families controlled companies that manufactured windows. Thus, they could rig the bids for installation contracts by charging inflated prices. If a company not owned by the Mafia submitted a bid, they would have to pay a penalty tax for each window they installed. Four families would share in all the profits. The housing authority typically would replace thousands of windows yearly, so the profits were quite lucrative. The workers who installed the windows were all members of Local 560, a union the Mafia controlled.

After they killed Spero, the capo in the Colombo family, a contract was issued on Pappa, and he was murdered. Savino thought he was next as he had participated in the Spero hit. He was summoned to meet with "Chin" Gigante and representatives of other families. Gigante assured him he was not in trouble. Gigante did confirm that they killed Pappa in retaliation for the murder of Spero, which was not sanctioned. He did not seem aware of Savino's involvement. Pappa had a direct role as a middleman with Gigante and the other bosses, funneling money to them from the windows scam, and they now wanted Savino to fill that role. Savino would report to Venero "Benny Eggs" Mangano regarding all decisions relating to the windows scam. Mangano, who attended the meeting, told him, "You now belong to the Genovese family." Spero concluded this opening phase of the debriefing by acknowledging that the meeting with Gigante began his involvement in this conspiracy.

Rudolph handled Savino for over a year and on numerous occasions, he wore a wire that recorded critical conversations with Mangano and Gigante regarding the windows scam. There was speculation that Mangano no longer trusted Savino, and Rudolph became concerned that they may be on to him, so he ended Savino's role. One night, agents showed up at his home and he and his family immediately entered the federal witness protection program. The next time Gigante and Mangano saw Savino, he appeared as a witness at their trial in federal court.

After a prolonged investigation by Pritchard's squad, Gigante and fourteen coconspirators were indicted for violations of the RICO statute. The indictment alleged that they had skimmed millions of dollars from contracts awarded to the New York City Housing Authority. A team led by Agent Rudolph arrested Gigante in his pajamas and bathrobe. That morning, agents also arrested a cross-representation of significant leaders of the other families, including Genovese underboss Venero "Benny Eggs" Mangano, capo Dominick "Baldy Dom" Canterino, Lucchese capo Peter "Fat Pete" Chiodo, and John Gotti's brother, Gambino capo Peter "One Eye" Gotti. Two additional subjects, Vittorio "Little Vic" Amuso and Anthony "Gaspipe" Casso of the Lucchese family, had also been indicted, but their whereabouts were unknown at the time of the indictments. At his arraignment, Gigante's attorneys argued that he was mentally incompetent and that the charges should be dismissed. The court ordered a competency hearing.

At this point, the FBI had three cooperative Mafia witnesses to offer to the court who could testify to Gigante's mental state: Sammy "the Bull" Gravano, Alfonso "Little Al" D'Arco, and Vincent "the Fish" Cafaro. They all testified that they had attended meetings when Gigante was present and they did not detect that he had any mental difficulties. After many delays, the court finally ordered that Gigante was competent enough and that the trial should proceed. Gigante and his coconspirators were convicted and received lengthy prison sentences. While in prison, he attempted to run the family through intermediaries, but was unsuccessful, before finally passing away in 2005. This was the final nail in the coffin for the leadership of the Genovese family. The family would never again rise to the level of power and corrupt influence it once exerted over the citizens of New York.

CHAPTER 15
The Bonanno Family

The FBI's history, compiled over the years from various sources regarding the five Mafia families, was quite revealing from an intelligence standpoint. It showed each family's inherent difficulties in operating an ongoing criminal enterprise and the ever-increasing tensions that developed within the family structure. One could surmise that, at times, the leaders felt more threatened from within their ranks than by the leaders of rival families. They were not overly concerned about investigations by the FBI or local police and ran their operations almost with impunity.

Joseph Bonanno, also known as "Joe Bananas," was appointed boss of the Maranzano family in 1931 when he was only twenty-six, the youngest of the five bosses at the end of the Castellammarese War and the emergence of the Five Families. Under his leadership, the family thrived over the next thirty years and became proficient engaging in illegal activities. Bonanno considered himself above all the other Mob bosses, probably due to his long tenure. The family focused on traditional organized crime activities, but he allowed members to engage in drug trafficking. Bonanno was a traditionalist and ruled the family much as they were governed in Sicily. He made it a point to develop close working relationships with the other families in New York and other East Coast cities. His son, Joseph, married the daughter of

Colombo boss, Joseph Profaci, which led to the Profaci-Bonanno alliance. Over the years, this alliance strengthened his position and influence.

After the Commission discovered that Bonanno was involved in a conspiracy to kill Carlo Gambino and Tommy Lucchese, they summoned Bonanno to a meeting. Fearing for his life, he fled to Arizona. He was formally expelled as boss of the Bonanno family after several years of war, in which his son Salvatore "Bill" Bonanno fought on his behalf. It was a lost cause.

Upon the departure of their long-standing leader, the Bonanno family fell into total confusion and disarray. One boss succeeded another. One murder followed another. After the death of the most recent boss, Natale "Joe Diamonds" Evola in 1973, the Commission appointed Philip "Rusty" Rastelli the following year. Rastelli and the existing family hierarchy were now the focus of Supervisor Lew Schiliro. The squad had a good mix of very experienced agents and some relative newcomers. They had successfully developed quality informants—it was just a matter of pointing them in the right direction. The objective was to take down the entire Bonanno enterprise, which no law enforcement agency had ever done.

Without informants and cooperative witnesses, there was no way an investigation of a Mafia family would succeed. There are two levels of informants. First, there were those who are more or less on the street, in and out of gambling locations and places where the members meet. They furnish information and, in return, receive payment for their services. They are not directly involved in criminal activity, but are on the outside looking in. Then there are highly placed informants who are members of a particular family, such as Sammy "the Bull" Gravano and Vincent "the Fish" Cafaro, who are extremely difficult to develop. Their only incentive to cooperate is to avoid a long-term prison sentence. These types of informants are rare. In the case of the Bonanno family, we had both types.

Rastelli had a long history with the Bonanno family. It seemed, however, that he had a hard time staying out of prison, having been convicted of one criminal offense after another. Carmine "the Cigar" Galante, a former family consigliere, began planning a coup on Rastelli to seize control of the family and assume the title of acting boss. At the time, Galante was in prison. The information available to us indicated he would utilize the support of the Sicilian faction to make this happen. Upon his release, Galante was ready to make his move. Rastelli's role as boss was temporarily interrupted and he was again sent back to prison for a parole violation. In his absence, Galante designated himself as acting boss without first getting authority from the Commission.

Our files contained considerable intelligence on Galante. He was nicknamed "Lilo," a Sicilian name for cigars. Whenever he was seen in public, he usually smoked a cigar. Galante had the reputation of quickly resorting to violence if he could not settle a dispute. He had been a suspect in numerous Mob hits over the years, but had never been convicted. Rastelli, of course, recognized that Galante could order his death at any time to seize control of the family, so he had to act. Galante also had a history of drug trafficking, which the Commission had forbidden. The bosses were concerned over Galante's aggressive attitude and also his recent attempts to take over the Sicilian faction of the family that operated a heroin importation network. Rastelli appealed to the Commission that Galante had to go. The Commission approved this request and gave the contract to the Gambino family's underboss, Aniello Dellacroce.

On July 12, 1979, Galante decided to hold a meeting with one of his closest supporters, Leonardo Coppola, a capo in the family. He likely intended to elicit Coppola's support in dethroning Rastelli one way or another. Galante met Coppola in the garden patio area of the Joe and Mary Italian Restaurant on Knickerbocker Avenue in Brooklyn, one of Galante's favorites. His cousin Giuseppe Turano, a Bonanno soldier, owned the restaurant. Baldassare "Baldo" Amato and Cesare Bonventre served as Galante's bodyguards and accompanied him. They were both members of the Sicilian Mafia faction. Galante chose to have lunch in the outdoor garden patio, which would afford them more privacy. Three masked gunmen entered the restaurant just as they were finishing their meal. Galante and Coppola were suddenly hit by a fuselage of bullets that nearly decapitated Coppola. The blasts were so forceful that Galante died with his cigar still in his mouth, clenched between his teeth. Turano was also killed, but Amato and Bonventre were not even wounded. Rastelli's problem was solved; he could now run the family unimpeded.

Witnesses to the shooting could not provide any information, yet a customer had overheard the manager of the restaurant addressing one of the shooters with the comment, "They are in the back, Sally." We were aware this was one of the nicknames for Salvatore Catalano, who was the head of the Sicilian Mafia group operating the international heroin distribution network. This was the same group that Galante wanted to take over. The reason for the hit was now making sense. The Commission had already made its peace with Catalano and allowed him to operate as long as it did not involve any members of their families, and he agreed to share the profits. Based on our informant's information, we concluded that Galante was hit for making a real push to dethrone Rastelli, and he also wanted to take over the Sicilian heroin importation network of Catalano. Witnesses outside the restaurant observed the shooters fleeing from the scene, driving a blue Mercury Montego. A short time after the shooting, the vehicle was located, and a forensic examination discovered a palm print on the rear door handle. It was only a partial print and could not be matched to any prints on file.

One of the questions the agents had related to Bonventre and Amato. If they were Galante's bodyguards, why didn't they act when the killers entered the patio area with guns drawn? Were they in on the planning of the hit? We didn't know much about either individual, but through highly placed informants, we were able to develop a limited profile of each suspect. Bonventre was a native-born Sicilian, a member of the Mafia, and had arrived in

New York with a reputation as a hit man and drug trafficker. Galante had sponsored him and he became the underboss of the Sicilian faction. He was a cousin of Amato, who also became a member of the Sicilian Mafia after he arrived in New York. Rastelli had to convince Bonventre and Amato to help set up Galante, or they would be in jeopardy.

Within an hour or so after the Galante shooting, agents were conducting routine surveillance of the Ravenite Social Club. Anthony "Bruno" Indelicato, a soldier in the Bonanno family and the son of Alphonse "Sonny Red" Indelicato, a capo in the same family, was observed exiting his car and walking to the club's front entrance. Dellacroce and Salvatore Catalano greeted Indelicato outside the club and shook his hand. Dellacroce kissed him on the cheek, customarily given as a form of congratulations or gratitude in Mob circles. Their body movements and reactions further suggested they were congratulating him. They talked for several minutes and Indelicato left. The meeting was photographed, but the agents did not grasp its significance. Later on, however, the meeting would strike a chord with the case agents of the Commission investigation.

Pat Marshall and Charlotte Lang, co–case agents assigned to oversee the Commission case, had begun to compile the evidence collected by each squad that hopefully would become the predicate for indicting the five Mafia bosses. They began reviewing the facts of the Galante hit years after it occurred and discovered that the issue of the palm print had never been resolved. There had been recent speculation from a highly placed informant that Indelicato was one of the three shooters, and they also had access to the results of the surveillance of Indelicato outside the Ravenite. Marshall and Lang served a subpoena on Indelicato, ordering him to report to our office and submit his fingerprints and palm prints. After obtaining his prints, they were sent to the FBI forensic laboratory in Washington, along with the palm print lifted from the Montego. The prints matched—they had just identified one of Galante's shooters. After learning of the results, Marshall and Lang rushed into my office and loudly announced, "Boss, we have a match. We know who killed Galante." Quite a bit of detective work on their part.

The prosecutive team was ecstatic at this news. They had been searching for evidence to tie in the Commission to the actual authorization of a criminal act by an individual family member. Informant information was one thing, but they needed evidence to present in court. The meeting Indelicato had outside of the Ravenite Club immediately after the shooting was critical in establishing this connection. It now could be presented to a jury that Indelicato was reporting to the underboss of the Gambino family, Neil Dellacroce, and Catalano, a high-ranking member of the Bonanno family's Sicilian faction, that the contract on Galante was successfully carried out. The Commission had ordered the hit on Galante, and the meeting outside the Ravenite established that Gambino and Bonanno family members were conspiring to kill Galante at the behest of Bonanno family boss Philip Rastelli.

Rastelli, however, faced a new immediate threat. While he was in prison, Joseph "the Ear" Massino and Dominick "Sonny Black" Napolitano, two prominent capos, maintained control of the family and were loyal to Rastelli. Another faction headed by Alphonse "Sonny Red" Indelicato, Dominick "Big Trin" Trinchera, and Philip "Philly Lucky" Giaccone conspired to kill them and take over the family in Rastelli's absence. Massino, the underboss, knew they had to strike first, and he had the blessing of Rastelli. Massino contacted Indelicato to set up a meeting to settle the dispute. Indelicato accepted and planned to take this opportunity to kill Massino and Napolitano. Massino must have suspected this might occur, so he and "Sonny Black" developed their own plan.

At this point, we were getting firsthand information on these fast-breaking developments from FBI Agent Joseph Pistone, who, years earlier, had penetrated the Napolitano crew by working in an undercover capacity. He had assumed the name of Donnie Brasco. He was now a trusted associate, being considered for induction into the family. His first contact in the family was with

Anthony Mirra, a soldier on the crew who took a liking to Pistone. He soon met Benjamin "Lefty" Ruggiero, a moneymaker for the family and a hit man. Pistone started working with "Lefty," gaining credibility, and Ruggiero eventually became his mentor and sponsor. He told Pistone about their troubles with Indelicato and that Rastelli and Massino had to do something.

Massino set up the meeting at the 20/20 Club in Brooklyn in the basement storage room with Indelicato and his top associates Trinchera and Giaccone. Before the start of the meeting, Massino had learned from his sources that they would be armed with automatic weapons. Ordinarily, when a sit-down meeting was called for within a family, those designated to attend would not carry a gun. Massino did not trust Indelicato and believed that he and his associates were planning to kill him and his team. He did not intend to allow that to happen. Massino had his team of four killers hidden in storage room closets, waiting for Indelicato and his associates to arrive. As they arrived for the meeting in the basement, Massino's men bolted from the closets and gunned down Indelicato, Trinchera, and Giaccone. The three bodies were taken from the club and buried in a vacant lot in Queens. FBI agents dug up the bodies years later after Massino confessed to the murders and testified to the events that took place in what is now known as the "three capos murder." Rastelli had now eliminated the last immediate threat to his position as boss.

Jules Bonavolonta, Deputy Chief of the Organized Crime Section at headquarters, monitored Pistone during his undercover assignment and frequently contacted him. Bonavolonta knew all the players in the family, having served in New York as a brick agent and later a coordinating supervisor. As Pistone had been able to penetrate the Napolitano crew so profoundly, they were considering making him a member. He would have to kill someone at their direction to qualify for membership. Pistone also had to be concerned about his vulnerability, as he was very close to key members of the crew, and he could be the target of a retribution attempt on his life in the aftermath of the murder of Indelicato and his associates.

Bonavolonta decided to end Pistone's undercover role. Jules called Joe and said, "It's time to go home." He had been working undercover for an incredible length of time away from his family, and to say he had done an outstanding job is not giving him enough credit. What he accomplished had never been done before in the history of the FBI. He would prove to be a valuable witness for the government in future court proceedings. Family members quickly became aware that Donnie Brasco was, in fact, FBI Agent Joseph Pistone and were in total denial. They could not believe that Pistone was an undercover FBI agent.

Rastelli had no more threats to deal with and remained the family boss. Massino continued as the underboss and members considered him, in a way, the street boss while Rastelli was in prison and not readily available to settle serious family issues. In 1985, Rastelli was indicted and convicted in the Commission investigation and received a lengthy prison sentence. Massino replaced him as the boss, which the Commission approved. The repercussions by the Commission after learning of Pistone's penetration of the Bonanno family came very swiftly. They ordered Massino to seek out those who allowed Pistone to breach the family and eliminate them.

Through available informant information and contacts with Pistone, the agents learned that contracts were out for Anthony Mirra, Benjamin "Lefty" Ruggiero, and Dominick "Sonny Black" Napolitano. Agent Doug Fencl was one of the agents who periodically debriefed Pistone when it could be safely arranged. He decided to visit Napolitano, as he had previously had cordial contact with him.

"Sonny Black" still did not believe that Pistone was an FBI agent working undercover and thought this was all a ruse that the FBI put out there to use as intimidation and flip Pistone's associates. Fencl reassured him that was not the case and showed him a photo that agents had taken of Pistone, Ruggiero, and other members when they were in Florida together. Napolitano stared at the photo and shook his head in disbelief. Fencl told Napolitano the FBI had reason to believe that he and others were in jeopardy as a result of Pistone penetrating the family. Through his long experiences with the Mafia, Napolitano had already surmised that would be the case, as Pistone had been a part of his crew. Fencl offered him the sanctuary of the witness protection program if he cooperated. He refused, accepted his possible fate, and decided to deal with it. Fencl hoped to save Napolitano's life and also obtain his cooperation. His effort, unfortunately, failed.

Anthony Mirra became the first target, since he had unknowingly brought Pistone into the family. When he first met Pistone, he was hanging around at one of their bars in Brooklyn, and Mirra approached him as he was a stranger and not one of them. Pistone impressed him and said he had dealt with stolen jewelry and was from Florida. Mirra then introduced Pistone to "Lefty" Ruggiero, who became Pistone's close friend and mentor. Mirra was elusive and assuming he would be a target, fled the area, so we had no chance to approach him. Massino thought Mirra might respond to a member of his family and gave the contract to Mirra's cousin, Joseph "Joey Mook" D'Amico.

D'Amico had been a member for several years, had a close relationship with Mirra, and had always admired him, but he now had to carry out an order he did not want. He contacted Mirra and offered to help him relocate until things settled down with the Pistone uproar. Mirra, needing some help, agreed to meet in a parking garage in Manhattan. D'Amico got into Mirra's car and suggested they move to another location. As Mirra drove out of the garage, D'Amico shot him in the side of the head two times. Mirra was gone. Our informants identified D'Amico as a possible suspect in Mirra's death, and he was subpoenaed before a grand jury. He was later indicted for perjury, and rather than risk a lengthy prison sentence, he became a cooperative witness and later testified to his complicity in the murder of Mirra. He also implicated Massino as being responsible for ordering the hit.

Benjamin "Lefty" Ruggiero, a close friend and sponsor of Pistone, was also targeted. By coincidence, agents arrested him for racketeering around this time, and he avoided Massino's hired guns. Pistone eventually had to testify against him at his trial, and "Lefty" still did not believe he had penetrated the crew as an undercover agent. He continued to imagine that Pistone was Donnie Brasco. After being convicted and sentenced to serve fifteen years, we can assume the truth must have finally settled in. At sentencing, he told the judge, "But he was my friend." This was the first time the FBI was successful in inserting an undercover agent into a Mafia crew. Pistone risked his life every day in his role, and although we covered him the best we could, there were many times he had to place himself in dangerous situations.

Dominick "Sonny Black" Napolitano, the capo of the crew, was kidnapped off the street, tortured, and murdered. FBI agents dug up his body in Staten Island and it was unrecognizable. Medical records confirmed it was his body. His hands had been severed. This was a message that Massino wanted to send, but the meaning of such a horrendous act was unclear to the agents.

The killings of Mirra and Napolitano were unexpected. Usually, if a member becomes an informant or a cooperative witness, the Commission will order their execution. That was not the case with Mirra and Napolitano. They would have been indicted in due time, just like their fellow members eventually were, so their murders did not make sense in our minds. But nothing made sense when you think about this whole Mafia thing.

Massino was now in complete control of the family and the sole focus of the Bonanno squad. After a lengthy investigation, Massino, his underboss Salvatore Vitale, and capos Frank Lino and Dan Mongelli were soon indicted. They were charged in an extensive RICO indictment with numerous federal violations, which included the murder of Dominick Napolitano. Vitale decided to cooperate rather than risk the death penalty. He admitted to eleven murders committed at the direction of Massino. When Lino found out that Vitale had flipped, the agents went to Lino and told Frankie that it "was come-to-Jesus time." Lino read the tea leaves correctly and he too agreed to cooperate and testify. Suddenly, Massino's family was turning on him and the walls were closing in. Massino was indicted and charged for the murders he had ordered, as well as additional RICO violations. Massino was now facing the death penalty.

After the jury had announced the verdict and Massino was being led from the courtroom, an agent noticed him talking to a US Marshal. The Marshal turned to the agent and motioned him to join the conversation. Massino was requesting a meeting with the presiding trial judge. A request such as this had never occurred. The judge was contacted and agreed to briefly meet with Massino as long as his attorney was present. The meeting quickly took place and Massino decided to cooperate with the government in return for being spared the death penalty. Department of Justice officials were contacted and agreed to consider this offer after evaluating a thorough debriefing of Massino.

Massino's interview occurred and the agents uncovered the answers to many unanswered questions. He also agreed to wear a recording device during future meetings with family members and associates. This was the first time the boss of a Mafia family had agreed to cooperate. He confessed to ordering the murders of Indelicato, Trinchera, and Giaccone and revealed their burial sites. We had already located Indelicato's body, but not those of his associates. He also admitted to ordering the hit on Gerlando Sciascia, who was one of the hit men in the Indelicato murder. He was concerned that Sciascia, who was a suspect, would flip and implicate him in the murder. Massino worked with the agents for a considerable period, and his cooperation led to additional family indictments. After receiving a reduction in sentence, he was released into the witness protection program, and he died a free man in 2023.

After Massino's reign, it was getting to the point that whoever stepped up to take over as boss of the family would immediately be the subject of an intensive RICO investigation and face possible indictment and ultimate conviction. One by one, they came and went, from Basciano to Vincent "Vinny TV" Badalamenti and Michael "the Nose" Mancuso. As with the other four families, the Bonanno family would no longer have the power they once held. The Commission had not anticipated the possibility of so many members cooperating with the FBI. One of their own Commission members, Massino, had betrayed them. They now had to be highly cautious moving forward, which played to our advantage. The silence of omertà was gone and they all knew it.

Since I arrived, the agents and supervisors had accomplished a great deal. I was very proud of them. However, I knew that more issues still needed to be addressed. After my battle with the ulcer and the grind of the job these last three years, I started to doubt myself somewhat and questioned whether I could continue to lead the effort we had undertaken.

All the murders we investigated and the unending depravity of the Mafia for the first time were starting to get to me. I talked with Damon Taylor, the supervisor of the Colombo squad, about my state of mind. We had developed a close relationship and I trusted his confidence. Damon understood my feelings and commented, "Boss, I have often felt the same way. Many of us have had the same feelings from time to time. You are not alone." We talked for several minutes, and it was a good back-and-forth.

I got up to leave and told Damon, "Thanks, it's time to get back to work."

CHAPTER 16
The Pizza Connection

Jim Kossler had mentioned that agents Charles Rooney and Carmine Russo were working on a case in Brooklyn involving several individuals who may have had ties to the Sicilian faction of the Bonanno family. "I am unsure of what they have, but it sounds interesting." The information they had developed was limited. Surveillance indicated that Giuseppe Ganci had been observed on several occasions meeting with Salvatore Catalano, who allegedly was a Sicilian Mafia member who might have been involved in drug trafficking. Catalano was also a suspect in the hit involving Carmine Galante. Another agent, Bob Paquette, was working a money laundering case out of New Rochelle, and one of the subjects had ties to Ganci. Jim did not have a good handle on this matter, as it was managed by two supervisors in separate offices. This sounded like something I wanted to jump into right away, so I called a meeting of all parties to brief me on the case. This lack of a coordinated effort was not going to work.

I drove to New Rochelle and met with Carmine Russo, Charles Rooney, and Bob Paquette. Russo and Rooney worked for Manny Gonzalez in the Brooklyn office, and Paquette was assigned to a white-collar crime squad in New Rochelle. Russo, a native Sicilian, began the meeting by explaining how a source had put him onto Catalano. The information they received was sketchy, but it appeared Catalano was involved in heroin importation and distribution. Paquette was investigating several individuals on Wall Street who were laundering money, and he had determined that the funds might be coming from a drug cartel in Brooklyn. Both inquiries were in the early stages, with no informant available to furnish specific details. The agents were progressing, but the investigation was in the embryonic stages.

There was critical information that had been developed during a previous investigation when undercover agent Joe Pistone had penetrated a Bonanno family crew. Pistone had been meeting with Bonanno family member Anthony Mirra at a location in Brooklyn that was used as a meeting place for the family. We always attempted to cover Pistone when he was moving around Brooklyn. Our surveillance team observed Mirra meeting with suspected hit man Cesare Bonventre and Catalano. As Mirra left the meeting, he shook Catalano's hand and kissed him on the cheek, which, in the tradition of the Mafia, was a sign of respect. This was very significant to us, since it indicated Catalano held a high position of authority. Another individual, later identified as Ganci, was with Catalano. Pistone later identified Catalano and Ganci as "zips," a term used to denote members of the Sicilian Mafia—a faction of the Bonanno family—for their rapid speech.

It was relevant that Bonventre was present at this meeting, as he was supposed to have been Carmine Galante's bodyguard when he was recently hit. Due to his lack of response during the incident, he was suspected of setting up Galante. The reason Galante was murdered related directly to his efforts to take over the heroin distribution network already in place, which Catalano controlled. The pieces were starting to come together. Could Catalano himself be involved in the hit on Galante? At the very least, he could have ordered it.

Based on this briefing, I believed there was something here we had to pursue. I instructed the agents to confer with Louis Freeh, now an assistant US attorney in Manhattan.

"We can't make any headway in this case unless we can develop enough probable cause for court-authorized wiretaps of Ganci's phone, which will be the starting point." The agents stared back at me as I rambled on, and then I realized that although I may be right, the agents must have been thinking, *How the hell will we make this happen?* I then explained to them the "dynamic probable cause" approach, where you take circumstantial evidence, put it together in an affidavit, and present it to the judge. Freeh knew how to do this, which would be the agent's next step. I drove back to Manhattan, thinking this case could develop into a significant investigation.

The FBI had recently been given concurrent jurisdiction with the DEA to investigate federal violations of drug trafficking. We had no experience in this type of investigation and had no guidance from headquarters on how to proceed. We were on our own. The Mafia at present did not condone drug trafficking, as I had discovered in Philadelphia during the investigation involving the Bruno family. So how were we going to jump into a major investigation involving a Sicilian Mafia international heroin distribution network? Could we apply the RICO statute as a basis for investigating this group? Why not? It was certainly a continuing criminal enterprise.

My next stop was to meet with the DEA. I contacted the office and set up a meeting with the special agent in charge, Bruce Jensen, and his assistant, Tom Cash. I was sure they would be a little concerned about my purpose since we were now working on a drug case, and we might be infringing on their authority. They were, however, very accommodating and we had a great meeting. They knew nothing about Catalano or Ganci and had been focusing more on the Colombia cocaine distribution networks operating in the city, which were, in their words, out of control. I suggested we work this case jointly since their agency had the expertise and international connections we would need as we moved forward. Cash responded, "I will give you my best man, Anthony Petrucci, to work the case, as he has expertise with heroin networks." This was more than I had hoped for, since both agencies would have to trust one another if this case were to have a successful outcome.

I then called Louis Freeh and gave him the details of our meeting in New Rochelle. Louis liked the idea and would look forward to hearing from the agents. He had nothing on his plate that would prevent him from working full-time on the investigation. Louis remarked, "Frank, this might just be the case for exploring the dynamic probable cause concept." Things were starting to fall into place, but a serious issue had to be addressed: Who was going to supervise and coordinate this investigation? I sat down with Sheer and Kossler and briefed them on our progress.

My idea was to roll this case under the umbrella of the Bonanno family investigation, but to set up a separate group of agents to investigate this particular drug trafficking network. The agents would work out of Manhattan, and Russo, Rooney, and Paquette would be the lead agents reporting to Lew Schiliro, the supervisor of the Bonanno squad. Kossler could not coordinate the investigation, as Jim had his hands full with the Commission case. We also had two squads working on other drug investigations that needed oversight. I told Sheer, "We have to bring in Tom Vinton." Tom, a veteran supervisor and the drug coordinator for the office working out of New Rochelle, would be perfect to coordinate the investigative effort. He certainly had the background for it and the respect of the agents. These were bold moves that might result in some pushback. Sheer said he would personally call Vinton regarding the proposal. They were fellow Marines and had a good rapport. I would meet with Schiliro.

I then called Sean McWeeney and requested he contact our legal attaché office in Rome and set up a meeting with Italian National Police officials who investigated the Mafia. I told him I planned to fly to Rome to determine if they were aware of a heroin importation network controlled by the Sicilian faction of the Mafia in New York. McWeeney called back and said, "The officials will happily meet with you."

I booked a flight to Rome, and Lee Flosi, the head of our Rome office, met me at the airport. He had set up a meeting with the chief investigator of the Italian National Police, Giovanni De Gennaro, who was in charge of Sicilian Mafia investigations. Lee also had arranged for me to meet with Giovanni Falcone, the chief magistrate in Mafia prosecutions. He observed, "Falcone is a very busy judge, and it is unusual for him to meet on such short notice."

De Gennaro had an outstanding reputation as a law enforcement official dedicated to his work. Lee informed me that he also had an outgoing personality. He greeted me openly with, "Francesco, how can I help you?" He acknowledged that they were aware of Salvatore Catalano, who had been involved in heroin trafficking for years. He was part of an international organization headed by Gaetano Badalamenti, Italy's most wanted Mafia boss. Badalamenti had been a fugitive for years, yet was still able to manage his organization effectively. He had significant contacts in New York, but had additional associates throughout the East Coast and the Midwest. They were members of the Sicilian Mafia and had allegiance to the Bonanno family, which went back many years to the days of Joseph Bonanno. "These are bad guys," he said many times during our discussion.

I gave De Gennaro a thorough briefing of what our agents in New York had uncovered, and he was very interested. He offered that if the FBI succeeded with the wiretaps, they might lead to Badalamenti's location. He stated, "Badalamenti is constantly moving and pinning him down will not be easy." He offered his complete cooperation and suggested we might need a few of his men to serve as translators because Catalano and his crew transacted their business in Sicilian. That was an issue I had not focused on.

After our meeting, Lee and I drove to Magistrate Falcone's office and had a cordial introductory discussion. He was intrigued by my presence, as he stated, "I have never met an FBI agent from New York." I gave Judge Falcone an overview of what we had uncovered to date. "This is fantastic that you are chasing the same mafiosi we are—very good." He was committed to prosecuting members of the Mafia. "I want to develop a closer relationship with the Department of Justice attorneys assigned to prosecuting the Mafia in the United States; please help me do that." I assured him I would inform the appropriate officials when I returned to New York.

Upon returning to New York, I contacted Schiliro and briefed him on where we stood with the investigation, including what I had learned in Rome. He listened attentively, but probably thought, *Why is he telling me all this?* I told him Sheer and I had decided he was the best supervisor available to lead this investigation and wanted him and his squad to move to the Manhattan office. Paquette from New Rochelle and Rooney and Russo from Brooklyn would also be assigned to his special team of agents.

Schiliro was unhappy with the idea: "Like, are you kidding me? This is crazy." He pointed out that "the agents would push back on this move. You'll extend their commute to and from work, which will also be a hardship for their families."

I understood his concerns, but concluded, "It's done—we are moving ahead." He left the meeting unconvinced.

I intended to gather all the agents affected by this decision to make my case. A few days later, all the agents and Schiliro assembled to meet with me in Manhattan. I had a straightforward conversation with them and offered them the challenge: "You have the opportunity to work on a case that only comes along once in a career; if ever, don't let this pass you by." I continued, "This is why you are carrying a badge." There was some grumbling, but their eyes never left me as I spoke, and I hoped they were on board. I further emphasized that they would assume their previous assignment upon completing the investigation. The mutiny was averted, or at least I thought. We were now ready to get to work.

My secretary Loretta White walked into my office the next day and commented, "You better look at this." She handed me a one-paragraph memo from Schiliro addressed to me, stating that he was stepping down as a supervisor. There was no explanation, just a short "How do you do? I will be seeing you."

My first reaction was, "What the fuck!" This was my best supervisor, who just assumed management of a once-in-a-lifetime case and was backing off. There had to be something that was driving his decision. I asked him to report to my office at 9:00 a.m. the following day. I contacted Sheer and brought him up to date. I began to doubt the wisdom of this new reorganization plan. Had I gone too far and not considered how this would personally affect the agents and supervisors involved? Upon reflection, I thought, *Wait a minute, damn it, they are FBI agents, and this is what they signed up for.* We all had to move forward together, or the investigation would fail.

I realized that the supervisors in Queens did not like the arrangement of reporting to a boss in Manhattan. That was a given. But Schiliro's decision appeared to be based on something troubling him. Schiliro sat down with me the following day and we had an open and candid discussion. It seemed he was just tired of the stress that came with the job more than anything else. He had prepared the memo in a moment of frustration and had not thought it through. He found it difficult to constantly respond to some of the complaints about the commute, the cost of living in New York, and the long hours on the job. He loved the challenge of his position and was excited about our plans for the future. He felt unsure of himself and unsure if he could continue as a supervisor.

I mentioned to him that I had walked in his shoes and I was now commuting to South Jersey four times a week to care for my family. "It's a bitch, believe me. New York is difficult, but you will not find more important investigative challenges anywhere in the Bureau. Let's get back to work. I am a phone call away if you want to talk."

He got up from his chair, began to leave, and said, "Okay, I am with you." My bottom line was that I could not afford to lose Schiliro.

Within a few weeks, Rooney, Russo, Paquette, and Freeh had assembled an affidavit setting forth sufficient probable cause to obtain authority from a district judge to monitor Ganci's home telephone. The court order was implemented almost immediately. An issue we had to deal with concerned translating the conversations that were taking place, the exact problem that De Gennaro mentioned we would encounter. Many of the conversations were in Sicilian or carefully scripted, so they had to be interpreted to some extent. Carmine Russo was Sicilian, but he was the only translator we had to use to listen to the tapes.

An office worker assigned to the case to handle administrative duties approached Rooney and told him a coworker, Florence O'Connor, understood the Sicilian language since her husband was from Sicily. Rooney approached Florence with the idea of her becoming a translator. Her first response was, "Oh, no, it is not right that you are listening to someone's phone conversation." After Rooney explained the nature of the conversations, she quickly agreed and became an excellent translator. During the translating of Ganci's conversations, she would often say, "You have to lock up this son of a bitch." This back-and-forth always brought some humor to everyone.

The callers to Ganci would use phrases such as "Do you have any tomatoes?" and "I need a new shirt. Do you have any?" DEA agents advised that this type of language was prevalent in drug buys. It was all very vague, but after a few conversations, our surveillance observed suspects pulling into Ganci's driveway. After greeting them, Ganci would open the garage door and place a brown paper bag in the trunk of their car. What was in the bag? Our educated guess was a kilo or two of pure heroin.

Carmine Russo called one morning. "Boss, I think I should go to Rome and meet with De Gennaro. The main players are Sicilian and I need to learn more about their past and how they operate."

I thought this was a great idea, so I told Carmine, "Say hello to Johnny for me."

Carmine's trip was very beneficial. Although he was Sicilian, learning more about how the Mafia thinks and runs its organization was crucial. De Gennaro committed to temporarily assigning a translator to New York to assist Carmine in reviewing the conversations in Sicilian. We were now conducting a transatlantic investigation, with the two lead investigators working together as a team. It didn't get any better than that!

The investigation then suddenly took on another dimension. An individual named Benny Zito called Ganci and began a very cryptic conversation similar to other discussions we had intercepted from suspected buyers. Zito said, "I need a new shirt." We later learned Zito was a relative of Ganci's and a native Sicilian. He operated a pizzeria in Philadelphia. Several calls were made back and forth before the deal was finalized and a price was agreed to. Zito traveled to New York and was surveilled and photographed at Ganci's home carrying a small box under his arm. He left five minutes later carrying a similar package and placed it in his car. We assumed the package contained the kilo of heroin. This was dynamite evidence.

We didn't know it at the time, but Zito was under investigation by the DEA in Philadelphia and an undercover agent was in the process of purchasing a kilo of heroin from Zito. Agents from the Philadelphia DEA office now had Ganci's telephone number, and they contacted their office in New York and spoke to Agent Petrucci. He informed them, "You walked into our investigation—hold off on further actions." Petrucci then alerted Schiliro and a meeting was arranged in New York with all parties involved. Sheer and Louis Freeh would attend.

A heated meeting ensued as representatives of the DEA and the US Attorney's Office in Philadelphia demanded that they be allowed to make arrests of Zito and Ganci and take their case down. We argued against this idea because we were investigating an entire network and were not interested in busting one or two players and letting everyone else walk. Tempers began to boil; the prosecuting attorney was adamant and unreasonable. We realized we would have to go over her head. During the meeting, Freeh excused himself and contacted DOJ officials from a private office. They supported our position. He returned to the meeting and conveyed the department's decision, and the issue was settled. He bluntly stated, "There will be no arrests in Philly."

We then began working on a joint investigation with our office in Philadelphia and their DEA counterparts. Additional buys from Zito were arranged and captured by our surveillance team. The buys involving Zito were critical evidence in the case and established that Ganci was, in fact, in the middle of an organized drug trafficking network. Over several months, the investigation spread to other cities and additional subjects were identified. The majority of the traffickers we identified were all members of the Sicilian Mafia and operated pizzerias as fronts for their main activities.

The investigation was expanding and we continued to develop new avenues to pursue. Vinton and Schiliro were still the lead supervisors and everyone was getting restless. Some thought the investigation was taking too long. This did not surprise me, as the supervisors and agents were not accustomed to long-term investigations directed toward a vast enterprise. One Saturday afternoon, Schiliro called me at home and stated that agents had just intercepted a conversation indicating that one of the main subjects would be picking up two kilos of heroin that evening from Ganci, and they wanted to make an arrest and seize the heroin as evidence. The plan was to create a routine traffic stop, search the car, seize the heroin, and make the arrests. My reaction was direct and to the point. "Over my dead body. I am on my way to the city and will be there in two hours."

Upon arriving in New York, I went straight to the office command center to communicate over the radio with Schiliro and the agents on the street. I also called Sheer and Louis Freeh and brought them up to date, and they concurred with my position. Schiliro was supervising the surveillance and we resumed our discussion. He had told the agents to stand by and not take any action. Freeh was able to join the conversation and emphasized we had to let the heroin walk and not make any arrests or seizures. The objective was to take down the entire organization responsible for importing hundreds of kilos into New York yearly. That put an end to this episode and we all went home.

One of the painstaking roles in the investigation was listening to the tapes and interpreting what was being discussed. Carmine Russo could speak Sicilian and listening to and interpreting the conversations was one of his primary responsibilities. Russo was reviewing an intercepted conversation that seemed a little different. Ganci called an individual named Pietro somewhere in the Midwest.

The conversation was very encrypted. Pietro kept referring to someone as "he," being very upset over what had happened, and "he" was trying to connect. Other parts of the conversation indicated that Pietro was involved with the network. A check of his telephone records determined the call had been placed to Pietro Alfano, who operated a pizzeria in Oregon, Illinois. Russo thought, *Where the hell is Oregon and what is his role in the organization?* Carmine fantasized that when Alfano mentioned "he" several times during the call, he might be referring to Badalamenti. As it would turn out, Russo was right.

The conversations we were intercepting regarding Alfano led us to believe that he was the contact Badalamenti used to communicate with all the key players in New York and elsewhere who were responsible for distributing drugs. On April 5, 1984, we intercepted a call from Badalamenti instructing Alfano to bring money to him in Madrid, Spain, the next day. We were anxiously waiting for this moment, since upon their meeting, we would take the case down. After talking to Badalamenti, Alfano called a travel agent and booked a flight to Madrid. Surveillance was placed on Alfano's every move; we could not afford to blow this opportunity. We planned to have two undercover agents on the plane with Alfano accompanying him to Madrid. We notified our legat office in Madrid of the situation and he arranged to have local authorities supply backup surveillance at the airport. Upon landing, we would follow Alfano to wherever he took us.

The next day, Alfano left his home, headed to O'Hare International Airport in Chicago, and boarded a flight to Madrid. One of our agents and a DEA agent were on the same flight. The flight was an overnighter and Alfano did not arrive in Madrid until the following day. Our weary agents were awaiting his arrival at the airport and upon landing, his every move would be observed. An unknown male greeted him and after picking up his luggage, the two entered a cab. We discreetly followed the cab and observed the passengers dropped off at an apartment complex outside the city and entering a building. A discreet perimeter surveillance system was set up, which lasted throughout the night.

When morning arrived, Alfano left the building accompanied by another unknown male who closely resembled Badalamenti. They casually walked into town, chatting as they proceeded without any suspicion that they were under surveillance. Both men were quickly arrested and transported to police headquarters. Alfano and Badalamenti were now in custody. The police returned to the apartment and arrested Badalamenti's son, Vito. Rooney and Russo were notified of the arrest. It was now late Saturday evening in New York. Schiliro called me at home with the good news and I contacted Sheer. The plan was to assemble in the morning and proceed with all the arrests and searches.

Twenty-two defendants had been indicted the previous week. Agents had been alerted in several field offices to be ready to act on a moment's notice that upon taking Badalamenti into custody, we were prepared to execute simultaneous arrests and search warrants. When I arrived at the office, key staff members and Sheer were already in the command center. Louis Freeh and his assistant were present in case any legal issues arose when we executed the warrants.

We had an open line to all the field offices involved. Approximately 150 agents were stationed at critical locations, ready to move quickly. You could feel the tension and anticipation present in the room. After two long years of discreet and tedious investigative activity, we were about to take down one of the most significant heroin distribution networks that ever existed. At the right moment, Sheer said, "Okay, let's do it." The agents immediately responded and began to carry out their assignments.

Agents awaiting the order to move quickly executed arrest and search warrants at JFK International Airport, Brooklyn, and Queens in New York, as well as Michigan, Oregon, Illinois, New Jersey, and Philadelphia. All the arrests were made without incident, although one subject confronted an agent with a shotgun and a gun battle almost ensued. Over $100,000 in cash was seized, along with shotguns, rifles, loaded handguns, drug paraphernalia, essential telephone numbers, and records tied directly to the investigation. Alfano's wife attempted to flee their home with a loaded revolver in her coat pocket and was taken into custody. Sheer and I looked at one another when it was all over and just smiled, more or less a sigh of relief. I walked over to where he was standing and gave him a high five. "We did it, Tom." I left the command center and wearily drove home. It was now up to the prosecutors to bring this case to its final conclusion.

Louis Freeh was the lead prosecutor and had a great team assembled. Richard Martin was his chief assistant. This was not a case they could afford to lose. The trial began in the United States District Court in Lower Manhattan on September 30, 1985. Rooney and Russo were in court almost daily, and agents were made available on a standby basis to help the prosecutors locate witnesses if necessary. Benny Zito was not on trial. He had disappeared and it was presumed he had been murdered because he had led us to Ganci. His body was never found. Cesare Bonventre was also not on trial, as his body had been found in an oil drum in Brooklyn a few months before the arrests. The reason for his murder was unclear.

The presentation of the case would focus on establishing that the group on trial was part of a Mafia enterprise responsible for the importation and distribution of heroin from Sicily to distribution networks in the United States. Pizza parlors located in various cities were the centers of the trafficking and sale of drugs, and the profits were laundered through banks and brokerage houses in New York. Over a span of nine years, it was estimated that $1.5 billion in heroin sales were consummated primarily in the northeast section of the country. This was a tall order for the prosecution to prove, but they had the evidence.

Upon the conclusion of opening statements, the prosecution called its first witness, Tommaso Buscetta, a top leader in the Sicilian Mafia. He had agreed to testify, was extradited to the United States, and entered the witness protection program. Buscetta was the highest-ranking member of the Sicilian Mafia to ever cooperate with law enforcement. He had been caught up in a war between various factions of the Mafia in Sicily, and his wife and two sons had been kidnapped and murdered by his rivals. That event forced him to turn his back on the Mafia and he surrendered to Italian authorities. Through our established relationship with Magistrate Falcone and the Italian National Police, we learned of his cooperation and after negotiations, he agreed to enter our program.

Buscetta was acquainted with Badalamenti and furnished detailed information to the jury regarding the inner workings of the Sicilian Mafia and their interactions with Cosa Nostra groups in the United States. He testified that Badalamenti would not have been able to engage in drug trafficking in the United States without the approval of one of the New York Mafia families. He was a valuable first witness who established the relationship between the Mafia in the United States and its counterpart in Sicily. Extra security was provided in the courtroom during his testimony and the jury never took their eyes off Buscetta as he answered one question after another presented by the prosecutor. The defense did not cross-examine him; the reason was evident to everyone sitting at the prosecutor's table and, I am sure, to the jury.

The recorded conversations between the defendants were critical to the government's case. The surveillance and photographs of the subjects meeting and conspiring with one another were also vital. Agent Joe Pistone provided valuable evidence. He had had many conversations with key members that established they were involved in drug trafficking.

It had been a long and grueling exercise for the prosecution team and the case agents. Two unexpected developments occurred just before the case was ready for the jury. Gaetano Mazzara, one of the key defendants, did not appear for trial the day after Thanksgiving. We first thought he had fled as his attorney was getting ready to address the court in his defense, but why would he try to escape at this point in the trial? Within twenty-four hours, we got the answer. Mazzara's battered and tortured body was found and identified by agents in Brooklyn. There was speculation on our part that he had been killed because one or more of his codefendants may have thought he would cooperate with the government at the last moment. In their eyes, he was a risk and expendable, so they killed him to protect themselves.

On February 11, 1987, Pietro Alfano and his wife went for a walk in Greenwich Village during a trial recess. It was a cold and brisk day, but he needed to escape the trial for at least a moment or two. Alfano must have felt uneasy about his status because, although unintentional, he had led the FBI to Badalamenti's doorstep. He had to find a way out of the situation he was now in, but where would he turn? Suddenly, two men approached them from behind and, without saying a word, shot him three times in the back. His wife screamed in horror as her husband fell to the ground. She was not injured. After being rushed to the hospital and treated for his wounds, he survived but was paralyzed. An investigation into the shooting resulted in the arrest of three prime suspects; however, they were not prosecuted due to lack of evidence.

The orders for the hit could have come from one of three sources: Catalano, Badalamenti, or one of the other subjects on trial. We never found out the motive; Alfano was not an informant, nor had he cooperated with the investigation in any way. The incident created havoc among the defense attorneys, who immediately filed motions for a mistrial, which were denied. The trial proceeded and we wondered if there would be any more acts of violence.

The prosecution and defense made their final presentations and the jury began deliberations. After a long and exhausting six days, they had reached a verdict. Eighteen of the twenty-two defendants originally indicted were convicted and remanded to the custody of the US Marshal. The son of Badalamenti was acquitted. Two of the defendants had previously pleaded guilty. The sentences the judge imposed were significant. Salvatore Catalano and Badalamenti were sentenced to serve forty-five years in federal prison. The other defendants received sentences ranging from twenty to thirty-five years. Rooney and Russo, the two game changers who started it all, were in the courtroom at the time of sentencing. They could not say much as they watched and listened to the proceedings. It was a great victory for them and a time to go out and have a beer and pizza at Nino's. The Pizza Connection case was over.

CHAPTER 17
The Commission Trial

The trial of the Mafia bosses was held in the US District Court for the Southern District of New York in Manhattan and began on September 18, 1986. It would last ten weeks. The official court docket read *United States v. Salerno, et al*, but the press commonly referred to the proceeding as the Mafia Commission Trial, or just simply the Commission Trial. Assistant US Attorney Michael Chertoff was the lead prosecuting attorney who reported directly to Rudy Giuliani. Eight leaders of the New York Mafia were on trial for allegedly violating the RICO statute. The original indictment had charged ten Mafia leaders. However, Paul Castellano was murdered in December 1985 and Aniello "Neil" Dellacroce, his underboss, had recently died. If convicted, each one of the leaders could face up to 100 years in prison. US District Judge Richard Owen presided. The trial was considered the most significant prosecution the government had ever undertaken in its yearslong battle against the Mafia. On opening day, the courtroom overflowed with spectators and news media. This would be the norm throughout the trial.

It took several days to select the jury of seven women and five men. They would not be sequestered, but their true identities would remain anonymous. There had been several incidents in the past where attempts by the Mafia to bribe jurors were successful. The Gambino family, in particular, had that reputation. Deputy US Marshals were present in the courtroom to maintain order. We also planned to have selective agents as attendees during the proceedings to determine if any Mafia members were spectators and would make efforts to stare down members of the jury. I recalled this tactic had been adopted by the Bruno family when Frank Sheeran was on trial in Philadelphia. I hoped to attend as many court sessions as possible.

As the defendants entered the courtroom, there was total silence. Those engaged in a conversation immediately stopped and their eyes were fixated on the Mafia bosses. For some, I imagined it was just the sense of what they were witnessing for the first time. Before them stood the leaders of organized crime in New York who were allegedly responsible for ruthless acts of violence to maintain their positions of power for so many years. This is an event you saw portrayed in a movie or read about in a book; you seldom had an opportunity to witness it playing out in real time. Judge Owen entered the courtroom and all attendees stood. The clerk called the trial to order and the proceedings began.

Michael Chertoff was the lead prosecutor and was assisted by prosecutors John F. Savarese and J. Gilmore Childers. Chertoff made the opening statement to the jury, which was flawless. He briefly summarized the charges the government would prove. He told the jury, "You will hear recorded conversations intercepted by the FBI of the defendants discussing criminal activities and specific references to their membership in the Commission." He also pointed out that victims of their extortion schemes would testify along with members of the Mafia, which would further prove the government's case.

Attorneys representing the defendants took a rather novel and unexpected approach. Attorney Samuel Dawson readily admitted to the jury the existence of the Mafia: "This case is not about whether an organization is in existence, known as the Mafia or La Cosa Nostra. There is right here in New York City." He continued as he addressed the jury, "Can you accept that just because a person is a member of the Mafia, it doesn't mean he committed the crimes charged in this case?" The look on Chertoff's face as Dawson made this argument was bewilderment, as one of his objectives would be to prove to the jury that the Mafia did exist. Dawson had done that for him.

Dawson continued, "Yes, there is a Commission." He added that the Commission's only function was to approve new members and resolve conflicts. He continued, "The Commission was not about extorting money from the construction industry but setting prices to avoid competition." The only problem with that argument was that the Commission was not competing in the open marketplace for business contracts; it was extorting contractors who bid on contracts. Dawson concluded by stating, "This is a bid-rigging case; the government has reached for more than what the evidence shows." There had never been another trial where an attorney defending a Mafia leader admitted the existence of the Commission. Things got more outrageous as the trial proceeded with additional presentations by defense attorneys.

The attorney for Ralph Scopo admitted to the jury that "Scopo did, in fact, accept some labor payoffs, but they were not accepted on behalf of the Mafia." In an unprecedented move, Carmine Persico, the boss of the Colombo family, advised the court that he would defend himself. His attorney sat beside him at the counsel table and remained silent throughout the trial. I assumed Persico still considered himself the boss and his attorney the consigliere. In his opening remarks, Persico attempted to portray himself as a victim and made references to the prosecutors that "their only intent was to persecute him for crimes he did not commit." He was dressed for the part and, by all appearances, presented a professional appearance. However, when he began to present his case, it was evident he offered a false narrative of the facts regarding the investigation.

The prosecution had all the tape-recorded conversations intercepted by the FBI over three years and they would be played for the judge and jury, as well as the defendants and their attorneys.

The jury placed headphones on so they could listen more attentively to the tapes that would be played. They also were individually furnished with a transcript of the pertinent conversation. Throughout the investigation, we instituted over fifty court-authorized electronic surveillances of various Mafia members and associates. The critical discussions would be played during the trial, and there were many. The results of essential surveillance observations were also presented, the most important of which related to the Commission meeting we witnessed on Staten Island. The photographs of the Mafia bosses leaving the meeting were compelling evidence to present to the jury. FBI Agent Joseph Pistone testified as an undercover agent and the jury listened intently to his testimony. They were mesmerized by the story of his role as an undercover agent who had successfully become a member of thc Napolitano crew.

One of the most crucial prosecution witnesses was Angelo Lonardo, a former underboss of the Cleveland Mafia. He agreed to cooperate because he faced multiple federal charges in Cleveland. He described the Mafia and his long history with the organization. It was unusual for a high-ranking Mafia leader to break the code of silence and testify in a criminal proceeding. Lonardo personally knew the defendants and stated that his family in Cleveland understood they had an obligation to report to them. He pointed to Salerno, who was sitting at the defense table as his representative on the Commission. "People used to refer to him as Fat Tony—he's a little thinner." Salerno began squirming in his seat and glaring at Lonardo as he did so. During Lonardo's testimony, the following exchange took place:

> Chertoff: "What are the Commission's functions within La Cosa Nostra?"
>
> Lonardo: "Well, if there is a dispute about anything, they get together and iron it out."
>
> Chertoff: "Are there any functions the Commission performs?"

> Lonardo: "They make all the rules and regulations, what you can do, what you can't do. Well, the rules are that they can kill a boss in other cities or in New York City without them knowing anything about it."

The conversation Salerno had in the Palma Boys Social Club with John Tronolone and Joe Pieri of the Cleveland family was played for the jury to support Lonardo's testimony. Tronolone and Pieri wanted Salerno to intervene in their leadership dispute within the family. Salerno emphatically told the two Cleveland Mafia members: "Let the Commission decide. Tell him it's the Commission from New York. Tell him he's dealing with the big boys now."

Salerno did not support Philip "Rusty" Rastelli's efforts to be appointed boss of the Bonanno family and thus become a member of the Commission. He knew Rastelli had allowed his members to engage in drug trafficking. Salerno was intercepted, emphasizing his views to Michael "Mickey Dimino" Generoso, a Genovese capo. This particular conversation was important in establishing the existence and power of the Commission: "I told the Commission, 'Ah, hey, listen, this guy wants to be the boss. He can be the boss as far as I am concerned, but he cannot be on the Commission.' One vote is enough to throw it out. Because the Commission thing, it's supposed to be such a sacred thing."

Chertoff had to convince the jury that the Commission comprised the boss of each family. Salerno's conversation with an unidentified member was recorded, in which he expressed further concern about Rastelli becoming a member of the Commission. In this conversation, Salerno unwittingly implicated Paul Castellano and Anthony "Tony Ducks" Corallo as members of the Commission: "Listen, we don't recognize him down there. I didn't want to meet, Paul did not want to meet. Tony Ducks told Rusty, 'Listen, take care of your family first. Straighten out your family and when you straighten them out, then we talk about the Commission.'"

One of the critical elements charged in the indictment was the illegal profits gained from creating the Concrete Club by Colombo capo Ralph Scopo. We recorded numerous conversations between Scopo and contractors in his Lincoln Town Car, and the tapes were played for the jury.

Scopo had agreed to meet with Salvatore D'Ambrosi, a concrete contractor. His company was not included in the Concrete Club. D'Ambrosi pleaded with Scopo to allow his company to be considered for concrete bids, as they were always competitive, and he wanted to negotiate. The following conversation that took place was introduced as evidence:

Scopo: "The concrete's gotta be twelve million."

D'Ambrosi: "Yeah, why can't I do the concrete?"

Scopo: "You can't do it. Over two million you can't do it. It's under two million, hey, me, I tell you to go ahead and do it."

D'Ambrosi: "Who do I gotta see? Tell me who I gotta go see?"

Scopo: "You gotta see every family. And they gonna tell you no. So, don't even bother. First of all, the job costs you two points."

D'Ambrosi: "Why two points?"

Scopo: "That's what they pay. Anything over two million. All the guys in the club who got so much out pay two points."

D'Ambrosi: "Uh-huh. Put two points into the job."

Scopo: "That's what I say, you gotta put it in ahead of time. You know, if I bring you a customer twenty yards and I tell you, Sally, the concrete is $60 a yard, the guy's gonna give you $63."

D'Ambrosi: "Three's yours."

Scopo: "Three you gotta give me. What do I give a fuck?"

D'Ambrosi: "What do I give a fuck for?"

Scopo: "You're getting your $60."

D'Ambrosi: "That's it. What the fuck is the problem?"
Scopo: "And meantime, I'm bringing you the customer."

After this conversation was played, Chertoff methodically explained to the jury that Scopo was outlining how D'Ambrosi could inflate his bid by three dollars per yard of concrete. He would then kick back the additional funds for receiving a contract under $2 million. Furthermore, he could not bid on a contract over $2 million unless he was a member of the Concrete Club.

The defense strategy had been to convince the jury that the crimes alleged in the indictments were isolated incidents and not related to a broader conspiracy by the New York Mafia. In his closing argument, prosecuting attorney Chertoff directly addressed this point: "Merely the fact that a person is a member of the Mafia does not make him guilty of the crimes. But part of the crime charged here is being part of the Mafia and part of the Commission of La Cosa Nostra. That is one of the elements, that is one half of the crime because the crime that is charged here is racketeering, and what racketeering is about setting up, joining, and associating with a criminal enterprise, organized crime activity, and using that organization to commit crimes like extortion and murder and loan-sharking."

Chertoff brilliantly attacked the defense's position when he continued, "So it is not true to say that this case had nothing to do with the Mafia or that the Mafia is irrelevant. The Mafia is very relevant in this case. The Mafia is relevant because it is the Mafia that makes possible this kind of concerted criminal activity. The Mafia is relevant because racketeering is the evil that racketeering laws are designed to prevent: people banding together in an organized and disciplined fashion for one purpose: to commit crimes."

The case was then sent to the jury to begin reviewing the evidence. During the trial, they sat patiently in the jury box and listened to over 150 tape recordings that the FBI had accumulated during their investigation. Eighty-five witnesses testified. It was an astonishing amount of evidence that they had to digest and evaluate. The jury deliberated for six days and notified the clerk that they had reached a verdict.

As they returned to the jury box from their final deliberations, they kept their heads down and quietly took their seats. There was absolute silence in the courtroom. Judge Owen asked the forewoman to read the verdict, encompassing over 100 counts of federal law violations. The forewoman did her best, but it took approximately thirty minutes to complete, and she grew weary toward the end of her presentation. The defendants were found guilty on all counts charged in the indictment. There was no reaction from the attendees in the courtroom, nor from the defendants, who stared transfixed at the jury. The judge remanded them to the custody of the US Marshal and set a date for sentencing. Just like that, it was over.

As I sat in the courtroom with Kossler and Pat Marshall, one of the case agents, I simultaneously felt a rush of elation and satisfaction. We had come a long way since my initial conference with the supervisors when I arrived in New York in 1982. I challenged them then that our goal was to take down the Commission and all the top Mafia leaders. I am sure many of them thought, *Oh, yeah, right, I don't think so.* Well, here we were. The Commission leaders had been convicted thanks to RICO, and the Mafia would no longer have the swagger and power it once possessed. The game changers had done their job and should have been proud of their accomplishment.

Two months passed and all the defendants appeared in court for sentencing. Judge Owen sentenced all the defendants, except Indelicato, to 100 years in prison without the chance for parole. Indelicato received a forty-year sentence for the murder of Carmine Galante. Judge Owen's closing remarks to the defendants were punctuated with direct reference to "the lifetime of terror that they had inflicted on the community for the sole purpose of financial gain."

Giuliani's team did an incredible job presenting this complicated investigation to the jury. Michael Chertoff, in particular, earned the praise of all. He later became the US Attorney for the Northern District of New Jersey and then the Assistant Attorney General of the Criminal Division at the Department of Justice. President George W. Bush subsequently appointed him Secretary of Homeland Security, and he continued serving his country until he retired.

CHAPTER 18
Section Chief

Floyd Clarke, the deputy assistant director of the criminal division, called one day and said, "You are being promoted to chief of the organized crime section at headquarters, and I wanted to give you a heads-up." I would report directly to him. He had an outstanding reputation in the Bureau and I was pleased with this opportunity. Sean McWeeney had been promoted to another assignment, and his deputy, Jules Bonavolonta, would be transferred to New York to relieve me. The move made sense in many ways, but this would again be an adjustment for Susan; however, we would still be close to Philadelphia and our families. Our son David was only three, so I was sure he would not mind the move.

I had so many mixed emotions about leaving New York. The agents had accomplished so much and I was very proud of them. How could I show my appreciation? Over the past three years, the cases they made received a lot of local and national publicity, and I saved many of the news accounts. One night, I gathered the clippings together and made a collage depicting the results of their accomplishments. I had a photographer make copies of the collage and, in individual squad conferences, presented each one of the agents with a copy. I also mailed a copy to Director Webster. As I write this book, I have it hanging on the wall in my office and it will always remain with me. I would assume most of my game changers may have done the same thing.

Within a few days, the transfer letter arrived, and Sue and I began preparing for another move. The agents organized a going-away luncheon for me at a restaurant across from the office. I was overwhelmed, to be honest. So much had been accomplished by these young agents with whom I was now sharing goodbyes. As I thanked everyone for coming, I paused for several seconds and could not speak. It was weird, in a way. I did not want to leave and was caught up in the moment. I looked out and saw the faces of the men and women who had gone through so much and realized I could never duplicate my time in New York. It was a tough assignment, but in so many ways, a rewarding experience. When I arrived home, I sat down with Sue and confided in her as I always did when faced with stressful moments. Sue always made things better.

We left for Washington a couple of days later, and we quickly discovered that the price of homes was beyond our reach, so we decided to rent a house in the Chevy Chase section of the city. It turned out to be an excellent choice. Sue loved the neighborhood and enrolled David in a pre-K program at a school a few blocks from home.

The FBI was recently given jurisdiction of investigating drug violations, a new ball game for us. None of our agents had any training or experience in exploring this type of criminal activity, so we had to start from scratch. We had, however, just completed the Pizza Connection investigation in New York, which took down an international heroin distribution network. Investigating organizations was now something we were good at, but that approach was new to the rest of the field offices. I met with the supervisors in the section to get a sense of the type of drug investigations they were monitoring in our field offices. The feedback I got was alarming, but not surprising.

The overall organized crime program was moving in the right direction nationally. I would still oversee the program in New York and offer whatever assistance the section could provide. My attention was also focused on the FBI's newly assigned responsibilities in drug enforcement. I met with Floyd and we discussed the idea of creating a national drug strategy for the FBI field offices to follow when initiating a drug trafficking investigation. The objective was to offer the field some guidance on what type of approach we should take that was separate from what other agencies had adopted. Floyd observed, "Our focus should be on the drug organizations and not solely on individuals distributing drugs. The FBI only has finite resources for this problem and we must use them effectively." Floyd gave me the green light to go forward.

My assistant section chief, Bill Esposito, coordinated our drug investigations from the headquarters level as best he could. Still, his job was tricky because no clearly defined targets existed. We were not even aware of what type of drug issues were out there in each field office. How could we appropriate resource requests to a particular office to work on drug investigations when we didn't know the issues in their territory? I discussed this with Esposito and he offered a great idea. "The field has never been officially requested to furnish specific information concerning drug trafficking issues. Let's send a communication to each field office and require them to do just that. We will then have a database to analyze as we develop a national strategy." I loved this suggestion and asked Esposito to assign that responsibility to one of his best analysts.

The next day, Supervisors Tom Kubic and Frank Quijada came by my office for a chat after talking to Esposito. I gave Tom and Frank a brief rundown of what I was thinking and I could tell by their reaction they liked the idea. Tom remarked, "This lack of direction has concerned me for some time, and I believe the field is waiting for headquarters to give them some direction." I knew we had twelve drug coordinators with some experience assigned to various field offices. What if we brought them back to headquarters temporarily to review all the data we received from the field, thus making this more of a priority?

Tom volunteered, "I will send the survey out and follow up

with a request for the coordinators to come to headquarters for a temporary assignment once we have received the survey results." Perfect! One of those coordinators, of course, would be my former assistant in New York, Tom Vinton, who had just finished the Pizza Connection investigation. I would put him in charge of the group.

About two weeks later, some survey responses began to arrive, and the rest soon followed. We had put a deadline on our request and the field always responded to deadlines. The coordinator's request was sent out and they all replied they were available. I designated a work area in the section that they could utilize during their analysis. Within a week or so, they all arrived and Esposito, Kubic, and I sat down with them and explained what we were attempting to accomplish. They all seemed enthusiastic and supported the idea of developing a national strategy.

I visited the organized crime section at the DOJ. I spoke to David Margolis, the lead prosecutor who ran the section and had been so helpful during the UNIRAC investigation. Dave's response was what I hoped it would be: "We are totally on board and will support you in every way." He suggested I have Kubic coordinate our effort as we proceeded with an attorney in his section. I readily agreed to this arrangement, as this was precisely what I was looking for. Even at this point, if we developed a national strategy and the director approved it, he would also want the concurrence of the attorney general. Little did I realize then that the chain of approval would not stop with the attorney general, but would eventually lead us to the White House.

After a week or so, I sat down with the team of coordinators who analyzed all the surveys the field had submitted. The group's consensus was nearly unanimous: "The field is working drug cases randomly. Except for the Miami and New York offices, there are no organized drug cartels under investigation." It was also unclear how many agents were involved in conducting investigations, as headquarters had yet to set a target staffing level approving a specific number of drug agents for each office. It was obvious that the agents working on these cases were relatively inexperienced in investigating violations of drug trafficking. The responses we received, however, formed a database regarding the particular areas of the country where drug trafficking was a serious problem.

It was evident that the move to bring the FBI on board to investigate federal drug violations had one purpose in mind: The overall issue of drug trafficking in this country was a significant problem and more resources were needed. The role the FBI was to play had not been defined for us, nor did we, up to this point, define it for ourselves. We now had an opportunity to do just that by creating an institutional approach and strategy to address this significant criminal problem. Tom and the team began to put their thoughts together and develop a blueprint for what would become known as the FBI's national drug strategy. Within four or five weeks, they had a proposal on my desk.

The strategy took a few options away from the field when initiating a drug investigation. Each office would be required to develop intelligence on the most significant drug problem in their area and identify the resources and approaches they would utilize to address the issue. There had to be sufficient justification to spend our limited resources on a particular investigation. We had identified several offices that had organized drug cartels in their cities, and they would receive a majority of the resources and support from headquarters. Offices with less of a problem were encouraged to work with and support local law enforcement in addressing significant groups involved in drug trafficking. The strategy also encouraged adopting the RICO statute as a basis for investigating organized drug cartels. We cited the Pizza Connection case as a model to follow. Many divisions believed that now that the FBI had jurisdiction to investigate drug trafficking, they were obliged to work whatever case came along. I emphasized to Esposito "that approach will no longer be authorized."

The strategy required each office to focus on the most significant drug trafficking problem in their jurisdiction and advise headquarters before initiating an investigation. As long as the problem was deemed important, resources could be applied. If the problem was not a significant issue but did deserve attention, the offices could work in concert with local authorities. Resources would be allocated to offices based on the degree of the drug problem and no longer assigned randomly.

I realized that many SACs of various field offices would push back against this new policy, as they believed it was their office and would run it as they saw fit. This new strategy would change that way of thinking somewhat. Tom prepared a communication to all field offices setting forth the new strategy. He suggested we have the exhibits section prepare a chart depicting the entire country and highlight those areas where the drug problem was most profound and would be the primary focus of our attention.

I sat down with Floyd Clarke. He liked the strategy and readily approved the recommendations. He set up a meeting with Buck Revell, the associate director. We met with Buck, who went over the entire strategy in detail. Buck commented, "The SACs will want me to fire you when you send this out." Nonetheless, he believed it was essential, but would have to be approved by Director Webster before it could be implemented.

Several days later, Floyd called and said that Director Webster wanted to meet with him, Revell, and me for a presentation regarding the FBI's national drug strategy proposal. He told me to be ready with my chart the following morning, as I would personally make the presentation.

The next day, we all met with Director Webster in his office. I placed my chart on an easel that had been placed in his office. I spoke for about ten minutes, explaining the strategy and why it was imperative for the FBI to adopt one now. "It would greatly benefit the field, establish us as a critical player in the war on drugs, and help our future resource requests before Congress." The director listened intently and directed a specific question to me. Mr. Revell began to answer for me, but the director cut him off and said, "Let Frank tell me what he thinks."

After I finished responding, he said, "I like it." He thanked us for our time and said we must run this by Attorney General Ed Meese. He also requested that we prepare a slide presentation depicting the strategy and present the slides to him before the meeting. He would select the particular slides that he would need for the presentation.

Kubic and I again met to address the director's request for a slide presentation. He again contacted the exhibits section and within a week, they prepared a very professional depiction of the strategy with thirty slides. We reviewed each one and agreed that the slides told the whole story. I contacted Floyd and said we were ready to go. Another meeting with the director ensued, and he went through each slide. He methodically selected the ones he wanted. He would arrange a meeting with Attorney General Meese and present the strategy for his approval.

Within a few days, we all went across the street to the DOJ and sat down with the attorney general and his staff. The attorney general's conference room was huge. My only responsibility was to operate the slide projector as the director spoke. When the director wanted to move on to the next slide, he would turn his head slightly to the right. Everything was going as planned when suddenly the projector shut down as the director had just finished making a point. No one noticed, but I certainly did. What was going on? I looked at the projector and saw that I had stepped on the extension cord, which popped out of the electrical outlet. My future career flashed in front of me. I quickly corrected the misstep and the projector lit up again. The presentation continued and the attorney general approved the strategy and thanked the director. As it would turn out, we still had not finished selling our new product.

The director's office called and requested that I meet with him immediately. I hustled up to his office, unaware of the reason for his call. He had been in touch with the attorney general, and he requested that we meet with President Reagan's chief of staff,

Jim Baker, and present our strategy to him as the drug problem was a priority with the president.

The next day, I accompanied the director and his security detail to the White House. Upon arrival, we were escorted into the Roosevelt Room. I had the slide projector with me and we had been through this routine a few times—we were ready. A Secret Service agent advised us that the president was in his office just down the hall. Mr. Baker entered the room with his staff and greeted the director. "This better go well" was my focus at that moment.

After some casual conversation, Mr. Baker spoke about the priority the administration was placing on the drug problem in the country, and he was pleased that the FBI was now addressing the issue. With that, the director introduced the strategy and began the slide presentation. The discussion back and forth between the director, Mr. Baker, and his staff lasted a good thirty minutes. Mr. Baker thanked the director for his time and commented, "I like this approach and will brief the president." We returned to headquarters and the director did not say much during our ride back to headquarters.

An hour later, a messenger arrived at my office and handed me a handwritten note from the director dated May 7, 1985, that read, "Nice job this morning, William H. Webster." I still have that note. Upon his final approval, the strategy was forwarded to all field offices.

Floyd and I soon began getting phone calls from several SACs in the field, as we had expected. They resented the oversight we were requiring of their management of drug investigations. Several calls, though, were just the opposite. They were complimentary toward the idea of a national strategy and welcomed the support from headquarters. SAC Jim Ahern of the Boston office called and said, "Frank, this is the finest policy directive I ever received from headquarters." When you make controversial decisions, you cannot please everybody, so the criticism did not bother us. If they had better ideas or suggestions, we would listen. None were forthcoming, so we moved on.

* * *

With the development of the strategy and the FBI's success in the Pizza Connection case, the Bureau began to obtain a more comprehensive footprint within the federal law enforcement community regarding their ability to investigate drug trafficking. Attorney General Meese had initiated a review to determine if the FBI and DEA should be merged, as there was a belief that the overall administration and investigation of cases would be more efficient and better coordinated. The FBI did not take a firm position on this idea; however, the DEA was totally against it, creating friction between both agencies, which went on for a year or so. The attorney general had established a working group to study the proposal and develop specific recommendations. In the interim, FBI executives were assigned to the DEA to direct the organization, which created more friction. It fostered an uncomfortable working arrangement at the time.

I did not let the merger issue interfere with the implementation of the strategy. My relationship with DEA representatives at the headquarters level was professional and very workable. I respected the efforts of the DEA and experienced firsthand their outstanding contributions in the Pizza Connection case. We began to attend meetings with the National Drug Enforcement Task Force headed by Frank Keating, a deputy assistant attorney general. The group comprised officials representing every federal agency involved in addressing the national drug problem and met once a month. Vice President Bush created the group at the direction of the president. I presented the strategy to the group and they were very supportive.

Buck Revell contacted me one Monday morning and stated that Attorney General Meese wanted to attend a meeting that the ambassador to Mexico, John Gavin, would host the following Sunday in his home in Cancún. He wanted me to attend and be prepared to make a presentation regarding our national drug strategy. We would fly to Mexico on an FBI jet, leaving National Airport at 11:00 a.m. That Friday, my boss, Tony Daniels, who was the deputy director of the criminal division, came charging into my office and announced, "Gordon has just been shot in a shoot-out." I almost jumped out of my chair. Daniels explained that "there has been a shoot-out in Miami and Gordon has been seriously wounded." Two agents had been killed and three others were in critical condition, including Gordon. The two bank robbers they were pursuing were also dead. At that moment, I lost my breath and could not believe the words that Daniels was pouring into my brain.

Gordon McNeill was one of my closest friends. We had gone to the same high school and were administrative assistants in the Philadelphia office when we were both in college. We had attended each other's weddings before going to the training academy. Later, we worked together under George Benjamin in the organized crime section, as did Tony Daniels. The information we had from Miami was sketchy. One of the agents killed was Ben Grogan, a former organized crime supervisor whom I had gotten to know very well when I monitored the program in Miami. He stepped down from that role, joined Gordon's bank robbery squad, and was a SWAT (special weapons and tactics) member. The other agent who was killed, Jerry Dove, was also SWAT-trained.

Details of the shooting continued to trickle into headquarters as the day progressed. Gordon was the supervisor of the bank robbery squad that had been investigating a series of robberies in which two bank employees had been killed. They had determined the make of the car used in the robberies and the license number that had been stolen. The robberies had occurred primarily in the Biscayne Boulevard area, always on Fridays when banks had the most cash. Gordon led a team of ten agents to patrol the area that Friday morning, hoping to spot the bank robbers. They successfully located the suspects, but they would not surrender, and a shoot-out occurred.

When I arrived at the airport Sunday morning for the flight to Cancún, I was advised that the attorney general wanted to visit the agents in the hospital in Miami before continuing the trip. Two hours later, we arrived at the Miami airport and were escorted to the hospital. Upon our arrival, we were greeted by what seemed like the entire Miami office. The first person I spotted was Gordon's wife, Elaine, who tearfully rushed to my side.

We were then escorted into the hospital rooms where the wounded agents were being treated. Gordon had already undergone surgery and was on the road to recovery. He was asleep as I entered his room. One of the agents, Ed Mireles, was in extremely critical condition. He was the last man standing during the shoot-out and finally had killed the remaining suspect while he reached for his shotgun. Both he and Gordon survived the shooting, but his prognosis was also uncertain.

As I began to leave, I hugged Elaine and she whispered, "Frank, I am not sure he is going to pull through." We both cried softly for a moment as I had to turn away. Our party had to leave the hospital and head to Cancún.

As I sat on the plane, staring into an open sky, I pondered what had happened in Miami the previous Friday. In this job, you do not focus on these events as possibilities. You go to work every day and react instinctively to dangerous situations. Many times, they are spontaneous, unpredictable, and beyond your control. Fortunately, this type of incident in Miami does not occur often, but other similar incidents have occurred more frequently lately. I drifted off to sleep and before I knew it, we had landed in Cancún.

Ambassador Gavin had invited representatives of several Mexican law enforcement agencies and a few government officials to meet at his home with the attorney general. He had a beautiful, spacious home on the outskirts of Cancún, which was heavily guarded. When we arrived, the ambassador greeted us at the front door and we could appreciate why he had become a successful movie star. He had a confident presence and demeanor. Our meeting in his conference room lasted a few hours, and as in most meetings of this type, nothing was resolved. However, it allowed parties to meet one another and obtain additional information about the fundamental issues we faced in combating the drug problem. I had no speaking role, which was fine with me because my mind was on Gordon, the wounded agents, and the families of Ben Grogan and Jerry Dove.

We departed Cancún early that evening and Susan was awake and waiting for me when I arrived home. She always worried when I traveled on business and did not like the idea of me going to Mexico. She was concerned about Gordon and relieved to hear he would survive. We sat, talked, and hugged one another close. I did not sleep well that night; my thoughts and concerns were with Gordon, his wife Elaine, and their two teenage daughters.

CHAPTER 19
The 'Ndrangheta

Michael LaScala felt desperate and had nowhere to turn. He was in ill health and out of money to cover expenses. He had just turned sixty. He was a member of the 'Ndrangheta, a Mafia-type criminal organization based in Calabria, Italy. The organization was involved in an international heroin distribution network. He was angry, as he had not been paid the money due to him from past transactions. He picked up the phone and called the Los Angeles office of the FBI, and agent Steven McCraw took the call. LaScala relayed his plight to McCraw, "I have to meet with you." McCraw met with LaScala at a rundown hotel in the city's poorest section where he had been living. LaScala began to tell McCraw a fascinating story about his present circumstances.

LaScala had dual citizenship in the United States and Italy. He had been a member of the 'Ndrangheta for quite some time and was closely aligned with the Cuntrera-Caruana family, operating in Venezuela, Italy, and Canada. While living in Venezuela, he had been contacted by police authorities. He told McCraw in a shaky voice, "They told me they had a warrant for my arrest and extradition to Italy and demanded money, or else they would serve the warrant." His 'Ndrangheta contacts would not provide him the money he needed to avoid arrest, so he fled the country and had arrived in Los Angeles several months ago. Members of the 'Ndrangheta were operating in Los Angeles and had also established a network in New York. He remained connected to that group, and as the organization's bookkeeper, he monitored all their financial transactions. "If I cooperate with you, I must be allowed to return to Italy and be with my family." He also wanted an outstanding warrant to be dismissed. He tearfully pleaded, "I am willing to testify and want to break all ties with the Mafia." Agent McCraw agreed to do everything he could to help LaScala and advised him he would have to speak to his superiors.

Unit Chief Bill Rice walked into my office after receiving a call from Agent McCraw and laid out the facts as he knew them. "Because LaScala is a fugitive from Italy and there is an outstanding warrant for his arrest, we cannot go forward and utilize him as a cooperative witness without the approval of the Italian government."

He acknowledged, "This is an excellent opportunity to neutralize another Sicilian group working in our country, and we cannot let it pass us by." I agreed, but we would have to contact our legal attaché in Rome and Magistrate Falcone to seek their help.

I called our legat Lee Flosi for his opinion and he agreed to contact Falcone directly. After being briefed and seeing the investigative possibilities of operating this witness, Judge Falcone decided to fly to Los Angeles and personally interview LaScala. Rice then coordinated the logistics of the meeting with Falcone and McCraw. Falcone subsequently met with LaScala and debriefed him as only a magistrate of his experience could. After the interview, Falcone told McCraw, "I will dismiss the arrest warrant as long as Mr. LaScala cooperates." After receiving this news, it was apparent to Rice that we were on the verge of investigating another highly sophisticated drug organization. We did not give this case a code name, but informally called it Pizza Connection II.

Los Angeles now had the go-ahead to launch an investigation utilizing LaScala as a cooperative witness who had agreed to testify in future court proceedings. Over the next eighteen months,

LaScala introduced an undercover agent to members of the Sicilian Mafia and 'Ndrangheta operating in the United States and Italy. Multiple heroin purchases were made and it was determined that the organization was supplying heroin to Alfredo Spavento, an alleged member of the Mafia located in New York. His name had come up in the Pizza Connection case, but insufficient evidence was developed to indict him. The New York office, however, now had probable cause to obtain court authorization to initiate electronic surveillance of Spavento.

As the investigation went forward, a money laundering operation was uncovered in Canada, and the subjects made frequent contact with coconspirators in Italy. Agent McCraw and LaScala traveled to Italy to meet with Inspector Johnny DiGiorgio of the Italian National Police (INP), who had conducted investigations of the Mafia and 'Ndrangheta. The focus was directed at a group operating in Calabria in southern Italy. They agreed that they would allow LaScala to contact his counterparts in Calabria. The FBI legat assigned agents to assist in monitoring the investigation with representatives of the INP. LaScala had several meetings over the next two weeks, which were all monitored, and police officials identified his contacts. Inspector DiGiorgio stated, "I am reluctant to have my officers conduct extensive surveillance in Calabria because members of the 'Ndrangheta are extremely violent." However, the evidence gathered in Calabria yielded sufficient evidence for future investigative actions and possible prosecutions.

The electronic surveillance of Spavento in New York was very successful. Spavento's base of operation was a retail store called the Garage Sale. An informant introduced an undercover agent to Spavento as a retail drug dealer. Over six months, the agent made multiple purchases of heroin from Spavento. The electronic surveillance identified his supplier and other retail dealers. The agent indicated that he wanted to purchase significant amounts of heroin. Spavento responded in the following recorded conversation: "I don't do this type of thing, but I know where to get three pairs of pants. You know, that's what we call it. And there are seven coming in. This guy usually gets $215,000."

Further incriminating conversations were recorded. Spavento subsequently introduced the agent to his associate Michele Modica, and they sold him a kilo of heroin for $195,000. Further purchases involved another Spavento associate, Emanuele Adamita. At this point in the investigation, discussions were held between the New York and Los Angeles offices to take the case down. Inspector De Gennaro was also a party to this conversation, as this would have to be a simultaneous event. We called for a meeting in Miami for all concerned parties to review the evidence and coordinate the indictments and arrests. Bill Rice, who was in charge of the investigation, would coordinate the agenda.

A week after the meeting, I got an unusual call from our press office. The next day, two representatives of the *New York Post*, reporter Brian Duffy and editor in chief Mort Zuckerman, walked into my office. After some initial pleasantries, they got to the point. "We have uncovered specific information regarding one of your major drug investigations and plan to write a story about what we've discovered." As they continued, I knew they were referring to the 'Ndrangheta investigation. They stated, "We wanted to consult with you about the ramifications this might have on your ongoing plans." I almost literally fell off my chair.

Gaining my composure, I said, "You cannot do that; it would cause significant damage to the case and we would have to move up our timeline prematurely." I offered them an alternative. I would give them advance notice when we made the arrests and provide them with details of our investigation. I mentioned they could meet me at headquarters and be on hand when the arrests were made. It became obvious to me that both reporters were men of integrity and were only interested in writing an accurate account of the investigation and not jeopardizing our future efforts. Mort got up from his chair, held out his hand, and proclaimed, "It's a deal." I told them I would be in touch and breathed a sigh of relief as they left my office.

I called Bill Rice into my office and told him we had a problem. Bill immediately thought a leak must have occurred at the recent conference held in Orlando. He contacted the Tampa office and requested they conduct an inquiry at the hotel where the meeting was held. Bingo, he hit the nail on the head. They located a maid who, while cleaning one of the rooms at the hotel, found a memorandum containing information about this investigation. She gave it to her husband because she was uncertain what to do with the information, and he contacted a local media representative. We let it go at that and never requested Duffy or Zuckerman to divulge their source, which they would not have done. There was no indication that the subjects were aware they were under investigation.

On April 1, 1988, we were ready to arrest all the subjects indicted in Italy and the United States. Logistically, this was going to be a difficult task, as the arrests had to be executed simultaneously because the subjects were still in contact with one another. I had already notified Duffy and Zuckerman of our intentions. The press office contacted the DOJ so a joint news conference could be scheduled in the aftermath of the arrests. We expected extensive interest from the press here and in Italy. Attorney General Meese's office then called Clarke and requested a meeting to discuss the case so he would be prepared for the press conference that afternoon. Clarke, Deputy Daniels, and I met with Mr. Meese and his staff in their conference room. He asked many detailed questions, and as I was in charge of the investigation, he relied on me to come up with the answers. We anticipated having the press conference in our auditorium; the director and DEA administrator, Jack Lawn, would also participate. This was going to be a big deal.

A total of sixty-two suspected members of the Sicilian Mafia were arrested in Italy. Thirty-two drug traffickers were arrested in New York and another eight in other cities throughout the country. Twenty-two kilos of heroin were seized in Italy, along with six kilos in New York. One of the subjects indicted was a Catholic priest, Lorenzo Zorza, who lived in New York and had been reported missing. That was not a good sign for Father Zorza. More subjects that had been indicted were still being sought by the FBI and the Italian National Police.

A press conference was held that afternoon and there must have been fifty or so reporters in our conference room. I sat up front with the attorney general, the director, and other officials. Rinaldo Petrignani, the Italian ambassador, and the US Attorney Rudy Giuliani were present. Mr. Meese began with an opening statement referring to the investigation as "the largest international drug case ever developed by the Department of Justice." The reporters present asked many questions. Mr. Meese felt uncomfortable with one particular question and called me to the podium to address the reporters.

I was unprepared for this role. I walked cautiously to the podium as the reporters' cameras taped my every move. As I began to respond to the question, I added that "today's arrest was the culmination of two years of an extensive investigation conducted by the FBI, DEA, and the Italian National Police." With that, the questions kept coming and Mr. Meese, standing by my side, did not attempt to take back the podium, so I spontaneously answered the questions. I began to feel comfortable in this role, as I knew the facts of the case so well. At that time, I was being considered for a promotion, and I even joked with the reporters that "I cannot afford to slip up." This brought some laughter and the tension in the room subsided. I ended my remarks by stating, "The Pizza Connection case taught us how to do it." The next day, my comment was quoted in *The New York Times*—it was pretty cool.

On April 11, 1988, *U.S. News & World Report* published a detailed accounting of the entire investigation and the arrests of the subjects indicted. It was the magazine's cover story. I am sure journalists Duffy and Zuckerman were pleased that we fulfilled our promise to them to obtain exclusive coverage of the case. Pizza Connection II was over, but I was sure other challenges would lie ahead. Several weeks after the investigation, Giovanni

De Gennaro called and stated that "Magistrate Falcone and his fellow magistrates desired to travel to Washington and meet with FBI and DEA representatives to discuss the progress in addressing the Mafia."

I told Johnny, "It will be our honor."

Magistrate Falcone and his party arrived at the FBI Academy in Quantico. De Gennaro and his staff also attended the conference. We began roundtable discussions about what had been accomplished and what remained to be done. I recall explicitly discussing the relationship between the Sicilian Mafia operating in the United States and the Cosa Nostra families located in all our major cities. Magistrate Falcone was so clear in his response that the "Sicilian Mafia group's allegiance is to the families in Sicily, and they operated only in cities like New York after La Cosa Nostra grants an accommodation." This accommodation included retributions that they had to pay to the families in the United States to operate their drug organizations. Now I understood; although they operated independently, they had to abide by the rules established by the controlling Cosa Nostra family in that city. This question had troubled us along the way, and his conclusion was consistent with what we were beginning to learn as we delved further into the workings of the drug organizations. The meeting lasted several hours and we adjourned so our guests could get some rest. A testimonial dinner in their honor was planned for that evening.

After dinner, Judge Rocco Chinnici was scheduled to address all the attendees. He was very close to Magistrate Falcone, and they had worked together on Sicilian Mafia prosecutions for many years. His presentation of the issues they faced in Italy was very personal and the longer he spoke, the more emotion he expressed. "They are destroying our country, and together, we must stop them, please." His voice cracked and tears flowed down his cheeks. Everyone in the room was silent and respectful. You could hear a pin drop. I had never experienced such a moment in my career and realized how important it was for the FBI to continue this fight. The director presented both officials with an honorary award, and we ended the evening embracing one another. Our meeting successfully established a closer working relationship as we continued to combat the Mafia here in our country and in Italy. We drove all our guests to the airport for their return flight home the next day.

Judge Chinnici was subsequently murdered weeks later in Sicily by the members of the Corleonesi Mafia. We were shocked, saddened, and alarmed at this news. Since the murder of his friend and associate Judge Chinnici, Judge Falcone now had to be more concerned for his safety, and the government provided bodyguards to protect him and his family. The Corleonesi Mafia family, however, was intent on killing him. On May 29, 1992, Judge Falcone and his wife, Francesca Morvillo, were returning from vacation to their home near Capaci in Sicily. His driver and bodyguards accompanied them. He was traveling on a highway he had taken many times before, as it was a direct route from the airport to his home. As they entered a tunnel underpass, an explosion was detonated, and Judge Falcone, his wife, and bodyguards were killed instantly. An investigation by the authorities determined that the Corleonesi Mafia family was responsible, led by Giovanni Brusca. They knew the route that Falcone would have to take from the airport to his home and had planted explosives in the tunnel to detonate when his car entered.

The director attended the funeral as the FBI representative to honor Judge Falcone. The FBI created a Giovanni Falcone Gallery at headquarters, and his sister Maria Falcone participated in the gallery's ceremonial opening, attended by numerous law enforcement officials. The murders of Judge Falcone and his wife deeply saddened me. During my career, I witnessed and participated in the investigation of at least fifty or more murders by members of the Cosa Nostra and the Sicilian Mafia. There had never been a judge, magistrate, or FBI agent assassinated in the United States.

During the investigations of the Pizza Connection case, we

were concerned about the reactions the Sicilian Mafia members here in the United States would have when they were under investigation and ultimately prosecuted. For this reason, the lead agents assigned to the cases were cautioned to keep a low profile and to be very cautious when contacting suspects directly. Fortunately, there were no repercussions directed at any agents or prosecuting officials. We had lost a great leader in the battle against the Mafia. The FBI and other law enforcement agencies were determined to continue the journey to eradicate this cancer from our society. That is what Magistrate Falcone would have wanted.

CHAPTER 20
The Kansas City Family

In 1988, I was transferred to Kansas City and appointed the special agent in charge of the division. The office covered all federal crimes within the FBI's jurisdiction throughout Kansas and half the state of Missouri—a lot of territory. This would be a new experience for Sue and me, as we had never visited the Midwest and had no family or friends in the community. I knew Brian Carroll, the assistant special agent in charge, having worked with him in Philadelphia. We picked out a lovely home near a beautiful park and close to a good school, as our son David was about to start first grade. Everything was okay until the day the furniture was to arrive from Washington. We went to the house that morning and waited on the porch, but the moving van never arrived. I finally called the company and they apologized for dropping the ball and missing our delivery date. The dispatcher said it would be there the following day. Okay, I thought, we're getting off to a good start. As they unloaded the furniture the next day, neighbors began visiting with coffee and a friendly "welcome to the neighborhood" greeting. This was a good beginning.

The next day, Sue dropped me off at the office, and I introduced myself to the receptionist. My assistant, Brian Carroll, greeted me, and I met Anne, my secretary, and began to settle in. It felt a little strange. This was my first assignment as the head of an FBI field office, and I was assuming a whole new role. I would rely on my inner voice: *Just play it by ear and let the chips fall where they may.* I had never visited Kansas City and did not know much of its history, but one event stood out in my memory. During my training at Quantico, one of our instructors had this account on his agenda when introducing us to the history of the FBI.

Kansas City played a unique role in the FBI's early years, and an event that occurred in the city many years ago would be a turning point in the FBI's investigative focus and manner of fulfilling its responsibilities. The Kansas City massacre that took place on June 17, 1933 would forever change the face of the FBI. On that fateful day, FBI agents and local police arrived at Union Station to await the arrival by train of an escaped federal prisoner, Frank "Jelly" Nash. He had escaped from the federal penitentiary in Leavenworth. Nash had been captured in Hot Springs, Arkansas and placed on a train bound for Kansas City, guarded by FBI agent Raymond Caffrey and two police officers. Upon his arrival, he would be transported to Leavenworth. The estimated arrival time was early in the morning, and the local FBI agent in charge, Francis Lackey, planned to meet the team of officers with Nash at Union Station and assist in the transfer. Several Mob associates of Nash had learned of his arrest in Arkansas and that he would be arriving at Union Station. They began making plans to intervene and force his release from custody. Charles "Pretty Boy" Floyd, another wanted fugitive, had organized a group of gangsters to help free Nash. His associates were later identified as Vernon Miller, Frank Mulloy, and Adam Richetti, who allegedly had links to the Mafia family in Kansas City.

As the train pulled into the station, the escort team of officers planned to walk Nash to a waiting police vehicle that would transport him to prison. FBI agents Lackey and Frank Smith greeted Agent Caffrey at the station platform and then escorted a handcuffed Nash to their cars in the parking lot. "Pretty Boy" Floyd and his gang were waiting for them. After Nash was placed in a vehicle, one of the agents observed two armed men jump from a nearby car carrying a machine gun and a shotgun. The words "let them have it" rang through the air as a fuselage of gunfire exploded. Two police officers fell to the ground, dead, along with Agent Caffrey. The chief of police from Hot Springs was also killed. FBI Agent Smith had been shot three times, but survived. Nash was caught up in the gunfire and was killed.

The shooters escaped, but not for long. They were soon captured, tried, and, in some cases, executed. After an extensive manhunt, Floyd was killed by FBI agents when resisting arrest.

At that time, the FBI had no authority to carry firearms and had limited federal jurisdiction in addressing interstate criminal activities. This event changed all that. The public and Congress demanded action, and several laws were passed to increase the FBI's ability to have a broader investigative responsibility. All agents were trained and authorized to carry a firearm. As time passed and more interstate crimes were identified, additional federal laws were given to the FBI to investigate. Their workforce grew along with their ability to solve major criminal problems. This progression ultimately led to the battle against organized crime, but it took a long time to get there.

In reviewing the history of the Mafia in Kansas City, I would not have suspected that it rivaled those Mafia families on the East Coast. The Mafia in Kansas City got an early start. In 1912, two members of the Sicilian Mafia fled Sicily and arrived in Kansas City. They soon organized a group to engage in illegal activities. When Prohibition arrived years later, their enterprise prospered. A new boss, John Lazia, succeeded them, and their influence grew as the city was wide open with little or no law enforcement interference.

An entrenched political machine headed by Tom Pendergast controlled the local government and police department. Lazia developed a close relationship with Pendergast and his political machine. Tom's brother Jim Pendergast had been elected as an alderman of the First Ward, which included an area known as Little Italy. Based on his relationship with the Pendergast brothers,

Lazia was able to place corrupt officers in the police department. At the time of the Kansas City massacre, there had been speculation that an officer of the department had notified "Pretty Boy" Floyd of the details concerning the arrival of Frank "Jelly" Nash. The FBI's investigation into the incident never resolved the question of how Floyd and his associates learned of the precise time of Nash's expected arrival.

Lazia expanded the operations of his enterprise to include legitimate businesses and gambling casinos that were allowed to operate in the city. He and Pendergast prospered until a rival eventually murdered Lazia. The organization he had built survived and was entrenched in the town's fabric. Following the 1950 murder of KC boss Charles Binaggio and the death of his successor Anthony Gizzo three years later, Nicholas Civella eventually became the boss and first came on the FBI's radar screen after he was arrested when he attended the meeting called by Vito Genovese in Apalachin, New York, in 1957.

Civella expanded the Mafia's interests and relationships with other families, particularly the one referred to as the Chicago Mob, or the Outfit, headed by boss Joseph "Joey Doves" Aiuppa. The office investigated these activities under the code name Operation Strawman. Through authorized intercepted telephone conversations and undercover agents, the FBI determined that Joe Agosto of the Tropicana Casino in Las Vegas was funneling money to Civella in Kansas City. Indictments were returned against Agosta, Civella, and his brother, Carl, and two additional members of the Civella family. He and his brother were convicted and sent to prison.

William "Willie the Rat" Cammisano became the boss and the subject of a new investigation. Although Operation Strawman was a success, I noted that it was only focused on one type of criminal activity. The enterprise continued to operate as usual despite Civella's incarceration. As we had discovered in New York, it was easy for the Mafia to replace the boss, but not the enterprise.

I met with Supervisor Mike Shanahan, who directed the organized crime squad. He was a seasoned veteran who had worked cases involving family members and had street experience. That is something I always looked for. You cannot be an effective supervisor without acquiring the knowledge gained by being a brick agent actually conducting investigations. He had recently been promoted to the position of supervisor. Shanahan had an aggressive style and was not shy about expressing his opinion. Another good quality. He was one of the first supervisors I met after I arrived, and we spent a couple of hours discussing the challenges ahead. Of course, I inserted my friend RICO into the conversation.

Shortly after my arrival, I met with the head of the Organized Crime Strike Force and his staff. Carroll and Shanahan accompanied me. It was customary to have a get-acquainted meeting with government officials after being appointed to my position, but I also had another objective. I had noted that there had not been a RICO indictment against the Civella family, and I was curious why this approach had not been taken. The strike force chief was aware of the RICO statute and commented that it had been utilized to prosecute individual members of the Mafia involved in the Strawman investigation. If we could develop sufficient evidence to support prosecuting the Kansas City family under RICO, his office would be on board. It was a good meeting. The ball was now in Shanahan's court and Mike was ready to play the game.

My role as the SAC was somewhat different from prior assignments. I was the face of the FBI in the community and a representative to other law enforcement agencies. I had to ensure we had good working relationships with all state and federal law enforcement agencies. I met with the chief of police, Larry Joiner, and his staff to get acquainted and discuss our investigative priorities. Larry did not show much concern about organized crime activities. His main issue was the influx of Jamaican posses into the city who were engaged in cocaine distribution. These gangs were causing havoc, were quite violent, and had been responsible for several homicides.

I offered to join forces in this effort, as the FBI now had jurisdiction in drug investigations, and he readily agreed. We then set up a task force of agents to work with the police department on this issue under the supervision of Shanahan's relief supervisor. They began making significant progress and the news media jumped on the positive developments, with frequently published articles giving the problem the attention it deserved. I soon responded to a request from *Good Morning America* for a televised interview about this emerging problem, so our efforts were paying off. Joiner and the task force were successful over an extended period in neutralizing the gangs, and many of the leaders were either arrested or fled the city.

The time for our all-agents conference was approaching. It was held annually and the topic normally centered around the division's investigative problems and administrative issues. It was normally quite boring. I wanted to take this opportunity to introduce a topic that would be more interesting to the agents so they could learn something from the discussion that would be of some benefit. I contacted Gordon McNeill and asked him if he would be available to address the conference and discuss the Miami shoot-out. He had been transferred at his request to San Francisco after the shooting and had responsibility for the organized crime program. He might also be available to sit down with Shanahan and offer assistance on Mike's ongoing investigation of the Civella family. Gordon said he would be more than willing to make the trip. I invited him to stay with Sue and me so we could catch up.

Gordon arrived and looked like his old self, though I knew he had not fully recovered from the wounds he'd suffered in the shoot-out. The mental scars would stay with him forever. Every agent that could be available was present for his presentation. When he began to speak, there was total silence in the room and all the agents listened intently. The shoot-out had occurred on the morning of April 11, 1986, in a subdivision outside the city of

Miami and was the most violent incident in the history of the FBI. Gordon was the supervisor of the bank robbery squad, and they were focused on two bank robbers who had robbed a series of banks and committed at least two homicides. Their identities were unknown, but the car they utilized had been identified. For some reason, the suspects focused on banks located off Biscayne Boulevard in a heavily concentrated business and residential area on the outskirts of downtown Miami. The plan was to have several agents surveil the area early on a Friday morning, as that was the day of the week when most of the robberies occurred.

Ten agents, including two SWAT team members, Jerry Dove and Ben Grogan, were strategically stationed along the boulevard. At approximately 9:30 a.m., they spotted the vehicle driving along Biscayne Boulevard with two white males in the front seat. Grogan alerted the other agents and everyone engaged in the surveillance. Grogan radioed McNeill and suggested they make a routine traffic stop of the vehicle to avoid a confrontation. The suspects must have suspected they were being followed, as they suddenly turned into a residential community.

The agents followed—they had no choice at this point. An attempt was made to stop their vehicle, but the suspects rammed the agent's car and disabled it. Both suspects bolted from the vehicle and began firing at Dove and Grogan, who were able to get out of the car and return fire, partially wounding one of the suspects. Both suspects had semiautomatic rifles, while the agents only had Smith & Wesson revolvers that held six rounds. One agent had the only 12-gauge shotgun. Dove and Grogan were armed with semiautomatic revolvers since they were members of the SWAT team. The scene of the ongoing shooting was a quiet residential street, and the gun battle would last approximately six minutes, which was a lifetime in that type of violent confrontation. Both suspects were formerly in the armed forces and were well-trained in firearms.

Grogan and Dove were both killed even though they successfully wounded both suspects. McNeill was critically wounded and four additional agents had been shot. Toward the end of the battle, one of the suspects had been killed. However, his partner was still firing. Somehow, Agent Ed Mireles, although suffering from severe wounds, had enough willpower and strength to engage the remaining suspect and finally kill him. The suspects were later identified as Michael Lee Platt and William Russell Matix. McNeill concluded his remarks by citing that the lessons learned from this incident caused the FBI to arm all its agents with more sophisticated and powerful handguns. Agents were also instructed to keep a shotgun in the trunk of their car when on duty. Simply put, the agents were outgunned that day, and FBI headquarters knew it and were forced to make policy adjustments.

During his remarks, Gordon's voice cracked somewhat at times, and it was evident that this was a difficult moment for him. The agents present gave him a standing ovation that lasted several minutes. We had a quiet dinner at home that night with Susan and talked about when we were clerks in Philly, still wet behind the ears. It was great to spend this time together once again. He left the next day for San Francisco. Gordon never fully recovered from his wounds. He died on January 2, 2004. He was only sixty-two years of age. I will forever cherish his friendship and his unquestioned bravery.

One afternoon, my assistant Brian Carroll rushed into my office and announced, "There was a shooting in St. Louis and an agent has been killed."

My secretary Anne gasped, "Oh, my God."

St. Louis was our neighboring field office and we often worked on joint investigations with their agents. The agent was identified as SWAT member L. Douglas Abram. I had visited the office the prior week to attend an FBI National Academy outing. Dave Binney, a former supervisor in New York who oversaw the Salerno investigation, was now the SAC.

The incident had just ended and the shooter had been killed.

This was a SAC's worst nightmare—having to tell a wife that her husband has been killed in the line of duty. I waited a few hours and then called Dave. The shooting had occurred on the first floor of a building where the suspect was hiding, and he would not surrender. The SWAT team made a forced entry and although Abram was wearing a bulletproof vest, the bullet that killed him entered his body just above the neckline of the vest. The gun battle continued until the agents were able to take down the suspect.

Abram's funeral was held several days later and Brian and I drove to St. Louis to attend. The acting director, John Otto, also attended. Abram was to be buried in his SWAT uniform. The entire day was full of sorrow and grieving. I can still picture his young son standing by his father's coffin, teary-eyed, with his mother by his side, trying to comfort him. It is moments like this where you ask yourself why.

The next day, I held an all-agents conference to inform everyone of the details of the shooting. We had a long moment of silence for our fallen hero, Doug Abram.

Shanahan and his squad successfully created a prosecutable RICO case against the Cammisano family. In 1990, he was convicted and sent to prison along with his top lieutenants. He had been involved in organized crime since he was very young and this is how it would end. Cammisano died in prison several years later. When I looked back at all the cases we worked on, I realized they all seemed to end the same way. The bosses were convicted, sent to prison for the rest of their lives, or rivals killed them. It made no sense.

I had just returned from lunch and Anne mentioned that Floyd Clarke had called from headquarters. I returned his call and he stated that the recent inspection in New York had not gone well and that management changes had to be made. I was being promoted to the position of deputy assistant director. I replied that I had not been in Kansas City that long and he commented, "Well, this is a development we did not expect, and we must make a move." Clarke ended the conversation by saying, "The ball is in your court." At first, I was unsure of what he meant, but upon reflection, I understood the comment.

When I broke the news to Sue, she was elated, as it would bring us closer to Philadelphia and be our last transfer. David was unhappy, as he loved his school and would miss his best friend, Taylor, who lived across the street. My son Trip was planning a wedding in Philly, which would take place in a couple of months, so the move would coincide with his big moment. The transfer had many positive aspects.

Now, if only the moving van would show up this time.

CHAPTER 21
Deputy

I was now back in New York as deputy assistant director in charge. New York had 1,200 agents assigned and was the largest field office in the country. I would report to the Assistant Director in Charge, Jim Fox. I was expected to oversee the division's administrative and investigative policy-related issues. In addition, I had management responsibilities over the Joint Terrorism Task Force, comprising three squads of FBI agents and an elite group of officers from the New York City police department. It was a handful, but I welcomed the challenge.

Due to issues arising during the last inspection, my predecessor had been transferred. I spoke to Clarke and Revell before I left Kansas City, and it was clear that they anticipated the assistant director would retire shortly and that I would be considered for that position. Being promoted and consistently moving up the line was never my goal. It was always about the job and a new challenge. Sue was looking forward to finally settling down in one particular spot, and as I was nearing retirement age, I believed this would be the last stop on my FBI journey.

We were still unpacking boxes in our new home when I received a call from the agent on duty at the office. He told me that "Meir Kahane, a rabbi and controversial activist, has just been assassinated while giving a speech at a downtown hotel in Manhattan. A suspect, El Sayyid Nosair, had been arrested while attempting to enter a cab outside the hotel fleeing the scene." At the time, I had no idea who Kahane was or the significance of this event. This time, I did not have to report to the scene, as the agents assigned to the task force immediately responded.

The following day, I met with Terry Cox, the supervisor of one of the terrorism squads. He had been on-site at the scene the night before and gave me a briefing of his initial thoughts. He was accompanied by his counterpart, a police detective and terrorism expert. They both felt this was an act of terrorism and intended to pursue that approach in conducting the investigation. There was something odd about Nosair's actions after the shooting that caught the investigating agents' attention. When he left the hotel, Nosair promptly went to a cab parked in front of the hotel. It appeared to witnesses that the cab was waiting for him.

Cox posed several questions: "How did he get to the hotel? Did he take that cab and who was the driver?" They believed the driver may have been an accomplice. The postal inspector who arrested Nosair had furnished a cab number and a partial New Jersey license plate. Before his arrest, Nosair had shot and wounded a police officer while attempting to flee.

I met with Chief of Detectives Joseph Borrelli to get his take on the incident. He was a seasoned department veteran and I quickly understood he had a territorial attitude. He believed the murder was just another random shooting with no apparent motive and did not consider it an act of terrorism.

His department had the shooter in custody, and he concluded, "We consider the case closed."

I disagreed with this assertion and informed him, "The Joint Terrorism Task Force will pursue the follow-up investigation." He wished me good luck and ended our meeting. I was not impressed.

The investigation determined that Nosair belonged to a mosque in Jersey City and he was a member of a radical Islamic cell. He was charged with the murder of Kahane, pleaded not guilty, and was acquitted. Kahane's family did not agree to an autopsy of his body; thus, police lab technicians were unable to examine the bullet fragments to confirm that they were fired from Nosair's gun. The jury felt this was critical evidence. Ironically, Nosair was convicted of shooting the police officer and received a lengthy prison sentence. The FBI concluded that this was a terrorist act committed by a member of the cell in Jersey City and continued to investigate Nosair's associates.

Jules Bonavolonta was still in charge of the organized crime program, and the agents had achieved outstanding accomplishments under his leadership. Jim Kossler remained the coordinating supervisor, contributing to the program as only he could with his vast knowledge and expertise. Many of the investigations regarding the Five Families were winding down due to all the successes that had been achieved. Kossler informed me that the families were now focused only on traditional criminal activities, such as running illegal gambling operations, loan-sharking, and drug trafficking, as the prohibition against that activity had been lifted. It was challenging to identify the new bosses because no one wanted to step forward publicly. Jim further explained that their control over the unions and related businesses was just about gone. The program continued to move forward.

One case I was paying attention to related to John Gotti, the boss of the Gambino family. He was on trial in Brooklyn, having been charged with violating the RICO statute due to an investigation by Mouw's Gambino squad. Sammy "the Bull" Gravano was now a potential key witness. He agreed to testify against Gotti and plead out for several crimes he had committed, which would result in his incarceration. He would be placed in the witness protection program upon his release.

During the trial, the strike force chief who was trying the case contacted me. He made an unusual request. He said, "At the last minute, Gravano is getting cold feet and he might be reluctant to take the witness stand and face Gotti in open court." His testimony was expected the next day. Despite his history as a tough guy and admitted hit man for the Gambino family, he believed "Gravano was intimidated by the aura of the federal courtroom and Gotti himself." Based on my previous experiences, the strike force chief suggested, "It might be helpful if you meet with Gravano before he is scheduled to testify."

I agreed and the following morning, I drove over to Brooklyn. Two FBI agents assigned to the case greeted me as I arrived at the courthouse and escorted me to the basement. The prosecuting attorneys and Gravano were present, and I was formally introduced. I walked over to Gravano, shook his hand, and thanked him for his cooperation.

We moved to a corner of the room and he paused momentarily and, with a blank stare, muttered, "I know who you are—we heard of you." A chill ran up my spine for a moment. The words were almost threatening and slightly angry, as only a hit man, I suppose, could say them. He must have been referring to my first tour in New York when I was in charge of the organized crime program. I was now standing next to a man who had confessed to our agents that he had killed over twenty individuals during his career as a hit man for the Gambino family.

I asked Gravano, "What about your family? You have a wife and two children to think about. Your days of being protected by the Mafia are over. It's time to start a new life and move forward."

He almost teared up and kept repeating, "I know, I know." We spoke for several minutes and he seemed more relaxed and composed. Finally, he said, "Okay, I trust you, I will do it." At that point, I shook his hand, wished him good luck, and departed. I will never forget that meeting.

The next day, I decided to attend the trial, anticipating there might be further issues with Gravano's testimony. The prosecution called him as their next witness, and two US Marshals cautiously escorted him into the courtroom. The clerk swore him in and he took the stand. All those in attendance knew who he was, as it had been well publicized that he was now a cooperative witness. Gotti sat at the defense table and just glared at Gravano. I sat up front, only about fifteen feet away. There was total silence on the part of the attendees, which is always a court requirement. The atmosphere was a bit different than you would typically find in a courtroom setting. All eyes were on Gravano, as if he were some mystical figure out of a gangster movie about to spill the beans on the boss.

The principal act charged in the Gotti indictment was the planning of the murders of Paul Castellano and Tom Bilotti outside of Sparks Steak House on December 16, 1985. Gravano provided a minute-by-minute account of the crime. The prosecuting attorney wanted the jury to listen to all the gory details, and Gravano was more than willing to offer them. It was Gravano's responsibility to put together the hit team, and he enlisted capo Frank DeCicco's help. Their group included Salvatore "Fat Sal" Scala, Edward Lino, and John Carneglia, the main shooters. Positioned further down Forty-third Street would be Angelo "Quack Quack" Ruggiero, Dominick "Skinny Dom" Pizzonia, and Anthony "Tony Roach" Rampino, who would be backup shooters if there was a misstep. Castellano and Bilotti would be shot as soon as they arrived at Sparks. They knew Castellano would not be armed, but Bilotti, as Castellano's bodyguard, might be. For that reason, one shooter was assigned to take Bilotti out as soon as he parked the car in front of the restaurant.

Gotti and Gravano had driven to Forty-third Street and Third Avenue and parked the car half a block down from Sparks so they could witness the shootings. He testified, "We were looking down at Sparks, and all of a sudden, Bilotti and Castellano drove right by us." Neither Castellano nor Bilotti noticed them as they drove to Sparks' front entrance. "I just turned and told John they were right next to us."

As both men exited the car, "the shooters ran over to them, started shooting right away," Gravano explained. After both Castellano and Billoti were shot, Gotti drove his Lincoln past the restaurant so they both could personally observe the scene of the shooting. Gravano continued that as they drove by the front entrance to Sparks, "I noticed. I looked down at Tommy Bilotti, and I said he was gone. We drove a little faster to go to Second Avenue. We made a right. We drove back to my office in Brooklyn."

The shooters just walked away among the Christmas shoppers and made their escape. Gravano further testified that he had committed numerous murders for Gotti and Castellano. His delivery had very little emotion or concern, and he seemed very relaxed and showed no remorse for what he had done. The jury was spellbound throughout this phase of his testimony, which would continue for several days. I left during the next break in the trial. On my way back to the office, I wondered, even with all this evidence, would the jury do the right thing and find Gotti and his codefendants guilty as charged?

On April 2, 1992, Gotti was convicted on all counts. At that moment, as Gotti sat at the defense counsel's table staring up at the judge, his defiance was gone, and I am told that the expression on his face was fixated. He had faced similar trials on three occasions and had always been acquitted. The press had referred to him as the Teflon Don. He publicly mocked the justice system. At an FBI press conference that afternoon, Assistant Director Fox could not resist. He stated, "The Teflon Don is gone; Gotti can now be called the Velcro Don"—a reference to the charges having finally stuck. After hearing the verdict, it is fair to assume that Gotti realized this might be the end of the line. He was remanded to the custody of the US Marshal and escorted from the courtroom. Weeks later, he received a life sentence. He spent his remaining years at the Marion, Illinois maximum security prison in solitary confinement. He died there in 2002 at the age of sixty-one.

On the date of Gotti's conviction, a retirement dinner was held for me at the New York Athletic Club. Many of my game changers, including Louis Freeh, were there. Several agents from the Bruno squad in Philadelphia had made the trip up the turnpike to attend. My mom and dad were there, as were Susan and my three children, Trip, Karen, and David. It was a great night and at the same time, I felt sad I was leaving. I almost began to cry as I addressed the attendees. It had been such a great job. Someone once told me, "If you are lucky enough to love your job, it's really like you are not working at all." That sums up how I felt about my career as an FBI agent.

It was my honor to serve.

AFTERWORD

There is a saying in the FBI that when you complete an investigation, you note that the case is closed. My battle against the Mafia was over, but the war would continue. The Mafia that I once knew would never be the same. There will always be remnants left, but the FBI now had the expertise and knowledge to address them when they raised their ugly head. As far as I was concerned, this case was closed.

After I retired, William Webster, the director of the FBI, made a national press release. He outlined the new policy the FBI had adopted institutionally in conducting investigations directed at criminal enterprises such as the Mafia by utilizing the RICO statute:

> *The FBI has determined that the most effective means of combatting this crime is to use the enterprise theory of investigation, which focuses investigations and prosecutions on entire criminal enterprises rather than individuals. Through this process, all aspects of the criminal operation can be identified. The theory supports not only the prosecution of the criminal enterprise but also the seizure of the enterprise's assets, which is intended to disrupt or dismantle entire criminal organizations.*

I hope all my game changers had the opportunity to read that press release. Their hard work, imagination, and resilience in adopting this new investigative solution ultimately destroyed the Commission and the Mafia in New York. This led to the FBI institutionally changing its policy on investigating organized criminal enterprises. A great deal was accomplished through their efforts and the ship was in good hands, moving in the right direction.

It now seemed the right time for my friend RICO and I to move on.

I will never forget any of it.

APPENDIX:
Mafia Boss Succession

Gambino Family

1931–1951: Vincent "The Executioner" Mangano
1951–1957: Albert "Lord High Executioner" Anastasia
1957–1976: "Don" Carlo Gambino
1976–1985: "Big" Paul Castellano
1985–2002: John "The Teflon Don" Gotti
2002–2011: Peter "One Eye" Gotti
2011–present: Domenico "Italian Dom" Cefalù

Lucchese Family

1930–1951: Tommaso "Tommy" Gagliano
1951–1967: Tommy "Three-Finger Brown" Lucchese
1967–1973: Carmine "Mr. Gribbs" Tramunti
1973–1986: Anthony "Tony Ducks" Corallo
1986–present: Vittorio "Little Vic" Amuso

Colombo Family

1928–1962: Joseph "Olive Oil King" Profaci
1962–1963: Joseph "Joe Evil Eye" Magliocco
1963–1971: Joseph "Joe" Colombo
1973–2019: Carmine "The Snake" Persico
2019–2022: Andrew "Andy Mush" Russo
2025–present: Theodore N. "Skinny Teddy" Persico, Jr.

Genovese Family

1922–1931: Giuseppe "Joe the Boss" Masseria
1931–1946: Charles "Lucky" Luciano
1946–1957: Frank "the Prime Minister" Costello
1957–1969: Vito "Don Vitone" Genovese
1969–1981: Philip "Benny Squint" Lombardo
1981–2005: Vincent "Chin" Gigante
2006–present: Liborio "Barney" Bellomo

Bonanno Family

1930–1931: Salvatore "Little Caesar" Maranzano
1931–1968: Joseph "Joe Bananas" Bonanno
1968–1971: Paul Sciacca
1971–1973: Natale "Joe Diamonds" Evola
1974–1991: Philip "Rusty" Rastelli
1991–2004: Joseph "the Ear" Massino
2004–2011: Vincent "Vinny Gorgeous" Basciano
2013–present: Michael "the Nose" Mancuso

Philadelphia Family

1931–1936: John "Nazzone" Avena
1936–1946: Giuseppe "Joseph Bruno" Dovi
1946–1958: Giuseppe "Joseph" Ida
1958–1959: Antonio "Mr. Miggs" Pollina
1959–1980: Angelo "the Gentle Don" Bruno
1980–1981: Phillip "the Chicken Man" Testa
1981–1990: Nicodemo "Little Nicky" Scarfo, Sr.
1990–1995: Giovanni "John" Stanfa
1995–1999: Ralph Natale
1999–2024: Joseph "Skinny Joey" Merlino
2024–present: George Borgesi

Kansas City Family

1931–1934: John "Brother John" Lazia
1934–1939: Charles "Charlie the Wop" Carrollo

1939–1950: Charles Binaggio
1950–1953: Anthony Gizzo
1953–1983: Nicholas "Nick" Civella
1983–1984: Carl "Cork" Civella
1984–1995: William "Willie the Rat" Cammisano
1995–2006: Anthony "Tony Ripe" Civella
2006–present: John "Johnny Joe" Sciortino

ACKNOWLEDGMENTS

It is nearly impossible to acknowledge all those who contributed to this incredible journey to take down the Mafia without inadvertently omitting a few. This work is a testament to the collective effort of many. I have highlighted the FBI agents and supervisors who were the actual game changers and were instrumental in the successes achieved. Equally important were the family members who stood by these agents, providing them with much-needed support and encouragement. On a personal note, my wife, Susan, was my go-to source to lean on when I needed to vent my frustrations or look for answers to what seemed like unsolvable problems. I could not have completed this work without her guidance and support.

I want to acknowledge the guidance and input I received from members of the Rehoboth Beach, Delaware Writers Guild during the writing of this story. In particular, President Mary Beth Fischer, along with Cindy Hall, Stella Marie Alden, Crystal Heibel, and Norton Beckerman, who provided so much support. Also, I must recognize in particular my wife, Susan, for being my in-home editor and advisor who lovingly encouraged me along the way. My sister Maureen Clare Matthews was also was very supportive.

Finally, the initial recognition I received from my Literary Agent Frank Weimann of Folio Literary Management LLC, and my Editor Jame Abbate of Kensington Publishing Corporation, made this work possible. Thank you all.

Bibliography

Books

Anastasia, George. *Blood and Honor*. Camino Books, 1991.

Blumenthal, Ralph. *Last Days of the Sicilians*. Times Books, 1988.

Bonavolonta, Jules and Brian Duffy. *The Good Guys*. Simon & Schuster, 1996.

DeStefano, Anthony M. *Gotti's Boys*. Citadel, 2019.

Gleeson, John. *The Gotti Wars*. Simon & Schuster, 2022.

O'Brien, Joseph F. and Andris Kurins. *Boss of Bosses*. Simon & Schuster, 1991.

Pistone, Joseph D. with Richard Woodley. *Donnie Brasco*. New American Library, 1987.

Raab, Selwyn. *Five Families*. Thomas Dunne Books, 2005.

Podcasts

Freeh, Louis J. "On the Waterfront Mafia Style." *Inside the FBI*. 2008.

Magazines/Publications

Caramandi, Nicholas and Richard Behar. "A Crow Turns Stool Pigeon." *Time*. June 17, 1991.

Cosa Nostra News

Hayde, Frank R. "The Story of the Kansas City Mob." *American Mafia*. 1998.

May, Allan. *Crime Magazine*.

Mob-Mad: Daily Excerpts on Gangsters, Outlaws, & Criminal Organizations.

The Mob Museum

Soccer, Nizza. "The Three Racketeers–Ralph Scopo." *Mafia Book Reviews*. October 2021.

Gangsters Inc.

Court Decisions and Transcripts

Spavento v. United States

US v. Anthony DiSalvo

US v. Local 359, United Seafood Workers Union

US v. Myles E. Billups

US v. Nicodemo Scarfo

US v. Orena

US v. Pasquale Amato

US v. Salerno (review of court testimony and transcripts of taped conversations recorded by the FBI)

US v. Scotto (progression of a waterfront corruption prosecution from investigation through appeal, including transcripts of court testimony)

Newspapers

National Registry of Exonerations

The New York Times

The Philadelphia Daily News

The Philadelphia Inquirer

The Washington Post

Index